# Population Estimation
# and
# Projection

# POPULATION ESTIMATION AND PROJECTION

*Methods for Marketing, Demographic, and Planning Personnel*

## James C. Raymondo

QUORUM BOOKS
New York • Westport, Connecticut • London

**Library of Congress Cataloging-in-Publication Data**

Raymondo, James C.
    Population estimation and projection : methods for marketing,
    demographic, and planning personnel / James C. Raymondo.
        p.    cm.
    Includes bibliographical references and index.
    ISBN 0–89930–663–2 (alk. paper)
    1. Population forecasting.  I. Title.
    HB849.53.R39      1992
    304.6′01′12—dc20        91–45709

British Library Cataloguing in Publication Data is available.

Library of Congress Catalog Card Number: 91–45709
ISBN: 0–89930–663–2

First published in 1992

Quorum Books, One Madison Avenue, New York, NY 10010
An imprint of Greenwood Publishing Group, Inc.

Printed in the United States of America

The paper used in this book complies with the
Permanent Paper Standard issued by the National
Information Standards Organization (Z39.48–1984).

10 9 8 7 6 5 4 3 2 1

# Contents

*Illustrations*                                                                    vii

*Preface*                                                                           ix

**1**   Population Estimates and Projections: Introduction
        and Overview                                                                 1

        Population Estimates and Projections                                         2

        Summary                                                                      9

**2**   Population Concepts and Measures                                            11

        The Base Population                                                         12

        The Classic Demographic Variables                                          12

        Summary                                                                     40

**3**   Survival Rates: Census and Life Table Methods                              43

        Census Survival Rate Method                                                43

        The Life Table                                                             47

        Life Table Survival Rates                                                  54

        Census Survival Rates Versus Life Table Survival Rates                     58

        Summary                                                                     60

**4**   Census Geography Concepts                                                   61

        Major Concepts of Census Geography for 1980                                62

        Additional 1980 Census Geography Concepts                                  68

        Major Concepts of Census Geography for 1990 and Changes
        Since 1980                                                                  70

|  | Additional 1990 Census Geography Concepts | 72 |
|  | Key Issues in Census Geography | 73 |
|  | Final Considerations | 79 |
|  | Summary | 79 |
| **5** | **Sources and Types of Data for Population Estimates and Projections** | **81** |
|  | Major Sources of Data | 81 |
|  | Summary | 97 |
| **6** | **Methods of Intercensal Population Estimation** | **99** |
|  | Methods of Intercensal Population Estimation | 100 |
|  | The Role of Interpolation in Intercensal Estimates | 101 |
|  | Producing Intercensal Estimates by Interpolation | 102 |
|  | Intercensal Estimates and the Closure Problem | 110 |
|  | Key Issues With Interpolation Techniques | 112 |
|  | Detailed Intercensal Estimates: The Forward/Reverse Survival Rate Method | 113 |
|  | Summary | 119 |
| **7** | **Methods of Postcensal Population Estimation** | **123** |
|  | Elementary Postcensal Methods of Population Estimation | 125 |
|  | Advanced Postcensal Methods of Population Estimation | 133 |
|  | Summary | 158 |
| **8** | **Methods of Population Projection** | **161** |
|  | Ratio Allocation Methods | 163 |
|  | Mathematical Methods | 165 |
|  | Econometric Models | 176 |
|  | Cohort Component Method | 178 |
|  | Summary | 189 |
| **9** | **Population Estimates and Projections: Putting It All Together** | **193** |
|  | Issues in Postcensal Population Estimation | 193 |
|  | Issues in Population Projection | 196 |
|  | Summary | 198 |
|  | *References and Suggested Readings* | 201 |
|  | *Index* | 205 |

# Illustrations

**Figure**

8.1  Population Projections                                          167

**Tables**

3.1  Life Table: Total U.S. Population, 1987                          55
6.1  Intercensal Population Estimates With Arithmetic and
     Geometric Rates of Growth                                      107
6.2  Intercensal Adjustment                                         112
6.3  The Forward/Reverse Survival Rate Method                       118
7.1  The Ratio Correlation Method                                   154
8.1  Population Projections Under Alternative Growth
     Assumptions                                                    168
8.2  Calculation of the 1990 Expected Population Through
     Application of Life Table Survival Rates to the 1980
     Population                                                     180
8.3  Calculation of 1980 to 1990 Migration Rates Through
     Comparison of Observed 1990 Population With Expected
     1990 Population                                                182
8.4  Detailed Population Projections: 1990 to 2000 Through
     the Cohort Component Model                                     186

# Preface

It is fitting that the World Series is in progress as I write the preface to this book, since in a convoluted way the book has something of a relationship to baseball. More accurately, the book has a relationship to the classic comedy routine by Abbott and Costello, "Who's on First?" In 1987 I wrote an article on population growth in the United States that appeared in a leading demographic magazine. I had analyzed population trends between 1980 and 1986 at the county level and had given the manuscript an appropriately academic-sounding title which the editors of the magazine promptly changed to "Who's on First?" It did not really bother me too much, after all my work was going to be published, and I was getting paid in the bargain.

Some months later I received a letter from Thomas Gannon, an acquisitions editor for Quorum Books. It seemed he had run across the article and was writing to see if I would be interested in preparing a book on the subject. I answered his letter pointing out that the topic was not really the kind of material that would be appropriate for a book-length project but that I did have something in mind for a book on methods of population estimation and projection. I also pointed out that I did not have the time to work on such a project because I was trying to change jobs and wanted to get back into academia. A year later I was successful in obtaining an academic appointment and joined the faculty of Union College. After two hectic years I finally had some time to devote to writing, and I contacted Tom Gannon to see if Quorum were still interested in the idea I had for the book. Fortunately, they were, and I thank Tom Gannon for his help and advice while I was preparing the manuscript. In addition, I would like to thank Angela Morrison who copyedited the manuscript for Quorum. Her efforts have improved the clarity of the final product in many ways. I also extend my appreciation to Deborah Ross who served as the production editor and shepherded the work through the conversion process from a manuscript to a published volume.

Much of my time during the past year has been devoted to the writing of this book. My goal was an ambitious one. I wanted to produce a book detailing the major methods of population estimation and population projection in a clear and concise way that would allow the book to serve as a guide or resource for the marketing and planning professionals who are the frequent users of population estimates and projections. At the same time I wanted to produce a book with sufficient technical detail and background in basic demographic concepts that would make it useful to the working demographer. Time will tell if I have succeeded.

In the meantime I would like to extend my thanks to Signe I. Wetrogan of the Population Division of the U.S. Bureau of the Census who was kind enough to send me copies of the Bureau's latest population projections. I also would like to thank Robert W. Marx, Chief of the Geography Division of the U.S. Bureau of the Census, who was kind enough to send me a wealth of material describing census geographic concepts and products for the 1990 census. I hasten to add that neither of them bears any respon-sibility for the content of this book, and any errors or omissions are solely my responsibility.

I would like to include a personal note of thanks to Donald W. Hastings, Professor of Sociology at the University of Tennessee, Knoxville. Chip Hastings served as my professor and dissertation director when I was in the graduate program at the University of Tennessee, where he taught me a little bit of what he knows about demography. More important, he has remained a good friend. I should point out that any deficiencies in this book are more a reflection of my shortcomings as a student many years ago rather than his as a professor. Finally, I would like to thank Paul S. Moore, Academic Vice President of Union College. I could thank Pete Moore for several things he has done for me over the past three and a half years, but I think I am most appreciative of his momentary lapse in judgment in 1988 that brought me to Union College.

# Population Estimation
## and
# Projection

# 1

# Population Estimates and Projections: Introduction and Overview

In a rapidly changing environment the useful life of population data may be quite short. Although it is well and good to know what the population *was* at the time of the most recent census, it is often necessary to know what the population *is* today and what the population *may be* at some point in the future. Demographic parameters play an increasing role in the decision-making process, heightening the importance of population estimates and projections for a wide variety of individuals, including the business professional, the marketing and advertising specialist, the governmental planner, and the school administrator, among others.

This book is intended to serve as a guide to the major methods of population estimation and projection that have been developed to meet the need for demographic information. It is written at a general level to serve as an information resource for the nondemographic professional, but with sufficient attention to technical aspects of population methods to meet the needs of the applied demographer. The book begins with an introduction and overview discussing the differences between a population estimate and a population projection; some general rules of thumb with respect to the nature of population estimates and projections; a discussion of some practical issues with respect to levels of geography and detail in demographic characteristics such as age, race, and sex; and identifies the major strategies of population estimation and projection.

Chapters 2 through 5 provide a foundation in demographic concepts and techniques related to the production of population estimates and projections. Chapter 2 discusses the three basic demographic variables of fertility, mortality, and migration. The basic methods of constructing rates to measure fertility, mortality, and migration are illustrated and discussed along with the major advantages and limitations of each type of demographic rate. Chapter 3 focuses on the converse of mortality—survival. Survival rates actually are more frequently employed in the production of population projections, and they may be derived from a census survival technique or a life table analysis. Both the censal survival rate method and the life table method are discussed in chapter 3. Chapter 4 presents a discussion of the basic concepts in census geography. Most population estimates and projections are produced for areas of geography consistent with U.S. Bureau of the Census definitions, and chapter 4 discusses the basic census geographic concepts for both the 1980 and 1990 censuses. Chapter 5 discusses the major types and sources of data employed in the production of population estimates and projections. A discussion of the general categories of data such as census data, sample survey data, vital registration, and special sources of data is presented along with suggested sources or outlets for demographic data. Included in the discussion are a description of the major data products from the 1990 census that may be of use in the production of population estimates and projections, and the major media through which 1990 census data are disseminated.

The discussion of major methods of population estimation and projection is presented in chapters 6, 7, and 8. Methods of population estimation are presented in chapters 6 and 7. Chapter 6 focuses on methods of intercensal population estimation, and chapter 7 focuses on methods of postcensal population estimation. Major methods of population projection are identified and discussed in chapter 8. Chapter 9 presents a concluding discussion in which the major methods of population estimation and projection are put into perspective. The discussion in chapter 9 focuses on practical considerations and provides suggestions for evaluating the various methodologies presented in the book.

## POPULATION ESTIMATES AND PROJECTIONS

The concepts of population estimate and population projection are often confused even though the distinction between the two is usually simple and straightforward. The concepts are similar in that they each involve generating a number that is intended to indicate the size of the population of a given area at a specific point in time. In a sense, both population estimates and population projections make use of the basic demographic equation:

$$P_1 = P_0 + B - D + I - O$$

Where:
- $P_1$    is the current population
- $P_0$    is the population at a previous point in time
- $B$    is the number of births since $P_0$
- $D$    is the number of deaths since $P_0$
- $I$    is the number of inmigrants since $P_0$
- $O$    is the number of outmigrants since $P_0$

The simple demographic equation expresses the population at any given point in time as a function of the population at a previous point in time plus the amount of natural increase and net migration during the interim. Natural increase is simply the number of births minus the number of deaths in the area, and net migration is simply the number of inmigrants to the area minus the number of outmigrants away from the area. The difference between births and deaths comprising the amount of natural increase is the subject of a vast vital registration network, resulting in a large amount of current data. Net migration made up of the difference between inmigration and outmigration is not the direct subject of official data collection, and as a result one must rely on alternative data sources making the measurement of net migration more difficult.

While population estimates and population projections are each based on the logic of the demographic equation, there are some important differences between them centering on two key factors. The first factor differentiating a population estimate from a population projection is the time period involved. In general, a population estimate refers to the size of the population of an area in the recent past, while a population projection refers to the size of the population of an area at some point in the future. The second factor involves the type of data used in generating the population value. Population estimates are generally based on direct components of population change, such as the actual number of births and deaths occurring between the date of the previous population and the date of the estimate; in the absence of direct data, a population estimate will be based on symptomatic indicators of the components of population change. Symptomatic data are those data that move in concert with the data of direct interest. For example, a change in the school enrollments or the number of motor vehicles being registered may serve as symptomatic indicators of migration. Since population projections refer to the size of the population at a point in the future, they cannot be based on actual data comprising the components of population change. Population projections must in one form or another be based on the extension of either current or expected population trends into the future. All things being equal, a population estimate for a given area for a given point in time is preferable to a population projection for the same area and time period.

## The General Nature of Population Estimates

Methods of population estimation are employed in two broad applications: intercensal estimation and postcensal estimation. More attention by far is given to postcensal estimates, but intercensal estimates are used in some cases. Intercensal estimates result when one has population totals for a particular area from two successive censuses for the census years but does not have population totals for the intervening years. Intercensal estimate methodologies provide a way of estimating the population of the area on a year-by-year basis for the intercensal period. Major strategies for producing intercensal population estimates are detailed in chapter 6. Postcensal estimates involve estimating the population of an area after the most recent census or some other base period up to a point in the recent past. In most applications a population estimate is produced for the previous year based on the latest data available. Postcensal estimates are more likely to be in demand by planners and other similar users of population data. The major strategies for postcensal population estimation are detailed in chapter 7.

A wide range of population estimation methodologies have been developed. In part, the variety of methods is a response to the differing needs of users of population data; in part, it is a response to technical factors such as data availability and the technical expertise of the persons providing the estimates. No single set of generalizations is applicable to all population estimation methodologies, but some general guidelines may be offered that will apply in most cases.

1. Population estimates tend to be more accurate when produced at the national level rather than for geographic subareas within the nation. The national population is less likely to be impacted by migration than are regional subdivisions such as states or counties. In some cases the national borders may be closed to migration thus virtually eliminating the problem of obtaining migration data. In cases where there is migration, one is more likely to have some

form of migration registration at the national level, but very few nations will have an extensive registration system to track migration within the nation. Finally, fluctuation in local conditions may have a major impact on the population in the immediate area but will have virtually no impact on the national population. The creation of a major source of new employment is likely to result in a large population gain for an area, but most of the gain will be from some other area within the nation rather than from outside the nation. The net effect on the national population is negligible.

2. The greater the level of detail in the population estimates, the greater the level of error. Population estimates of the total population are generally more accurate than estimates that include some form of population detail such as age, race, or sex. Detailed population estimates require a greater level of data and more complex methodology than estimates for population totals only.

3. Estimates produced through the use of direct demographic data will be more accurate than estimates produced through the use of indirect or symptomatic data. Direct data are those involving any of the three parameters of population change: fertility, mortality, and migration. Potential indirect data sources would include a large number of variables such as school enrollments, automobile registrations, voting records, utility service hookups, and a variety of others. If given the choice, no one would choose to employ indirect data over direct data, but indirect data are often the only data available. The migration component of population change is especially likely to be estimated only through indirect data, particularly when population estimates are made at subnational levels of geography.

4. Beyond the issue of direct versus indirect data, the higher the quality of input data, the higher the quality of the resulting estimates. Most estimation methodologies begin with a base population at a previous point in time. A base population consisting of the most recent census is of higher quality and will yield better current estimates than a base population consisting of a previous estimate. A similar argument can be made for other data sources. Data resulting from official sources whose collection is mandatory will almost always be of higher quality than data collected on an informal basis.

5. The longer the period of time between the enumeration of the base population and the estimation date, the greater the degree of error in the estimate. Estimates made for shorter periods of time—for example, for 2 to 3 years past the base period—will generally be more accurate than estimates made 8 or 9 years past the base year. Ironically, the need for current estimates is more critical the farther one moves from the base period. Most planning and marketing needs may be met by using census data that are only 1 or 2 years old. The same cannot be said when the most recent census data are 8 or 9 years old.

6. In the most general case, the simpler mathematical methods of population estimation will produce results with greater error than the more complex methods of estimation. Simpler mathematical methods of population estimation include interpolation, extrapolation, and proration. Interpolation techniques are most often used for intercensal estimates where the population is known at a beginning point and an end point but not for the intervening years. Extrapolation methods are essentially a simple type of population projection technique, and proration methods involve allocating the known population of a larger area among the several smaller subareas comprising the larger area. More complex methods of population estimation will include cohort techniques where each major age group of the population will be estimated separately, ratio correlation techniques which involve the development of a statistical regression equation, and several others.

The mathematical methods will usually result in estimates of poorer quality than the more complex methods, with mathematical extrapolation techniques resulting in the least accurate estimates. It should be noted, however, that the use of a more complex method does not necessarily guarantee a quality result. The more complex the method, the more demanding the data requirements, and in some cases the required data will simply not be available or will be of poor quality. No method of population estimation based on poor quality data will produce an accurate result, and complex methods of estimation are no exception. In fact, in the absence of quality data, a simpler method of population estimation may be the best choice.

7. No single method of population estimation will always be the best choice. Over time, one will achieve better results from a program of population estimation by employing a variety of estimation techniques. Using multiple techniques will provide a means of checking the validity of the estimate since similar results obtained from a variety of different methods tend to suggest the overall accuracy of the result. In many cases, one will be well served by averaging the results of several estimates to obtain the final population estimate.

## The General Nature of Population Projections

It has been pointed out that population projections are based in one form or another on extensions of current trends or the application of expected population trends into the future. Actually, each strategy results in a slightly different type of product. Population projections traditionally are based on the extension of current population trends into the future or on the application of an alternative set of population trends to the base population. The typical situation is one where the projections are based on the assumed continuation of the current situation, or perhaps on a high-growth scenario, or on a low-growth scenario, and so on. In none of these cases is there an explicit expectation that the result of the projection process will actually equal the population of the area in the future. Naturally, one would hope that the projections are accurate, but in a real sense the nature of population projections is that of a "what would happen if . . . ?" exercise. For example, "What would happen to the population if current trends continue," or "What would happen to the population if growth rates increased by 10%," or "What would happen to the population if mortality rates declined by one-third?"

In contrast, the application of *expected* population trends to a base population is generally regarded as a population forecast. In the case of a population forecast there is an implied expectation that the forecast population value will closely approximate the value of the population at a future date. Some regard the distinction between a population projection and a population forecast as trivial, but in many ways the distinction is a valid one. Population projections are more the result of a technical process. In one sense, if the procedure is done correctly, there is no such thing as an incorrect population projection. Should it turn out that the projected value of a population is significantly too high or too low, one simply acknowledges that the assumptions upon which the projection was based were wrong. Technically the projection is correct even though it may turn out to be far different from the actual population observed at the end of the projection period. A population forecast may be done in a technically correct fashion but may turn out to be incorrect since there is an implied judgment behind it. While the distinction between a projection and a forecast is sometimes vague, further confusing the issue is the fact that the methodologies of projection and forecasting are the same.

The general methodological strategies for producing population projections fall into four basic categories: (1) ratio allocation methods, (2) mathematical extrapolation methods, (3) econometric methods, and (4) cohort component methods. Ratio allocation and mathematical extrapolation methods are simpler strategies for producing population projections. Ratio allocation methods are used to allocate an existing population projection for a larger area among the subareas that comprise it. For example, a state population projection may be allocated among the various counties that comprise it, resulting not only in the original projection for the state but in individual projections for each county. Mathematical extrapolation methods involve the application of a selected growth rate into the future.

Econometric methods and cohort component methods are somewhat more complex strategies for producing population projections. These methods not only require additional technical expertise but require a great deal more input data in order to complete the projection process. Econometric methods project population as part of an overall forecast of the economy in an area and usually generate a population projection by linking future population to expected future employment. Cohort component methods project population by examining separately for each cohort (or age group) in the population the three major components of population change: births, deaths, and net migration. In some applications, the results from these more complex methods are likely to be more accurate compared with the simpler approaches, but the real advantage is in the greater detail that is available in the final data product. Cohort component methods generally result in population projections with the highest level of detail by age, race, and sex of any projection method.

The choice of a projection methodology should be based on several factors, including the geographic level of the projection, the length of the projection period, the desired level of detail in the projection, and the availability of input data. The simpler methods of projection have a wider range of application and may be used to produce population projections at almost any geographic level. Econometric and cohort component strategies have more extensive data demands and are less appropriate for smaller areas of geography. The length of the projection period may vary from relatively short-range projections of under 10 years, to middle-range projections of 10 to 25 years, to long-range projections of over 25 years. In some applications, projections have even been produced for over a 100-year period. Any of the methodological strategies may be used for short-range projections, and all should produce acceptable results provided the data requirements have been met and the projections are done in a technically correct manner. Middle-range projections are more appropriate for the more complex methods that take into account some of the underlying population processes that result in population change. Again, it is assumed that the data requirements may be met and that the methods are applied correctly. Long-range projections are a problem for any methodological strategy, particularly in cases where the projection period is over 50 years. For highly detailed population projections by age, race, and sex, the clear choice is a cohort component method. Econometric methods result in some detail by age, but not as much as cohort component methods. The simpler projection techniques result in little if any detail beyond the population total. Finally, all too often the real determinant of methodology will be the availability of data. Econometric methods and cohort component methods have extensive data requirements; unless they are met, one must simply choose an alternative methodology.

While there are exceptions to any set of generalizations, the following points tend to be descriptive of the discussion of the major methods of population projection presented in chapter 8.

1. Results of any methodological strategy are likely to be better the shorter the length of the projection period. Population change is a dynamic process with change sometimes occurring in ways that are unanticipated. The longer the length of the projection period, the more time will be available for the unanticipated to occur.

2. Population projections tend to be more accurate for areas that have low levels of vital rates such as fertility and mortality. There are far fewer examples of areas with low rates of vital events turning dramatically higher than there are of areas with high rates of vital events turning dramatically lower. The population of areas with rates of vital events already low will be more predictable as a result.

3. Results of population projections will tend to be more accurate the larger the area of geography analyzed. Several factors operate to improve the results for large areas. Population processes are volatile at times, but subarea fluctuations tend to be averaged out as one moves to a larger area of geography. For example, unusually high rates of population growth in one area will often be matched by unusually low rates of growth in another. In addition, migration represents one of the most difficult population processes with which to deal. As the area of geography increases, the problems due to migration decrease.

4. Results of population projection tend to be more accurate for areas that grow at a stable and moderate rate. Areas that experience unusually low rates of growth or unusually high rates of growth are more difficult to project than areas with moderate growth. The worst results are likely to be seen in areas with extreme rates of growth that fluctuate from time to time. Projecting population is analogous to trying to hit a moving target: It is generally easier when the target is moving at a moderate, predictable rate over time.

## SUMMARY

Population estimates and population projections play an increasingly important role in the strategic decision-making process of business professionals, planners, educators, or anyone concerned about the current or expected size of the population. This chapter discussed the similarities and differences between population estimates and population projections, and the distinction that is often made between a population projection and a population forecast. Some generalizations concerning the nature of population estimates and population projections were offered. Finally, the chapter provided a brief overview of what is to follow in the remainder of the book.

# 2

# Population Concepts and Measures

This chapter introduces the major population concepts of fertility, mortality, and migration which are each involved in the production of population estimates and projections. Included is a discussion of the major methods of measuring the basic demographic variables and some of the issues one must consider when selecting a technique to measure fertility, mortality, or migration.

Many different methodologies may be used in the estimation and projection of populations, and each has its own special demographic data requirements. Some methodologies also require data of a non-demographic nature such as school enrollment figures, driver's license data, or the number of medicare recipients in a particular area. Non-demographic data sources will be discussed later as selected methodologies are described and illustrated. This chapter focuses on the major demographic data concepts and measures employed in the production of population estimates and projections. Included in the discussion is the base population, which one may think of as the starting point of the estimation or projection process, and the demographic concepts of fertility, mortality, and migration. The latter three concepts constitute the dynamic variables of population change which determine additions or subtractions to the base population.

## THE BASE POPULATION

Central to most methods of population estimation and projection is the concept of a base population. The base population may be considered the starting point of the estimation or projection process. It is the known population at some point in the past of the geographic area to be estimated or projected. Most often the base population will be taken from the most recent decennial census. The population of the United States is enumerated once each decade in years ending in zero, and the resulting census figure becomes a reliable base from which to estimate or project populations at a later time. On occasion, a special census may be conducted for a particular geographic area prior to the regular national census. A special census is normally conducted at the request and expense of the political jurisdiction to be enumerated. Most often the request is made for areas that have experienced unusually rapid population growth since the last decennial census. When available, the special census count provides an excellent figure to use as a population base for purposes of later estimation or projection.

## THE CLASSIC DEMOGRAPHIC VARIABLES

The field of demography focuses on the three classic demographic variables: fertility, mortality, and migration. In more common words, these are, respectively, the number of people being born, the number of people dying, and the number of people moving from place to place. The following discussion of the major population concepts and measures is organized along the lines of the three demographic variables.

### Fertility

Demographers have constructed literally scores of fertility measures, and each has its own special purpose. Fortunately, fertility measures employed in methods of population estimation and projection are usually selected from a far smaller group. This discussion of fertility measures focuses on four key fertility indicators: (1) the crude birth rate, (2) the child woman ratio, (3) the general fertility rate, and (4) the age specific fertility rate.

*The Crude Birth Rate.* The crude birth rate (CBR) is the most basic measure of fertility in general use. The CBR is defined as the number of births per year for each 1,000 people living in a given geographic area.

The midyear population is most often used as the base upon which the rate is calculated. The formula for the CBR is as follows:

$$CBR = \frac{\text{number of births in the year}}{\text{midyear population}} \times 1,000$$

The calculations are straightforward and relatively easy as illustrated by the hypothetical data below.

| Midyear Population | | Births |
|---|---|---|
| White | 488,750 | 7,090 |
| Nonwhite | 86,250 | 1,910 |
| Total | 575,000 | 9,000 |

In this example, the crude birth rate for the area of interest would be calculated by dividing the number of births occurring during the calendar year by the total midyear population of the area and multiplying the result by 1,000.

$$CBR = \frac{9,000}{575,000} \times 1,000 = 15.65$$

Similar calculations can be made for the white and the nonwhite population:

$$\text{White CBR} = \frac{7,090}{488,750} \times 1,000 = 14.51$$

$$\text{Nonwhite CBR} = \frac{1,910}{86,250} \times 1,000 = 22.14$$

The CBR is based on vital registration data which are usually readily available on an annual basis, and it is easy to calculate. Ironically, the numerator consisting of the number of births in an area is based on data gathered from vital registration information, while the denominator consisting of the midyear population is usually the product of a current population estimate. The CBR may also be calculated for a variety of geographic levels and for a variety of racial categories.

One disadvantage of the CBR is that it is a crude rate—fertility is calculated based on total population size without taking into account the age or sex structure of the population. The lack of specificity with respect to population characteristics increases the risk of upward or downward bias when the CBR is used in methods of population estimation or projection. The problem will arise when the characteristics of the population to be estimated or projected differ in some substantial way from the characteristics of the population serving as the basis for the calculation of the crude birth rate. It is therefore critical that the CBR be calculated from a population similar to that which is to be estimated or projected in order to avoid the introduction of bias into the results.

*The Child Woman Ratio.* The child woman ratio (CWR) is a censal measure of fertility; it is based on census data collected every 10 years rather than on vital registration data which may be collected every year. The CWR is defined as the number of children under 5 years of age per 1,000 women aged 15–44 years. The formula for the CWR is as follows:

$$\text{CWR} = \frac{\text{number of children under age 5}}{\text{number of women aged 15–44 years}} \times 1,000$$

Calculation of the CWR is not difficult, but it does require detailed population data specified by at least age and sex and by race if one desires to calculate a separate CWR for each racial category. The following data may be used to illustrate the calculation of the CWR.

|  | | | | Race | | |
|  | Total | | White | | Black | |
| Age | Male | Female | Male | Female | Male | Female |
|---|---|---|---|---|---|---|
| Under 5 | 1,312 | 1,241 | 1,303 | 1,222 | 154 | 168 |
| 5–9 | 1,452 | 1,374 | 1,439 | 1,358 | 9 | 14 |
| 10–14 | 1,543 | 1,372 | 1,528 | 1,365 | 13 | 6 |
| 15–19 | 1,443 | 1,480 | 1,415 | 1,460 | 25 | 12 |
| 20–24 | 1,210 | 1,282 | 1,182 | 1,260 | 24 | 20 |
| 25–29 | 1,106 | 1,166 | 1,090 | 1,158 | 14 | 6 |
| 30–34 | 1,044 | 1,114 | 1,037 | 1,101 | 4 | 8 |
| 35–39 | 875 | 948 | 872 | 936 | 1 | 11 |
| 40–44 | 745 | 769 | 737 | 759 | 4 | 8 |

These data are typical of what might be reported in a census summary table for a county, although the full data table would include persons of Spanish origin, which would account for the discrepancy between the total population reported and the sum of the white and black population. The child woman ratio would then be calculated for the total population by dividing the number of children under age 5 by the number of women aged 15–44 years and then multiplying the resulting value by 1,000.

$$\text{CWR} = \frac{2,553}{6,759} \times 1,000 = 377.7$$

A separate CWR could be calculated for each of the two racial categories of white and black.

$$\text{White CWR} = \frac{2,525}{6,674} \times 1,000 = 378.3$$

$$\text{Black CWR} = \frac{23}{65} \times 1,000 = 353.8$$

The CWR is easy to compute and the data are readily available from census sources. In addition, the measure may be computed on a variety of geographic levels making it appropriate for a number of methods of population estimation and projection. The CWR may also be calculated easily for different racial categories.

There are some disadvantages associated with the CWR. The most serious problem is the fact that children under age 5 are more likely to be under-enumerated in a census than are women aged 15–44. The resulting bias tends to underestimate the amount of fertility present in an area. Further, the CWR does not take into account the fact that levels of fertility vary widely across the female's reproductive life span. For example, the overall fertility rate in 1988 was 67.2 births per 1,000 women aged 15–44 years. Fertility rates ranged, however, from a low of 4.8 births per 1,000 women aged 40–44 years to a high of 113.4 births per 1,000 women aged 25–29 years. Using the CWR may result in the introduction of bias if the population for a particular geographic area to be estimated or projected has an unusually large concentration of females in a critical age group.

An additional limitation is illustrated by the data used in the above example. The black population reported for the hypothetical county is relatively small compared to that of the white population. The resulting problem with respect to the calculation of the CWR is that the end result is subject to distortion and may yield an unreliable CWR. The addition or subtraction of as few as five black children under age 5 would have a significant impact on the size of the resulting CWR since the base population of women aged 15–44 is so small. For example, five additional children under age 5 would increase the black CWR from 353.8 to 430.8 (an increase of over 21%), while the subtraction of five children under age 5 would reduce the black CWR to 276.9 (a decrease of over 21%). Finally, the CWR is limited in that as a censal measure of fertility it is calculated using data that are collected only once every 10 years. The 10-year interval between censuses is more likely to be a problem in those areas where underlying fertility patterns are changing rapidly than in areas characterized by stable fertility patterns.

*The General Fertility Rate.* The general fertility rate (GFR) is a measure of fertility that overcomes one of the disadvantages associated with the crude birth rate since the GFR does take into account the sex structure of the population. The GFR is defined as the number of births per year per 1,000 women aged 15–44 in the population. Unlike the CBR, the general fertility rate is calculated using the population that is most likely to give birth (women aged 15–44). It is therefore a more sensitive indicator of fertility. The formula for the general fertility rate is as follows:

$$\text{GFR} = \frac{\text{number of births}}{\text{midyear female population aged 15–44}} \times 1,000$$

Calculation of the GFR is relatively easy but does require population data detailed by age and sex. The GFR is also unique with respect to the fertility measures discussed up to this point in that its data requirements may represent a hybrid between current vital statistic data and decennial census data. The number of births will be obtained from current vital registrations, but the midyear female population may be obtained from census data or in some cases from current population estimates detailed by age and sex. In most cases detailed population data by age are available only from the census, but the population of some geographic areas will be estimated with detail by age and sex periodically.

Detailed age data similar to those provided for calculation of the CWR are summarized below and may be used to illustrate the calculation of a GFR with the addition of the following hypothetical annual birth data:

**Midyear Population of**
**Females Aged 15–44**                          **Births**

| White    | 26,767 | 1,687 |
|----------|--------|-------|
| Nonwhite | 3,653  | 316   |
| Total    | 30,420 | 2,003 |

$$\text{White GFR} = \frac{1,687}{26,767} \times 1,000 = 63.0$$

$$\text{Nonwhite GFR} = \frac{316}{3,653} \times 1,000 = 86.5$$

$$\text{Total GFR} = \frac{2,003}{30,420} \times 1,000 = 65.8$$

Use of the GFR will generally provide superior results to that of the crude birth rate. There are, however, potential limitations in using the GFR. The GFR is a measure of fertility requiring greater knowledge of the population, and that information may not be available in all cases. Further, as was the case with the child woman ratio, fertility levels vary over a female's reproductive career, and this fact is not taken into account with the GFR. Still, the GFR remains one of the more important fertility measures when estimating or projecting populations. It may be computed for a variety of geographic areas and for multiple racial groups.

*The Age Specific Fertility Rate.* The age specific fertility rate (ASFR) is an extension of the general fertility rate, but the ASFR provides an even greater level of specification in the population base used in the fertility calculation. The age specific fertility rate is defined as the number of births per year per 1,000 women of a specified age group in the population. Age specific fertility rates will usually be calculated for each 5-year age group of women beginning with the 15–19-year-old group through the 40–44-year-old group. The formula for the age specific fertility rate is as follows:

$$\text{ASFR} = \frac{\text{number of births}}{\text{midyear female population of selected age group}} \times 1,000$$

Typically, a schedule of age specific rates will be produced with a separate rate reported for each cohort or age group in the population. Hypothetical data are reported below, but the resulting ASFRs are compatible with current U.S. fertility levels.

| Age | Female Population | Births | ASFR |
|---|---|---|---|
| 15–19 | 9,990 | 535 | 53.6 |
| 20–24 | 13,850 | 1,544 | 111.5 |
| 25–29 | 11,320 | 1,279 | 113.0 |
| 30–34 | 9,115 | 675 | 74.1 |
| 35–39 | 6,375 | 180 | 28.2 |
| 40–44 | 5,240 | 25 | 4.8 |

The age specific fertility rate overcomes one of the major disadvantages seen in other measures of fertility by using a more narrowly defined age group in its calculation. The result is to control bias that may be introduced by the variation in fertility levels that occur over the reproductive span. A schedule of age specific fertility rates will generally be the most sensitive indicator of fertility in a given area. Separate schedules of ASFRs may be computed for each racial category desired in the analysis, provided the required detailed population and vital registration data are available.

A frequent disadvantage of the ASFR is that the detailed population data required for its calculation may not be available. This is likely to be a problem as one deals with smaller areas of geography in the production of population estimates and projections. One may still encounter problems with the ASFR even in instances when the required data are available. For example, a relatively small number of women in one or two of the age groups for which the ASFR is calculated may lead to unreliable estimates of fertility for those age groups, since the change of a few births either way will have a greater impact on the resulting rate. The problem is not likely to occur in large geographic areas such as states, but use of the ASFR at the county or subcounty level may be problematic. Bias from a small population base is more likely to occur when ASFRs are computed for more than one racial group, since the total female population is being allocated among an increasing number of categories.

Each of the fertility measures described in this section is appropriate for use in the production of population estimates and projections. The crude birth rate is perhaps the easiest to calculate and has the least demanding data requirements. The CBR may also be calculated for separate racial groups with little difficulty. As a crude rate, however, it is not as sensitive an indicator of fertility as some other choices. The child woman ratio requires more detailed population data than the CBR, but the data are readily available from census sources. A major advantage of the CWR is that it is based on census data that may be reported for a wide range of geographic areas and racial subgroups. The CWR, however, is perhaps the least sensitive of the fertility measures discussed in this section. Census data are collected only once every 10 years, so the validity of the CWR is likely to diminish over time. The problem of underenumeration of young children also reduces the utility of the CWR. Yet, in the absence of current vital registration data, the CWR may be the only fertility measure available.

The general fertility rate and the age specific fertility rate provide increased sensitivity to fertility measurement. Calculation of each of these measures of fertility is based on the population that is genuinely at risk of childbirth, resulting in more precise indicators of fertility than the CBR or the CWR. The general fertility rate is perhaps the most versatile of the three. The GFR combines the advantage of an accurately specified population base with minimal additional data requirements. The result is a sensitive fertility measure that is still applicable for a large number of population estimation and projection methodologies.

The age specific fertility rate possesses all of the advantages of the GFR and extends them by providing greater specificity in the population at risk. This is not a trivial issue as examination of the schedule of age specific fertility rates presented in the previous example will demonstrate. Fertility levels do vary widely over the course of a female's reproductive life span, and the ASFR is ideally suited to measure the variation. Ostensibly the result will be a set of highly sensitive indicators of fertility, and in some applications this may be the case. The creation of a schedule of fertility rates each calculated on a relatively small population base, however, is not without a potential risk. The smaller the population base used to calculate the ASFR, the greater the instability of the rate and the greater the likelihood of bias as a result. The ASFR may be used for geographic areas with a total large population with little chance of bias. Problems are more likely to arise when one attempts to produce a set of ASFRs for a smaller geographic area below the state level, such as a county or a town.

### Mortality

The second of the three classic demographic variables considered in this section is mortality. Levels of mortality are equally as important as those of fertility when estimating or projecting a population. Mortality may be measured in a number of different ways, but only a few are of interest in this discussion. Of primary interest are the following measures of mortality: the crude death rate, the age specific death rate, and the infant mortality rate. Demographers construct a variety of additional mortality measures such as cause specific death rates, which provide information on numbers of deaths due to a specified cause such as heart disease or cancer, but cause specific rates are not required in the production of population estimates and projections.

*The Crude Death Rate.* The crude death rate (CDR) is a measure of mortality that is directly analogous to the crude birth rate measure of fertility. The CDR is defined as the number of deaths per year for each

1,000 people living in a given geographic area. The midyear population is most often used as the base or denominator, and the actual number of deaths in the calendar year comprises the numerator. The formula for the CDR is as follows:

$$\text{CDR} = \frac{\text{number of deaths in the year}}{\text{midyear population}} \times 1,000$$

The calculations are straightforward and relatively easy, following the same pattern as the crude birth rate. Hypothetical data below may be used to illustrate the calculation of a CDR.

| Midyear Population | | Deaths |
|---|---|---|
| White | 488,750 | 4,423 |
| Nonwhite | 86,250 | 647 |
| Total | 575,000 | 5,070 |

The overall crude death rate is obtained by dividing the number of deaths for the calendar year by the total midyear population as follows:

$$\text{CDR} = \frac{5,070}{575,000} \times 1,000 = 8.82$$

Similar calculations can be made for the white and the nonwhite population:

$$\text{White CDR} = \frac{4,423}{488,750} \times 1,000 = 9.05$$

$$\text{Nonwhite CDR} = \frac{647}{86,250} \times 1,000 = 7.50$$

Nonwhite mortality as measured by the crude death rate is usually at levels below that of white mortality. The differential in mortality levels between the white and nonwhite population does not reflect a health advantage for the nonwhite population. To the contrary, any health advantage associated with one racial group or the other would tend to favor the white population. One would hasten to add that in most cases the health advantage of whites compared with nonwhites is a function of status differences and is not biologically or genetically based. The fact that crude rates imply lower mortality among the nonwhite population is a function of the differences in the respective age structures of the white and nonwhite population. One may recall from the previous discussion on fertility that birth rates for nonwhites were higher than those for whites. The result of the fertility differentials is to have a larger proportion of nonwhites in the younger age groups which are in turn less likely to die in any given year. Conversely, the white population with its lower birth rate has a greater proportion of its population in the older age groups, and the probability of death in any given year increases with age once one survives the first few years of life. As a result, the total population of whites appears to have a higher single year death rate than the total population of nonwhites.

It is frequently desirable to calculate crude death rates for each sex in addition to the calculations by race. The crude rate mortality differentials by sex are often as large or larger than those by race as the U.S. mortality data for 1988 presented below indicate.

### Crude Death Rates

|          | Female | Male | Total |
|----------|--------|------|-------|
| White    | 8.60   | 9.52 | 9.05  |
| Nonwhite | 6.52   | 8.72 | 7.58  |
| Total    | 8.27   | 9.40 | 8.82  |

In each case the female crude death rate is below that of the corresponding male rate. It is remarkable that female crude death rates are below that of males since there is some bias introduced in the rates by the relative age structures of the male and female populations. A larger proportion of the female population is located in the older age groups which normally are subject to a higher probability of mortality in any given year. The bias resulting from the age structure should operate to reduce the apparent CDR of males to a level at or below that of females much in the way that nonwhites have a lower CDR than whites. The fact that the female CDR remains below that of males indicates the considerable difference between mortality levels of males and females.

It is possible to adjust the data statistically and control for the effects of age in the respective crude death rates. The resulting age adjusted death rates indicate what the respective crude death rates for males and females would be if both groups had an identical age structure; that is, if there were the same proportion of males and females in each age group. Actual U.S. mortality data for 1988 are presented below to illustrate the age adjusted mortality differentials by sex (National Center for Health Statistics, 1990b).

| Age Adjusted Crude Death Rates | | | |
|---|---|---|---|
|  | Female | Male | Total |
| White | 3.84 | 6.64 | 5.10 |
| Nonwhite | 5.24 | 9.04 | 6.93 |
| Total | 4.04 | 6.97 | 5.36 |

The results are rather dramatic. Male crude death rates are approximately 1.7 times those of females in each category. Note also that controlling for the effects of the age structure had the effect of reversing the relationship between white and nonwhite crude death rates.

The crude death rate is easy to calculate much as its fertility counterpart is. In addition to the ease of calculation, the CDR is often a wise choice for estimation or projection methods in areas plagued by a shortage or lack of vital registration data. Certainly in most areas of the developed world, vital registration data are usually readily available and, in fact, may even be a little more accurate than those available for fertility. Mortality almost always comes to the attention of the authorities and is registered in the vital statistics data, while fertility may occasionally go unreported for an extended period of time. The CDR may be calculated for multiple levels of geography, for a variety of racial groups, and by sex assuming the requisite data are available. Like any crude rate, however, the CDR is likely to result in bias if the base upon which it is calculated is substantially different from the population to which it is applied.

*The Age Specific Death Rate.* The age specific death rate (ASDR) provides a measure of mortality for narrowly specified age groups. The ASDR is directly analogous to the age specific fertility rate discussed previously. The ASDR is defined as the number of deaths per 1,000 population for a particular age group. The formula for an ASDR is as follows:

$$\text{ASDR} = \frac{\text{number of deaths}}{\text{midyear population of selected age group}} \times 1,000$$

In some applications the ASDR will be reported for each 100,000 persons in the population, in which case one would simply substitute 100,000 for 1,000 in the formula. Hypothetical data are provided below to illustrate the calculation of the ASDR per 1,000 population:

| Age | Population | Deaths | ASDR |
|-----|-----------|--------|------|
| 5–14 | 7,690 | 2 | .26 |
| 15–24 | 6,865 | 7 | 1.02 |
| 75–84 | 1,535 | 97 | 63.20 |

While the data employed to illustrate the calculation of the ASDR are hypothetical, the resulting values for the death rates are in line with current U.S. mortality patterns. The example also illustrates the desirability of reporting the ASDR per 100,000 persons. Using the larger multiplier will have the effect of increasing the reported ASDR by a factor of 100 and would eliminate the fractional number for the 5–14 age group. One should also note that the ASDR may be calculated for a variety of age groupings. The current example reports results for three cohorts consisting of a 10-year age interval, but the rate may just as easily be calculated for 5-year cohorts or even for single years of age provided the required data are available.

Age specific death rates vary considerably across the life span as illustrated by the U.S. mortality data for 1988 presented below. The ASDR is expressed per 100,000 population rather than the 1,000 population base used in the previous example (National Center for Health Statistics, 1990b).

| Age | ASDR |
|-----|------|
| Under 1 | 1,008.3 |
| 1–4 | 50.9 |
| 5–14 | 25.8 |
| 15–24 | 102.1 |
| 25–34 | 135.4 |
| 35–44 | 219.6 |
| 45–54 | 486.2 |
| 55–64 | 1,235.6 |
| 65–74 | 2,729.8 |
| 75–84 | 6,321.3 |
| 85 and older | 15,594.0 |

The pattern of variability in age specific death rates is remarkable for a number of reasons. One of the most striking features is the relatively high risk of death among infants as indicated by the ASDR for those under 1 year of age when just over 1,008 infants out of every 100,000 infants is expected to die within one year of birth. It is not until the age 55–64 cohort that the risk of mortality exceeds that faced by those in their first year of life. For this reason it is customary to present an ASDR for the first year of life and then for years 1–4 before presenting the data in 5- or 10-year cohort intervals as illustrated above.

In many respects it is more important to be aware of variation in mortality rates as expressed by the ASDR than it is to be aware of variation in fertility rates. To use the simplest case of population estimation or projection by focusing only on fertility and mortality, one may envision the problem as an exercise in taking a known population at a particular point in time and then adding the appropriate number of new members due to fertility and subtracting the appropriate number of members due to mortality. It is true that fertility rates vary across the female reproductive period; however, all of the new members that are produced representing additions to the population enter the current population at the same point—that is, we are all born at the same age of zero, so the only question is one of volume. How many births will occur at a particular point in time? There is no allocation problem in terms of where in the age structure to put the new additions; they all go into the youngest cohort identified. The case of mortality represents a greater challenge. One must not only know the volume of mortality but must also know how to allocate the population loss since one may die at any age. In the case of mortality it is not enough to know how many people will die in a given period. One must also know from what age groups they will die.

Separate age specific death rates may also be calculated by sex and racial groupings. As the crude death rates illustrated, there are important mortality differentials by race and sex in addition to those by age. The calculations involved in creating highly detailed ASDRs to include sex or race are not difficult and simply follow the same pattern of the basic ASDR. A major problem may be finding the detailed population and vital event data necessary for the calculations. Even the data requirements, however, may be met with little difficulty, although not all levels of geography will be covered by detailed vital statistics reporting.

The major challenge in attempting to create highly detailed ASDRs is that the population base one uses in the calculation of the rate becomes increasingly smaller as greater detail is added. The smaller the base population, the greater the likelihood of bias since the change of one or two deaths either way will have a greater impact on the resulting rate. Detailed mortality data are desirable, but there are limits to how small a population base one should be willing to accept in the calculation of the rates. ASDRs specified by sex and race should be employed only when examining geographic areas with a large total population and sufficient numbers within each subgroup to avoid the introduction of bias.

The ASDR overcomes the primary disadvantage of the crude death rate which tends to apply too broad a brush to estimates of mortality. A schedule of ASDRs will more accurately portray mortality in a given area by taking advantage of the variation in mortality rates represented by each of the age specific death rates. One does run the risk, however, of overextending the population base by creating too many age specific death rates and encountering the resulting introduction of bias when too small a subpopulation base is used in the calculation of an ASDR. In such cases, a small fluctuation in the number of deaths will result in a disproportionate change in the resulting ASDR.

*The Infant Mortality Rate.* The final mortality rate considered in this section is the infant mortality rate (IMR). Infant mortality is of vital importance in the calculation of many types of population estimation and projection techniques. The discussion of age specific death rates highlighted some of the dramatic differences in mortality rates one may observe by age, and one of the most remarkable results was the high risk of mortality for those in their first year of life. It is not surprising then that rates of infant mortality often play a major role in the estimation or projection of a population.

Infant mortality refers to mortality of infants within the first year of life. The conventional infant mortality rate is defined as the number of deaths of infants per 1,000 live births in a given calendar year. The formula for a conventional infant mortality rate is as follows:

$$IMR = \frac{\text{number of deaths to infants}}{\text{number of live births}} \times 1,000$$

An infant mortality rate defined in these terms is relatively easy to calculate given the hypothetical data below. Just as in previous examples, the data have been constructed to result in infant mortality rates indicative of the current U.S. mortality patterns.

| Calendar Year Births | | Infant Deaths |
|---|---|---|
| White | 311,659 | 2,593 |
| Nonwhite | 74,353 | 1,298 |
| Total | 386,012 | 3,891 |

Conventional infant mortality rates for the total population would be calculated in the following manner:

$$IMR = \frac{3,891}{386,012} \times 1,000 = 10.08$$

Separate rates for the white and nonwhite population would be calculated in a similar fashion.

$$\text{White IMR} = \frac{2,593}{311,659} \times 1,000 = 8.32$$

$$\text{Nonwhite IMR} = \frac{1,298}{74,353} \times 1,000 = 17.45$$

The IMR discussed thus far has been referred to as a conventional infant mortality rate. Conventional measures of infant mortality do not measure infant mortality as precisely as they may first appear. A true infant mortality rate would be based on the actual mortality experience of a specific cohort of infants traced throughout their first year of life. The difficulty in constructing such a rate is the fact that infants born in any given year may die in either of two calendar years and still die within the first year of life. Consider the example of an infant born on the first day of November. That infant has 2 months of exposure to mortality during the calendar year of his birth, and 10 months of exposure to mortality during the next calendar year. As long as the infant dies prior to his first birthday, his death should be classified as an infant death. But if one examines the formula for the conventional infant mortality rate, it is clear that the numerator, or number of infants dying during the calendar year, is actually made up of two different birth cohorts. Some of the deaths are to infants born in the current calendar year, and some are to infants born in the previous calendar year. The infant born on the first of November would be classified as an infant death only if he died during November or December since those are the only 2 months of exposure to mortality during his calendar year of birth.

It is possible to calculate a true infant mortality rate and overcome the bias introduced by a conventional mortality rate. The difficulty in doing so is in obtaining the necessary vital statistics data. One must have access to mortality data with exact age at death and then combine mortality records for two successive calendar years. One would then be able to calculate accurately the rate of mortality for a given cohort of infants over their first year of life. In many cases one will not be able to meet the strict data requirements necessary to calculate a true infant mortality rate. An alternative solution is to employ a separation factor on the number of infant deaths in a given calendar year. The result is to allocate a portion of a particular year's infant deaths to one birth cohort and the remainder of the infant deaths to the next birth cohort. The size of the separation factor is usually based on previous empirical studies that have examined monthly infant mortality data in detail. The solution is not perfect, but the results are acceptable in most cases.

The concept of infant mortality is of such importance that it is frequently separated into two major components. Neonatal mortality refers to infant deaths within the first 28 days following birth. Postneonatal mortality refers to infant deaths following the first 28 days of birth but within the first year of life. Each of these rates is computed on a conventional basis just as the total infant mortality rate is; taken together, the neonatal mortality rate and the postneonatal mortality rate will sum to the total infant mortality rate. Data presented below indicate the current levels of infant mortality per 1,000 live births in the United States (National Center for Health Statistics, 1990a).

|  | **Infant** | **Infant Mortality** Neonatal | **Postneonatal** |
|---|---|---|---|
| White | 8.51 | 5.36 | 3.15 |
| Male | 9.52 | 5.95 | 3.57 |
| Female | 7.44 | 4.75 | 2.69 |
| Nonwhite | 15.04 | 9.66 | 5.38 |
| Male | 16.21 | 10.49 | 5.72 |
| Female | 13.82 | 8.80 | 5.02 |
| Total | 9.95 | 6.31 | 3.64 |
| Male | 10.99 | 6.95 | 4.04 |
| Female | 8.86 | 5.65 | 3.21 |

As the data indicate, it is possible to calculate the range of infant mortality rates for a variety of race and sex categories. Similar data are available for blacks in addition to the nonwhite category. As is the case with many of the vital rates discussed in this chapter, the problem is not one of difficult calculation but one of data availability. National data for the United States are readily available, but in general one will find that the smaller the level of geography, the less detailed data will be available.

Each of the measures of mortality discussed in this section may be employed in the production of population estimates or projections. The crude death rate is the most basic measure of mortality. The CDR is also the easiest to calculate, and it makes the least demanding data requirements. It may also be calculated separately for males and females and for different racial groups. The CDR is characterized by a lack of sensitivity as any crude rate is; however, in many applications the lack of sensitivity represented by a crude death rate is not nearly as problematic when measuring mortality as a crude birth rate is in measuring fertility. While age differentials in mortality are worth noting whenever possible, the crude death rate does make a valuable contribution to the measurement of mortality in the production of population estimates or projections, and the CDR remains a robust measure of mortality.

There are situations that require detailed mortality data beyond the capacities of the crude death rate, and age specific mortality rates are ideally suited to meet that need. The ASDR is easily calculated, and separate rates may be calculated for males, females, or certain racial groups. The major disadvantage is the stringent data requirements that must be met in order to complete the calculations.

Infant mortality rates constitute a specialized type of age specific mortality rate that often make a valuable contribution to the estimation or projection process. The risk of mortality in the first year of life is high, and the IMR provides a simple and effective way to assess that risk and its subsequent impact on the population. There are certainly limitations associated with the IMR, such as the difficulty in calculating a true rate as opposed to a conventional rate and the problem of underregistration of vital statistics data. The IMR, however, remains a useful tool in the measurement of mortality.

### Migration

The third and last of the classic demographic variables considered in this chapter is migration. Migration involves the movement of population from one area of geography to another, and it is the process of migration that makes the task of population estimation and projection a difficult one. In the absence of any migration, one requires only knowledge of fertility and mortality in order to estimate or project a population. One would simply begin with the base population and proceed to add in the appropriate number of new members as a result of fertility and subtract the appropriate number of current members due to mortality. The population estimation or projection would be a simple matter since fertility and mortality are the subject of a relatively extensive vital statistics data collection and reporting process. In addition, while there may be periodic fluctuations in mortality and fertility levels, the overall trends in mortality and fertility are relatively stable and therefore predictable.

Migration is the variable that complicates the entire process. There are two ways to enter any given population: birth and migration. Similarly, there are two ways to exit any given population: death and migration. While fertility and mortality may be the subject of extensive vital statistics data collection, migration is not. In fact, neither the federal government nor any state or local jurisdiction collects systematic data on population migration within the United States. The overwhelming majority of the approximately 250 million individuals living in the United States are free to move from place to place without prior notification to any reporting agency at their place of origin and are not required to check in with any reporting agency at their place of destination. Individuals with a serious criminal conviction and certain resident aliens comprise some of the exceptions, but for the most part U.S. residents are free to migrate at will.

There are a number of data sources that one may turn to in order to estimate migration volume within the United States, and these data sources are discussed briefly in this section. The topic is explored in detail in chapter 5 where major sources of data for population estimates and projections are discussed. Briefly, in the absence of official data on migration one must turn to symptomatic indicators of migration—that is, an examination of other types of data that might serve as an indicator of migration. These are called symptomatic indicators since they may be symptoms of migration just as certain physical conditions may be symptomatic of a particular disease.

The major sources of symptomatic data on migration come from those things that one might do when first moving to a new location. For example, most states require new residents to obtain a valid driver's license within 30 to 90 days after moving into the state. A large increase in the number of driver's licenses being issued over a particular period of time may then be symptomatic of a large number of new residents moving into the area. Unfortunately, it may also reflect an unusually large number of 15-year-olds turning 16 and obtaining a driver's license for the first time.

A similar data source is represented by automobile registrations. Again, most jurisdictions require a new resident to obtain a local automobile registration within a relatively short period of time after moving into the area. Of course, this is not a perfect data source for migration. An upsurge in registrations may represent migration, or it may represent existing residents purchasing more automobiles. In addition, not all new residents will comply with the registration laws. This is particularly a problem in states where automobile registration is relatively expensive.

One of the most extensive data sources on migration is also one of the most difficult to access. Tax data are particularly useful in tracking migration. The Internal Revenue Service is quite adept at keeping track of the place of residence of all taxpayers (as well as those who choose not to be taxpayers). A comparison of addresses from one tax year to the next tax year provides a valuable estimate of migration. Again, it is not a perfect source since not everyone is required to file a tax return, and not all those who are required to file actually do so. Additional symptomatic data sources may be identified, and all of these are discussed in detail in chapter 5. In the balance of this section some of the key migration concepts and rates are identified and discussed.

One may speak of migration at two major levels: international migration, which involves a movement of population from one country to another, and internal migration, which involves a movement of population from one area within a country to another area within the same country. Each of these concepts is of importance in estimating or projecting population, and each is plagued by data problems. International migration is the subject of official data collection and reporting. The Immigration and Naturalization Service (INS) collects data on the number of individuals who enter and exit the United States. One may not enter the United States from a foreign country without passing through the maze of official paperwork. On the surface then, it would seem that international migration is the subject of relatively accurate data collection. There is, however, one major problem. Not all of the individuals who enter the United States do so legally. The United States serves as the destination for a large number of undocumented aliens each year (individuals who in the past were referred to as "illegal aliens"). A reasonable estimate of the number of undocumented aliens entering the United States per year is in the range of 250,000 to 400,000. Undocumented aliens obviously are not the subject of any official data collection, although official efforts have been made to estimate their number.

*International Migration.* International migrants entering the United States, or any other country, are referred to as immigrants, while those exiting a particular country are referred to as emigrants. A single individual then is both an emigrant with respect to country of origin and an immigrant with respect to country of destination. An elementary method of remembering the difference between an immigrant and an emigrant is that the *i* in *immigrant* stands for *in*, and the *e* in *emigrant* stands for *exit*.

While the respective migration flows represented by immigration and emigration are of interest to demographers for a variety of reasons, the total flows are not the major factor of interest when producing population estimates or projections. The net migration volume is the primary factor of interest and represents the difference between total immigration and total emigration. In some applications one may be interested only in the international net migration volume. This point is developed in more detail following the discussion of internal migration.

*Internal Migration.* Internal migration involves population movement from one political jurisdiction to another. The standard Bureau of the Census definition requires change of residence across a county line to qualify as migration. A change of residence within a county results in one being classified as a mover, not as a migrant. Discussions of internal migration do not make use of the immigration and emigration terms employed in estimates of international migration. Similar concepts, however, are adopted. Those moving into a new political jurisdiction are generally referred to as inmigrants, and those moving out of a political jurisdiction are referred to as outmigrants. Any given internal migrant is simultaneously an outmigrant with respect to place of origin and an inmigrant with respect to place of destination.

The migration factor always plays a role in the production of population estimates and projections, but how large a role varies with the degree of detail one wants in the final product and the level of geography one examines. As a general rule, the larger the level of geography to be examined, the less of a problem one encounters with estimating migration. For example, at the geographic level of the United States, internal migration is irrelevant. When estimating or projecting the total population of the United States, one does not need to take into account any factors other than births, deaths, and international migration. The fact that some individuals may move from Wyoming to California is unimportant since no relevant political boundary has been crossed—Wyoming and California are each part of the same political jurisdiction called the United States.

If one is producing estimates or projections for the state of California, however, the issue of internal migration becomes a relevant one. One must be aware not only of births and deaths in the state but also of the net migration. By shifting to a smaller level of geography one must now attempt to track the number of residents moving into the state and the number of residents moving out of the state. In addition to the problems of internal migration, one is faced with a more difficult problem related to international migration. It is no longer sufficient to know total net international migration—that is, the difference in the number of individuals who enter the United States and the number who exit the United States; one must also attempt some realistic estimate of the portion of net international migration locating in the area under estimation or projection. Shifting the level of geography to a smaller unit results in an increasingly difficult problem with respect to migration. Further, as the unit of geography becomes even smaller—for example, the county level—the migration problem continues to increase.

In actual practice one does not normally distinguish between international and internal migration at the state or local level. In most cases the source of migration, whether it be internal or international, is not at issue; the point is that both international and internal migration may be factors in the population gain or loss for an area. Both types of migration are represented in the overall net migration values that one will attempt to measure.

### Calculating Migration

A variety of migration indicators may be employed in the production of population estimates and projections. There are two migration measures that may be of importance in the production of population estimates and projections: the crude net migration rate and the migration ratio. Each of these measures may be applied to the estimate of international migration and internal migration. In addition, there are two major methodological strategies for estimating migration: the intercensal component method and the reverse survival rate method. Again, each strategy may be applied to both international and internal migration. The most common approach is to calculate a particular measure of migration based on one of the methodological strategies without differentiating between international and internal migration. In most cases it is sufficient to estimate the effect of total net migration irrespective of the source.

*Crude Net Migration Rate.* The crude net migration rate (CNMR) serves as an indicator of net migration, and it may be applied to international migration data or internal migration data. The calculation of the crude net migration rate follows the same general logic as other rates that have been examined. The formula for the CNMR is as follows:

$$\text{CNMR} = \frac{\text{immigrants} - \text{emigrants}}{\text{total population}} \times 1,000$$

The result is a gross migration rate per 1,000 population. Current U.S. migration data estimate an annual immigration of approximately 750,000 persons and an annual emigration of approximately 160,000 persons. The net immigration total is approximately 625,000 persons; when that value is divided by the total U.S. population and multiplied by 1,000, the resulting CNMR is approximately 2.6.

Current estimates of immigration and emigration include a factor for undocumented aliens. Net immigration statistics have been adjusted by 200,000 persons annually since 1980 as an estimate for undocumented immigration. Estimates for emigration have been increased from 36,000 persons per year to 160,000 persons annually in conjunction with the increase in the immigration statistics (U.S. Bureau of the Census, 1987). Undocumented aliens often enter the United States for a period of time for work and then return to their place of origin; the increases in estimates of immigration and emigration reflect this propensity.

A CNMR of 2.6 to 2.7 per 1,000 population has been representative of the migration experience of the United States since the early 1980s. Rates were generally lower in the 1970s. The only noteworthy increase in recent history was in 1980 when the net migration rate jumped to 3.7 per 1,000 population due to the large influx of Cuban and Haitian immigrants that year. Similar CNMRs may be calculated for states or other levels of geography provided the requisite data are available. Lack of appropriate data becomes increasingly common as the chosen level of geography is reduced.

*Migration Ratio.* The migration ratio differs from a migration rate in that it represents net migration in the context of natural increase—the difference between the number of births and deaths—as opposed to the amount of migration in the context of the total population. The formula for a migration ratio is as follows:

$$\text{Migration Ratio} = \frac{\text{net migration}}{\text{births} - \text{deaths}} \times 1,000$$

Conceptually, we are expressing net migration as a ratio per each 1,000 units of natural increase. The resulting value provides not only an indication of migration but also an indication of the relative impact of migration versus natural increase. Migration ratios may be calculated for various levels of geography and for both international and internal migration. As was the case with the CNMR, however, in the production of population estimates or projections we are most often interested in an indication of total net migration irrespective of the source.

Both the crude net migration rate and the migration ratio are representations of the amount of net migration occurring in a given area to a particular population. The underlying logic of calculating these measures is similar to that of fertility and mortality rates examined previously. The factor that makes migration rates or ratios different is the relative lack of widespread data collection with respect to migration. One is seldom in a position to turn to an extensive database reflecting migration data. The alternative is to make the calculation of summary statistics on migration, such as rates or ratios, through the use of estimates of migration. These estimates are produced using a variety of methodological strategies; two of them, the intercensal component method and the reverse survival method, are discussed below.

*Intercensal Component Method.* The intercensal component method of estimating migration makes use of what demographers refer to as the population balancing equation. This equation represents the difference in population at two points in time as a function of births minus deaths plus inmigration minus outmigration. Symbolically, the balancing equation may be written as follows:

$$P_1 - P_0 = B - D + I - O$$

Where:    $P_1$   is the current population

         $P_0$   is the population at a previous point in time

         $B$    is the number of births since $P_0$

         $D$    is the number of deaths since $P_0$

         $I$     is the number of inmigrants since $P_0$

         $O$    is the number of outmigrants since $P_0$

The balancing equation represents population increase as a function of its two major components: natural increase, or the difference between births and deaths; and net migration, or the difference between inmigration and outmigration.

The intercensal component method of estimating migration makes use of the balancing equation by rewriting the equation in the following form:

$$I - O = P_1 - P_0 - B + D$$

By rewriting the equation, one is able to estimate net migration, the difference between inmigration and outmigration, for any given period of time as a function of the current population minus the previous population minus births during the time interval plus deaths during the time interval.

The technique is referred to as the intercensal method since the two most recent census counts of the population are used in the equation. Birth and death statistics are usually obtained from vital statistics registration information for the period between the two censuses. The following hypothetical data may be used to illustrate the calculation of net migration through the use of the intercensal component method.

| | |
|---|---|
| Population 1980 | 65,257 |
| Population 1990 | 72,486 |
| Total Births 1980 to 1990 | 10,115 |
| Total Deaths 1980 to 1990 | 5,810 |

Applying the data to the rewritten form of the balancing equation ($I - O = P_1 - P_0 - B + D$) would yield the following results:

$$\text{Net Migration} = 72,486 - 65,257 - 10,115 + 5,810 = 2,924$$

One may wish to calculate a migration ratio based on the resulting estimate of net migration obtained from an intercensal component estimate. The final estimate of net migration along with the birth and death data used in the calculation of the intercensal component method may be used in the calculation of the migration ratio. Recall the formula for the migration ratio:

$$\text{Migration Ratio} = \frac{\text{net migration}}{\text{births} - \text{deaths}} \times 1,000$$

Using data from the previous example, one would calculate the migration ratio as follows:

$$\text{Migration Ratio} = \frac{2,924}{10,115 - 5,810} \times 1,000 = 679.2$$

The intercensal component method of estimating net migration is relatively easy to calculate and is an extremely flexible technique. The method may be applied to a variety of geographic areas provided the required population and vital statistics data are available. In fact, the intercensal component method would seem to be ideal for the calculation of net migration. Unfortunately, there are a few problems associated with the method.

One of the major disadvantages of the intercensal component method involves a problem of validity. Quite simply, the intercensal component method does not measure exactly what it purports to measure. The value resulting from the calculation of the revised balancing equation measures net migration as intended; however, the value also contains some other effects that are not intended. Included with net migration in the result are errors in coverage from each of the two censuses and the vital statistics data.

As most people know, the census of population is intended to count each and every resident of the United States. As most people might suspect, any undertaking so ambitious is bound to fall short to some degree, and the fact is that the census does not count each and every person. The failure to count everyone in the census is referred to as undercount or, more generally, as a coverage error. For our purposes, in trying to estimate net migration by using the observed change from one census to another, the existence of a coverage error does not cause the major problem. The far greater problem occurs when the degree of coverage error changes from one census to the next. For example, suppose the coverage error for the 1980 census is at a level different from that of the 1990 census. The difference between the two population values represents change due not only to natural increase (the surplus of births over deaths) and net migration (the difference between in-migration and outmigration) but also to the fact that more of the people who actually lived in the area were counted in one census compared to the other. Using the balancing equation to estimate net migration results in the problem of attributing all of the apparent population change due to coverage error to net migration.

*Reverse Survival Rate Method.* The reverse survival rate method of estimating net migration represents an alternative to the intercensal component method. The reverse survival rate method is a more flexible method of migration estimation since it may be used to produce net migration estimates by age, race, and sex groups as opposed to the total net migration estimate resulting from the intercensal component method.

The reverse survival rate method of estimating net migration shares some similarities to the intercensal component method in that each technique employs data from the two most recent decennial censuses. The difference in the two techniques is that the reverse survival rate method proceeds on a cohort-by-cohort or age-group-by-age-group basis. Estimates of net migration are then produced by applying 10-year survival rates to the number of individuals in a particular cohort enumerated in the earlier census in order to predict the number of members of that cohort who should survive to the next census. The 10-year survival rate, as its name may imply, is an estimate of the proportion of individuals of a particular age group who are expected to survive for the next 10-year period. Survival rates are discussed in detail in chapter 3.

An example of the application of the reverse survival rate method involves the use of 1980 and 1990 census results and a set of 10-year survival rates. The technique may be represented by the following formula:

$$\text{Net Migration} = P_1 - (S \times P_0)$$

Where: $P_1$ is the population for a cohort at the current time

$P_0$ is the population for the cohort at a previous time

$S$ is the 10-year survival rate for the cohort

One takes a particular cohort of individuals—for example, males 20–24 years of age in 1980—and applies a 10-year survival rate specific to that group to the number of males 20–24 years of age counted in a particular area in the 1980 census. The resulting product represents the number of males 20–24 years of age that one expects to survive to 30–34 years of age in 1990. One then examines the number of males 30–34 years of age actually counted in the area in the 1990 census. We move to an examination of 30–34-year-old males in the 1990 census since the group we began with as 20–24-year-olds in 1980 has now aged 10 years. The number of males 30–34 years of age counted in the 1990 census represents the survivors from the 20–24-year-old cohort from 1980. The estimated number of survivors obtained by applying the 10-year survival rate to the number of males 20–24 years of age enumerated in the 1980 census is then subtracted from the number of males 30–34 years of age enumerated in the 1990 census. The difference between the estimated number of 30–34-year-olds and the actual number of 30–34-year-olds is attributed to net migration. The following hypothetical data may be used to illustrate the calculations.

| Age | 1980 Actual Population | 10-Year Survival Rate | Age | 1990 Population Expected | Actual | 1980–1990 Estimated Migration |
|-----|-----|-----|-----|-----|-----|-----|
| 20–24 | 13,402 | .983073 | 30–34 | 13,175 | 14,025 | 850 |
| 25–29 | 10,829 | .983026 | 35–39 | 10,645 | 9,885 | −760 |
| 30–34 | 8,654 | .979804 | 40–44 | 8,479 | 9,050 | 571 |
| 35–39 | 6,107 | .970050 | 45–49 | 5,924 | 5,905 | −19 |

The resulting estimates of net migration may be used as the basis for calculating an overall net migration rate for the population. In most cases, however, one would want to continue the analysis in a more detailed fashion and produce at the very least age specific net migration rates for the population. In some applications it may even be desirable to produce net migration rates with greater detailed characteristics, such as by race and sex in addition to the age detail. The decision as to the appropriate level of detail in producing net migration rates is best made after taking into consideration some of the same issues examined earlier with respect to detailed fertility and mortality rates. One is faced with a trade-off between the added advantage of more detailed data—for example, by age, race, and sex—and the disadvantage of errors introduced into the analysis by stretching the existing population base too thin when trying to estimate net migration rates for too many subgroups.

The same rule of thumb for detailed fertility and mortality rates also may be applied to net migration rates; the larger the population of interest, the more detailed the analysis may become without introducing bias from the examination of multiple subgroups. State populations easily should be large enough for the calculation of net migration rates by age, race, and sex. Most county-level populations also should provide a large enough population base for detailed rate calculations, although some county populations will be too small overall or too small with respect to some population subgroups to allow for the desired detail in all cases. There are alternative strategies one may adopt should a particular geographic area, such as a county, be too small for the calculation of a full set of net migration rates. Several contiguous counties may be grouped together to form a region with a larger population base for the purpose of calculating detailed net migration rates, and then the same set of regional rates may be applied to each of the counties in that particular region. Alternatively, counties of a particular type based on certain key characteristics, such as age or racial distribution, may be combined to form a more artificial type of grouping. Again, one would combine the similar counties to create a larger population base for the purpose of calculating the net migration rates. As a final alternative, one might choose to apply state-level net migration rates to those geographic areas that appear too small for the calculation of their own separate net migration rates.

The reverse survival rate method of calculating net migration provides an opportunity to calculate detailed net migration rates in a manner not permitted by the intercensal component method, and in some cases it represents an improvement over the results from the intercensal component method. The reverse survival rate method, however, shares a disadvantage with the intercensal component method. The reverse survival rate technique is hampered by some of the same problems of validity seen earlier in the intercensal component method. Comparison of the expected censal population with the actual censal population reveals much more than just net migration. Changes in coverage from one census to the next are also present in the final value that is considered to be net migration. In the case of the hypothetical example employed above, an improvement in population coverage for the 1990 census compared with the 1980 census would result in an inflated estimate of net migration. For example, more 30–34-year-old males than expected would be counted in the 1990 census due to a better job of counting rather than to inmigration of members of that cohort since the 1980 census was conducted.

An additional problem may be identified for the reverse survival rate method. Mortality rates, which serve as the basis for the survival rates used in the calculation of the net migration rates, may change over time. There would be an upward bias in the amount of net migration from one census to the next if there is a general reduction in the level of mortality over the 10-year period between the censuses. In most cases, the added detail made possible by the reverse survival rate method in the calculation of net migration will be worth the risk of the added bias. Migration patterns vary by age, race, and sex, and migration differentials are especially noteworthy by age and sex.

The importance of accurately estimating migration for the production of population estimates and projections cannot be overemphasized. Yet data for the migration component of population change are the most difficult to obtain. The two major strategies discussed in this section each have their advantages and, unfortunately, their disadvantages. The use of symptomatic data to indicate migration may be a viable strategy in some cases. Changes in selected data series such as driver's license applications, automobile registrations, voter registrations, utility service hookups, and the like do serve to indicate movement of population. Unfortunately, changes in these types of data also may reflect a variety of other population or economic changes taking place in the area under study.

The other strategy employed to estimate migration involving more detailed demographic methodology represents an alternative to the symptomatic data approach, and in some cases it may be more accurate. The intercensal component method employs more standard demographic data sources through the use of the two most recent census enumerations and through the use of vital statistics data on births and deaths. One should not be deceived into thinking that a valid measure of net migration will automatically result. The underlying logic of the intercensal component technique is quite sound. Current population minus former population plus deaths minus births occurring during the interval between census enumerations should equal net migration, and in fact it does—in a perfect world. Unfortunately, the world is not perfect; with respect to demographic data, this results in undercount of population of varying degrees in the census and incomplete registration in vital statistics data. The former represents a far greater challenge than the latter to the validity of the net migration estimate.

The validity of net migration estimates based on the reverse survival rate method is similarly affected by the problems of undercount in the census. Overall, the reverse survival rate is based on slightly weaker methodological assumptions than the intercensal component method in that survival rates from a previous time are extended into the future as a means of estimating the number of survivors to the next census by cohort. There is no reason to assume that mortality rates, and conversely survival rates, will remain constant; yet that is precisely the assumption that is made in the reverse survival rate method. The added assumptions of the reverse survival rate method represent an increased challenge to the validity of the net migration estimates resulting from it, but the technique is not without its advantages. The primary advantage is the added richness of detail in the net migration rates. Net migration rates specified by age, race, and sex are often invaluable in the production of population estimates and projections.

## SUMMARY

This chapter discussed the basic demographic concepts of fertility, mortality, and migration that in part form the foundation of population estimates and projections. Several measures of fertility were discussed, including the crude birth rate, the child woman ratio, the general fertility rate, and age specific fertility rates. Each of these measures has advantages and disadvantages associated with it, and each may be employed in the production of population estimates and projections.

A variety of mortality measures also was discussed in this chapter. The crude death rate, age specific death rates, and infant mortality rates are among the major measures of mortality from which one will select when producing population estimates or projections. Again, each of these measures has its advantages and disadvantages, and there is no simple answer to the question "Which measure of mortality is the best to use?"

The discussion of migration measures completed our consideration of the three classic demographic variables; as in the situation with fertility and mortality, there are choices to make with respect to measures. Data availability plays more of a role in the selection of a migration measure than it does for fertility or mortality. The intercensal component method and the reverse survival rate method were each discussed, and either may be acceptable choices for population estimates or projections that do not require detailed results. The production of detailed population estimates or projections will usually require the use of the reverse survival rate method.

## The Final Choice of Measures

There is no simple single choice of a population indicator that will be considered the best measure in all situations. Choosing from among the fertility, mortality, and migration measures involves a consideration of several factors, including desired level of accuracy, ease of calculation, desired detail in the population estimates or projections, and data availability. For example, producing population estimates or projections with detail by age, race, and sex will require some type of detailed measurement of fertility, mortality, and migration. Detailed population measures such as the age specific fertility rate or age specific mortality rate, however, require extensive vital statistics data for their calculation. When the requisite data are not available, one simply cannot produce the age specific rates required as inputs for the population estimation or projection model. Similarly, one may have the data necessary, but the accuracy of the population measures becomes questionable when one attempts to produce highly detailed rates for small areas of geography. While this list by no means includes all of the issues one needs to consider in selecting a fertility, mortality, or migration measure, it does provide a representative range of factors that impact the decision.

In the final analysis, the choice of fertility, mortality, or migration measures employed in the production of population estimates or projections will almost always involve a trade-off of some sort. Level of accuracy, data availability, and the composition of the final product will usually be the chief determining factors in the selection process.

# 3

# Survival Rates: Census and Life Table Methods

This chapter discusses the concept of survival rates and examines the production of two types of such rates: census survival rates and life table survival rates. In one sense, the chapter is an extension of the discussion on mortality begun in chapter 2. Mortality plays an important role in the production of population estimates and projections; however, equally interesting is the number of people who survive from one time period to another. After all, it is the number of survivors along with new additions by birth and migration that is actually estimated or projected. Survival rates serve as an indication of the survivors of a particular cohort from one time period to the next.

Survival rates are generated through the use of two major methodological strategies: the census survival rate method and the life table method. The census survival rate method involves an analysis of the two most recent decennial censuses on a cohort-by-cohort basis. The life table method involves an analysis of mortality and survival probabilities represented in the life table. Each of these techniques is discussed below, along with a detailed explanation of the life table itself.

## CENSUS SURVIVAL RATE METHOD

The census survival rate method requires data from two successive censuses. The resulting survival rate may be more accurately referred to as a survival ratio since it is based on the number of members of a particular age cohort in the most recent census divided by the number of members in the same cohort in the previous census. The formula for a census survival rate ($S$) may be represented in the following manner:

$$S = \frac{\text{population age } X + n \text{ in year } T}{\text{population age } X \text{ in year } T - n}$$

Where:   $X$   is the age of the cohort being examined
         $n$   is an interval of time usually set at 10 years representing the period of time between the two most recent censuses
         $T$   is the year of the most recent census

Logically, we are comparing the observed number of individuals of a particular age cohort from one census to the number of individuals in that same cohort in the next census. The size of the age cohort may be a single year of age, or it may be a larger interval of 5 years of age or 10 years of age. Survival rates would be produced for each cohort in the population.

Survival rates produced by the census method are easy to calculate as illustrated by the hypothetical data below.

| Age | 1980 Population | Age | 1990 Population | Survival Rate |
|-----|-----------------|-----|-----------------|---------------|
| Births | — | 0–4 | 1,248 | .987075 |
| Births | — | 5–9 | 1,298 | .984171 |
| 0–4 | 1,312 | 10–14 | 1,306 | .995427 |
| 5–9 | 1,452 | 15–19 | 1,444 | .994490 |
| 10–14 | 1,543 | 20–24 | 1,524 | .987686 |
| 15–19 | 1,443 | 25–29 | 1,419 | .983368 |
| 20–24 | 1,210 | 30–34 | 1,189 | .982645 |
| 25–29 | 1,106 | 35–39 | 1,085 | .981012 |

For example, the 10-year survival rate for the 5–9-year-old group surviving to age 15–19 would be calculated by dividing the 1990 15–19-year-old population by the 1980 5–9-year-old population as follows:

$$\text{Survival Rate} = \frac{1,444}{1,452} = .994490$$

The calculations would continue for all age cohorts up to a terminal cohort of usually age 75+ in 1980. The two youngest cohorts in 1990, the 0–4 age group and the 5–9 age group, represent individuals who were not alive in 1980 so they are not present in the 1980 census counts. Survival rates for these two cohorts are based on births that occurred within the most recent 5-year period and the period from 5 to 9 years past, respectively. The example illustrates the calculation of survival rates using cohorts of 5 years, but it is just as easy, although more time consuming, to calculate the survival rates for single years of age.

A separate schedule of survival rates may be calculated for males and females and for various racial groups. Survival rates will vary by race and sex to the same degree that mortality rates do, since survival rates are the converse of mortality rates. The range of variation in survival rates may become quite large in some cases, so the development of separate schedules by race and sex is desirable whenever possible. Naturally, the data from two successive censuses must be available in the detail desired in order to calculate survival rates by race and sex, but in most cases this will not be a problem.

Obtaining census data with sufficient detail to calculate the survival rates is seldom a problem since in most cases one will use only national-level data for the production of census survival rates. National-level data are used to avoid the introduction of bias resulting from migration. Comparison of population totals from two successive censuses will not result in valid survival rates unless one controls for the effects of population change due to migration. The logic of calculating a census survival rate assumes that the size of the terminal population represents the initial population minus any losses due to mortality. The assumption is valid only if the terminal population has not suffered losses due to outmigration in addition to the losses due to mortality, or if the terminal population has not experienced additions due to inmigration. It is far easier to control for migration at the national level than it is at a smaller level of geography such as a state or substate area. At the national level one must only adjust the data for international migration. While adjustments for international migration are not simple, they are far easier than the adjustments that one would have to make for internal migration.

Some of the problems inherent in using census data were discussed previously in the examination of migration rates, and many of these same problems apply to the calculation of survival rates. One major problem with using census data in the calculation of survival rates concerns coverage error. No attempt at conducting a census is ever entirely success-ful; some individuals will always be missed and will not be represented in the population figures. Coverage error would not be a problem if it were constant across time and age groups. For example, if we knew that each census undercounts the population by 5% we would simply inflate the final count by 5% and have an accurate census. Similarly, if all age groups were to have the same probability of undercount, we would simply inflate each age group by the same amount and have an accurate count of the population. In fact, for the purpose of calculating survival rates, we would not need to adjust the figures for undercount at all if the undercount were constant from census to census and across age groups. With a constant undercount the numerator and denominator for the survival rate would be deflated to the same degree, so the resulting survival rate would be identical to one produced with perfect data.

Unfortunately, we have neither perfect data nor a constant undercount in the census. The degree of undercount changes from census to census. In most cases we observe a smaller undercount with each successive census, although the 1990 census may be an exception. Further complicating the problem is the fact that some members of the population are more likely to be undercounted than others. As a general rule for the total population, those at the very extremes of the age distribution along with those in their middle years are more likely to be undercounted. Undercount is more likely to occur to those individuals under age 10 or over age 85 and to individuals between the ages of 35 and 54. Males are more likely to be undercounted than females, and the range of middle-aged males subject to undercount is broader, extending from age 25 to age 65 for males compared with a relatively small cohort of 35–39-year-old females along with females at the extremes of the age distribution. Middle-aged females are somewhat less mobile than males and as a result are less subject to coverage error in the census.

A similar differential in completeness of coverage exists with respect to whites and blacks. As a general rule, whites are less likely to be under-counted than blacks. White males are subject to undercount in the middle years between the ages of 25 and 59 and above age 85. White females are most subject to undercount between the ages of 35 and 39 and above age 80. In comparison, blacks are likely to be undercounted in almost all age cohorts with the exception of the 15–19 age group and those between the ages of 65 and 79. Blacks in all other age groups are likely to be the subject of undercount to some degree.

The tendency for males to be subject to greater coverage error than females is also present among blacks, resulting in the highest rate of coverage error for black males. It is estimated that as many as 16% of black males between the ages of 35 and 49 were missed in the 1980 census. (The discussion of estimates of census coverage for the 1980 census is based on Appendix F in U.S. Bureau of the Census, Current Population Reports, Series P-25, No. 952, May 1984. Comparable estimates by age for the 1990 census were not available at the time of publication of this book, but the total undercount for the 1990 census is estimated at just over 5 million persons.)

After one is reasonably confident that the pattern of coverage errors between the two most recent censuses is similar, or at least that it does not matter if it is not, one is usually in the position of making a number of assumptions when applying census survival rates. By far the greatest assumption made is that the national-level survival rates are applicable to smaller areas of geography. Of course, this is not a problem if one is producing only national-level population estimates or projections. In such a case the population serving as the basis for the survival rates is identical to the population being estimated or projected so there is no question as to the applicability of the survival rates.

In other cases one may be estimating or projecting a population for a smaller area of geography such as a state or a county. There is an implicit assumption that survival rates for the nation are similar to those in the smaller area of geography. In many cases the assumption will be false. Survival rates will vary across the country and, unfortunately, there is no practical way to produce an alternative set of local survival rates. Much of the geographic variation in survival rates, however, may be due to different concentrations of minorities in various regions of the country. The total survival rate for particular areas may differ from the national rate, but the difference may be due to the composition of the population. The specific age, race, and sex survival rates for the local area and the national area may be quite similar. Using national survival rates is not as great a problem in such a case since it is the age, race, and sex specific rates that are actually used.

## THE LIFE TABLE

An alternative to producing survival rates through the use of two successive censuses is to make use of survival information present in the life table. Life tables are analytical devices that summarize the mortality experiences of a segment of the population. The life table begins with a group of individuals at birth and traces their mortality experience through time. More and more of the initial group is removed from the life table as mortality rates are applied first to the initial group and then to the survivors. Eventually, the entire cohort will experience mortality. Life tables are categorized with respect to two different concepts: the type of mortality experience represented in the life table and the degree of age detail present in the life table. Each of these concepts is discussed below.

### Generational and Current Life Tables

Generational or cohort life tables represent the mortality experiences of an actual cohort of individuals. The mortality experience of a group of individuals born during a specified time is traced from the birth of the cohort through the death of the last member of the cohort in the generational or cohort life table technique. The production of a generational life table is not an easy task as one might imagine. Even more demanding are the data requirements necessary for a generational life table. One must follow the mortality experiences of a specific cohort—for example, all those individuals born in the year 1895—through time until all members of the cohort have died. Consequently, data must be collected for an extended period of time. The construction of accurate generational life tables is not possible for recent cohorts since all of their members have not yet died. As a result, the generational life table is a technique more often applied to historical periods.

The current life table is the alternative to a generational life table. The current life table represents the mortality experience of a hypothetical cohort, eliminating the need for tracing an actual group of individuals through time. Current life tables are produced by applying a schedule of current age specific death rates to the beginning hypothetical cohort termed the *radix*. Since the cohort is hypothetical its beginning size is arbitrary and a matter of choice. The beginning size of the cohort in a current life table is conventionally set at 100,000 persons, although in some applications a beginning radix of 10,000 is used.

Applying the current age specific death rate for 1-year-olds to the initial radix will result in the number of survivors to age 1. Applying the current age specific death rate for 2-year-olds to that group of surviving 1-year-olds will result in the number of 2-year-olds. The process continues until all of the initial 100,000 individuals have experienced mortality and there are no survivors. Implicit in the current life table is an assumption that current mortality patterns represented by the schedule of age specific death rates will remain constant and will therefore provide a reasonable representation of the mortality experience of the cohort. Of course, this assumption will not be entirely valid, but by making it one is able to avoid the requirement of having to trace the actual mortality experiences of a cohort.

## Complete and Abridged Life Tables

The second concept used to categorize life tables deals with the level of age detail represented in the life table. Complete life tables are those that represent the mortality experience of the beginning cohort on a year-by-year basis. Complete life tables will represent the cohort as it moves from birth to age 1, age 2, age 3, and so on up to a terminal age of usually 85 years.

Abridged life tables represent the mortality experience of a cohort through the use of age categories. Most often, 5-year age groupings are used with an exception being made for the first age grouping. Most abridged life tables using 5-year age groupings will subdivide the first 5-year age group into two categories: the 0–1-year-old group and the 1–5-year-old group. The 0–1-year-old group is singled out even in the abridged form of the life table due to the relatively high rate of mortality experienced during the first year of life. The reader may recall from the previous discussion of mortality rates that the first year of life represented a risk of mortality that was not equalled by most groups until middle age. In the case of the abridged life table, assuming a 5-year age grouping, the mortality experience of the cohort is traced from birth through age 1, then age 1–5, age 5–10, age 10–15, and so on until a terminal age of usually 85 years.

As is the case with so many concepts involved in the production of population estimates and projections, there is no single choice that may be considered appropriate for all situations. In general, one is not likely to be using a generational life table in the production of population estimates or projections. Most often we are interested in estimating or projecting a current population, so the data required for a generational life table simply will not be available for many years to come. As a result, a current life table almost always will be used.

The issue of age detail in the life table required for the production of population estimates or projections is handled in an equally practical manner. Whether one employs a complete life table or an abridged life table will usually depend on the level of age detail desired in the final product. Population estimates or projections produced with single year of age detail are best made with a complete life table; estimates or projections reported in age groups are best made with an abridged life table. An abridged life table may be used even for the production of estimates or projections reported in single years of age, provided one is willing to apply the resulting survival rates for the 5-year age group to each of the single years of age represented by the cohort. For example, the single survival rate for the 20–25-year-old cohort from an abridged life table may be applied to 20-, 21-, 22-, 23-, and 24-year-olds separately. Naturally, there is some degree of error introduced in the process, but in most cases it will be slight. In the absence of an acceptable complete life table, applying the 5-year survival rates to single years of age represented by the cohort may be the only viable option.

### The Life Table Explained

The standard life table represents the mortality and survival experiences of a cohort of individuals. A current abridged life table will be used in the following example, but the underlying logic is similar to that of a complete life table. The life table itself consists of the following seven columns:

| Column | Symbol | Definition |
|--------|--------|------------|
| (1) | $x$ to $x + n$ | Period of life represented by the age interval $x$ to $x + n$ |
| (2) | $nq_x$ | Proportion of persons alive at the beginning of the age interval but dying during the age interval |
| (3) | $l_x$ | Number of persons alive at the beginning of the age interval |
| (4) | $nd_x$ | Number of persons dying during the age interval |
| (5) | $nL_x$ | Number of persons alive in the age interval, assuming the birth of 100,000 additional persons each year |
| (6) | $T_x$ | Number of persons alive in this and all subsequent age intervals |
| (7) | $e_x$ | Average number of years of life expected to remain for those at the beginning of the age interval |

The symbol $x$ represents some value of age, and the symbol $n$ represents some interval of time. Most abridged life tables use a 5-year time interval. The $n$ subscript applied to the $nq_x$, $nd_x$, and $nL_x$ columns indicates that the values present in these columns represent a 5-year experience. Respectively, the columns indicate a 5-year mortality rate, the number of individuals of the indicated age group dying over 5 years, and the total number of persons of that 5-year age group who would be alive at any given time assuming the addition of 100,000 persons each year at the initial stage of the life table. Complete life tables represent single year experiences, so there is no need to include the $n$ subscript. Some life tables also will present an additional column containing the schedule of age specific death rates which serve as the basis of the cohort mortality probabilities represented by the $nq_x$ column. A more complete explanation of the columns of the life table is given below.

Column 1 simply provides the age interval for each respective row of the life table. Abridged life tables will usually be based on a 5-year cohort with the first age period of 0–5 years broken down into two components: age 0–1 and age 1–5. The remaining age categories will follow in a standard fashion of 5-year increments through the terminal age interval at the end of the life table. The final age category is usually represented as an open interval of age 85 and over.

Column 2 represents the proportion of individuals alive at the beginning of the respective age interval who will be expected to die by the end of the age interval. The $nq_x$ column represents the risk of mortality as a proportion. For example, a $nq_x$ value of .0040 for the 15–20 age group indicates that 4 of every 1,000 individuals alive at age 15 will die by the time the survivors of the age 15–20 cohort reach the age of 20. The $nq_x$ column is the key element of the life table, and the values in all of the other columns are determined by the $nq_x$ values.

The values represented in the $nq_x$ column are based on actual age specific mortality rates ($nM_x$) for the population, but the $nq_x$ values for any age group are not exactly equal to the respective age specific mortality rates for that age group. The discrepancy between the $nq_x$ values and the $nM_x$ values is due to the fact that the former represent the probability of dying for the cohort represented in the life table while the latter represent the annual mortality rate for individuals of the ages listed in the life table. The difference is a subtle one similar to the problem of actual versus conventional infant mortality rates discussed in chapter 2. For example, deaths occurring to individuals of age 25 in any given calendar year may actually represent deaths to individuals of two separate and distinct birth cohorts. For this reason it is necessary to adjust the $nM_x$ rates to reflect the probability of death for members of a specific cohort as represented by the $nq_x$ values. Several methods are available to convert conventional mortality rates into life table mortality probabilities. In most applications a good approximation may be made by using the following formula:

$$n q x = \frac{2 \times M_x}{2 + M_x}$$

This approximation assumes that one is calculating a single year life table survival rate from appropriate single year mortality rates. An abridged life table containing age intervals of perhaps 5 years will require a slightly different adjustment, but it is still a relatively simple matter involving the addition of a constant multiplier into the above formula equal to the number of years in the age interval in the life table. In the general case, the formula would be adjusted as follows:

$$n q x = \frac{2n \times {}_n M_x}{2 + (n)_n M_x}$$

For example, an abridged life table consisting of 5-year age intervals would require the following conversion:

$$n q x = \frac{2(5) \times {}_n M_x}{2 + (5)({}_n M_x)}$$

Column 3 represents the number of persons alive at the beginning of the respective age interval. The $l_x$ value for the 0–1 age interval in an abridged life table will indicate the size of the base population used in the calculation of the life table. In most applications, the base population will consist of 100,000 persons.

Column 4 represents the number of persons dying during the respective age interval. The $_n d_x$ column is calculated by multiplying the proportion dying during the age interval (the $_n q_x$ column) by the number of individuals alive at the beginning of the age interval (the $l_x$ column). The resulting product represents the number of individuals who will die during the given age interval. The number who will die during that age interval is then subtracted from the number of individuals alive at the beginning of the age interval represented by the $l_x$ column, and the result of that subtraction yields the value of the $l_x$ column for the next age interval.

Column 5 and column 6 represent the size of the stationary population. The values in column 5 (the $_n L_x$ column) and column 6 (the $T_x$ column) are based on the assumption that an additional 100,000 persons are added to the life table annually at age 0 and subjected to the mortality rates in the $_n q_x$ column. For example, the value of the $_n L_x$ column for the 30–35 age group represents the number of individuals who would be alive between the ages of 30 and 35 if 100,000 persons were added to the population each year at age 0 and subjected to the age specific probabilities of dying represented in the life table. Another way of interpreting the values in the $_nL_x$ column is to view them as "person years" lived by the members of the particular age group. Person years lived is a concept analogous to "man-hours" for a work project. For example, a project said to comprise 1,000 man-hours would take one man 1,000 hours to complete or 1,000 men 1 hour to complete, or any combination in between. In the life table one might prefer to think of 100,000 persons added each year to the life table experiencing 483,310 person years lived between the ages of 30 and 35.

In a complete life table representing the population experience in single years of age, the $_nL_x$ column is usually calculated by taking the number of survivors at the beginning of the age interval (the $l_x$ column) and subtracting one-half of the number of deaths (the $_nd_x$ column) expected to occur to that group over the next year. The resulting $_nL_x$ value represents the number of individuals on average expected to be alive at any particular age at midyear. In effect, we are assuming that the deaths expected to occur during the year will occur in a smooth, even fashion during the course of the year. The precise calculation of the $_nL_x$ column in an abridged life table is somewhat more difficult. The value of the $_nL_x$ column represents the cumulative experience of an additional 100,000 individuals over 5 successive years. To precisely calculate the $_nL_x$ values, one must take into account the fact that the first cohort of survivors will be exposed to the risk of mortality for 5 years, the second cohort of survivors will be exposed to the risk of mortality for 4 years, the third cohort of survivors will be exposed to the risk of mortality for 3 years, and so on. Further complicating the calculations is the fact that the risk of mortality indicated by the $_nq_x$ column represents a 5-year mortality risk. Therefore, it is not possible to calculate exactly the values of the $_nL_x$ column with the information present in the abridged life table. It is possible to provide very close approximations for the $_nL_x$ values by means of one of the two methods below:

(1)
$$_nL_x = 5 \times \frac{(l_x + L_{x+n})}{2}$$

(2)
$$_nL_x = 5 \times [l_x - .5(_nd_x)]$$

Either approximation will yield the same results, and each is very close in most cases to the exact $_nL_x$ values that would result from calculations made from a complete life table.

Column 6 (the $T_x$ column) is also a measure of the stationary population based on the assumption of an additional 100,000 persons each year subjected to the probability of dying as represented by the $_nq_x$ values of the life table. The $T_x$ column of the life table for a particular age group represents the total size of the population in that and all subsequent age intervals. The $T_x$ column for a particular age interval is calculated by summing the values of the $_nL_x$ column for that and all subsequent age intervals.

The $T_x$ column alternatively may be thought of as the total person years lived for a particular age cohort if it were to progress through the remainder of the life table. This alternative interpretation provides a clue to the ultimate utility of the $T_x$ column. The $T_x$ column represents the total person years lived for a particular cohort from the present to the end of its life span and, as such, may be used in the calculation of life expectancy.

Column 7 (the $e_x$ column) represents the remaining number of years of life expected for the particular age group. The life expectancy column ($e_x$) is calculated by dividing the $T_x$ column by the $l_x$ column. In effect, one is dividing the total number of person years of life for a particular age group (the $T_x$ column) by the number of survivors in that age group at the current time (the $l_x$ column). The result is the remaining number of years of life expected for the age group. The values in the $e_x$ column for the youngest age group represent the life expectancy at birth. Life expectancy values at birth represented by the $e_x$ are the most often cited results from a life table analysis.

An abridged life table for the total U.S. population (all races and both sexes) for the year 1987 is represented in Table 3.1 (National Center for Health Statistics, 1990c).


## LIFE TABLE SURVIVAL RATES

The life table represents a powerful tool in demographic analysis with functions that extend far beyond applications in population estimates and projections. The previous discussion of the life table is intended to provide an overview of the logic of the life table and to introduce its use in the production of population estimates and projections. In this context, the real contribution of the life table is in the calculation of survival rates. The life table method of calculating survival rates represents an alternative to the census survival rate method, and in many respects the life table method may be preferable. One key advantage of the life table method is that

**Table 3.1**
**Life Table: Total U.S. Population, 1987**

| x to x+n | $_nq_x$ | $l_x$ | $_nd_x$ | $_nL_x$ | $T_x$ | $e_x$ |
|----------|---------|-------|---------|---------|-------|-------|
| 0-1   | 0.0101 | 100,000 | 1,011  | 99,135  | 7,496,306 | 75.0 |
| 1-5   | .0020  | 98,989  | 201    | 395,485 | 7,397,171 | 74.7 |
| 5-10  | .0012  | 98,788  | 121    | 493,611 | 7,001,686 | 70.9 |
| 10-15 | .0013  | 98,667  | 131    | 493,081 | 6,508,075 | 66.0 |
| 15-20 | .0042  | 98,536  | 414    | 491,741 | 6,014,994 | 61.0 |
| 20-25 | .0057  | 98,122  | 555    | 489,250 | 5,523,253 | 56.3 |
| 25-30 | .0060  | 97,567  | 587    | 486,366 | 5,034,003 | 51.6 |
| 30-35 | .0073  | 96,980  | 707    | 483,174 | 4,547,637 | 46.9 |
| 35-40 | .0093  | 96,273  | 900    | 479,243 | 4,064,463 | 42.2 |
| 40-45 | .0124  | 95,373  | 1,178  | 474,130 | 3,585,220 | 37.6 |
| 45-50 | .0191  | 94,195  | 1,798  | 466,809 | 3,111,090 | 33.0 |
| 50-55 | .0307  | 92,397  | 2,841  | 455,329 | 2,644,281 | 28.6 |
| 55-60 | .0473  | 89,556  | 4,240  | 437,789 | 2,188,952 | 24.4 |
| 60-65 | .0736  | 85,316  | 6,276  | 411,740 | 1,751,163 | 20.5 |
| 65-70 | .1059  | 79,040  | 8,368  | 375,183 | 1,339,423 | 16.9 |
| 70-75 | .1585  | 70,672  | 11,203 | 326,327 | 964,240   | 13.6 |
| 75-80 | .2292  | 59,469  | 13,630 | 264,101 | 637,913   | 10.7 |
| 80-85 | .3407  | 45,839  | 15,619 | 190,359 | 373,812   | 8.2  |
| 85+   | 1.0000 | 30,220  | 30,220 | 183,453 | 183,453   | 6.1  |

survival rates may be calculated for small area geographies, provided one is able to acquire or calculate a schedule of age specific death rates. The flexibility of the life table allows the production of survival rates specific to the area of geography being estimated or projected. Theoretically, the same may be said of the census survival rate method, but in most cases one will find it problematic to produce suitable survival rates below the national level due to the confounding influence of migration.

## Complete Life Table Survival Rates

Survival rates produced through the complete life table are calculated based on values in the $L_x$ column of the life table which represent survivors to each age. The survival rates produced through the complete life table may be for any interval of time from 1 year to multiple years. Survival rates in the general case are calculated by dividing the appropriate $L_x$ value for the terminal age by the $L_x$ value of the initial age. The survival rate is logically the number of survivors at the end of an observation period divided by the number of survivors at the beginning of the observation period.

The 1-year survival rate for 25-year-olds surviving to age 26 would be obtained in the following manner:

$$S_{25} = \frac{L_{26}}{L_{25}}$$

The resulting value would indicate the proportion of 25-year-olds expected to survive to age 26. A 10-year survival rate for 25-year-olds would be obtained in a similar fashion by simply substituting the $L_x$ value for the 35-year-old age group into the equation:

$$S_{25} = \frac{L_{35}}{L_{25}}$$

Survival rates of any duration may be calculated in a similar fashion. Population estimates and projections are usually based on 1-, 5-, or 10-year survival rates with 5- or 10-year rates more common. The 10-year time period is a particularly popular one for population projections in part due to the 10-year time interval between censuses and in part due to a general bias toward round numbers.

### Abridged Life Table Survival Rates

Survival rates calculated from an abridged life table are, in most cases, based on values in the $_nL_x$ column. The exceptions are survival rates for the youngest age groups, those aged 0–1 and 1–5, and those in the terminal or last age group. In most cases, survival rates from an abridged life table will be calculated the same as those from a complete life table. A prefix indicating the length of the age interval represented by the $_nL_x$ value will be added, but in all other respects the calculations are identical. For example, the 10-year survival rate for those 30–35 years of age surviving to 40–45 years of age is calculated as follows:

$$S_{35} = \frac{_5L_{40}}{_5L_{30}}$$

Conventionally, the initial age of the interval is provided as the suffix $(x)$ for the $_nL_x$ value, and the prefix $(n)$ indicates the size of the age interval represented by the $_nL_x$ value. In the present example, a 10-year survival rate is being calculated for those aged 30–35 surviving to age 40–45.

An exception in calculating survival rates from an abridged life table is made for the youngest two cohorts. Recall that even in an abridged life table the 0–5-year-old cohort is divided into two parts—the 0–1-year-old group and the 1–5-year-old group—due to the relatively high rate of mortality in the first year of life. A survival rate for the 0–5-year-old group is calculated by first summing the $_nL_x$ values for the 0–1-year-old group, symbolized by $L_0$, and the 1–5-year-old group, symbolized by $_4L_1$. The sum of the two $L_x$ values represents the total number of survivors for the first 5-year cohort, symbolized as $_5L_0$. Ordinarily, one then would divide the number of survivors by the $_nL_x$ value for the earlier number of survivors. With the initial age cohort of the life table, however, there are no earlier $_nL_x$ values. The solution is to divide the $_5L_0$ value by 500,000, which is the number of individuals who would have been introduced into the life table over the 5-year period following the standard assumption that 100,000 individuals are added per year.

Survival rates for the 5–10-year-old age group are calculated in a similar fashion. The survival rate is calculated by dividing the $_5L_5$ value by 500,000. One does not divide the $_5L_5$ value by the $_5L_0$ value, the sum of the $L_0$ value and the $_4L_1$ value. It might seem logical to divide the number of survivors in the 5–10-year-old age group by the number of survivors from the combined previous age groups of 0–1 and 1–5, but the resulting survival rate would be inaccurate. A survival rate calculated on such a basis would be biased because the 0–1-year-old group has only been subjected to the risk of mortality for one year, and because that group is subjected to an extremely high mortality rate. The more logical alternative is to use the 500,000 figure, representing the number of individuals who would have been introduced into the life table over 5 years, as the base when calculating the $_5L_5$ survival rate.

The final exception to calculating survival rates from abridged life tables involves the two oldest age cohorts represented in the life table. Survival rates for the second to oldest age group may not be calculated in the standard fashion since the $_nL_x$ value for the terminal age group is somewhat misleading. An assumption usually is made in the construction of a life table regarding the mortality rate of the terminal age group. The terminal age group is usually an open interval; that is, rather than beginning at an exact age and ending at an exact age, such as 70–75 or 75–80, the final age interval will be 80 and older or 85 and older. Adopting an open interval for the final age group allows one to avoid the creation of age intervals to accommodate the relatively few members of the original cohort who will live to advanced ages. The assumption made for the mortality rate for the terminal age group is to apply a mortality rate of 1.00; in effect, all surviving members of the cohort are assumed to die in the final age interval.

Calculation of a survival rate for the terminal age interval becomes moot since a mortality rate of 1.00 is assumed for that group. As a consequence, the resulting $_nL_x$ value for the terminal age interval becomes misleading and as such is unsuitable for calculating a survival rate. The solution is to use the $T_x$ values for the two oldest age groups in the abridged life table. The $T_x$ values represent the number of survivors in the particular age group and all older age groups, and use of the $T_x$ values for the two oldest age cohorts will yield a more accurate survival rate for the next to last age group. The survival rate may be calculated in a manner similar to that of the other survival rates:

$$S_{75} = \frac{_5T_{85}}{_5T_{75}}$$

The number of survivors at age 85 and older is divided by the number of survivors at age 75 and older. The resulting value serves as a survival rate for the 75–80-year-old age group.

## CENSUS SURVIVAL RATES VERSUS LIFE TABLE SURVIVAL RATES

Census survival rates and life table survival rates are each suited for use in the production of population estimates and projections, and each technique has its own advantages and disadvantages. Census survival rates are relatively easy to produce, and they are based on census data that are readily available in published form. In most cases, one will work with census survival rates based on national-level data to avoid the confounding influence of migration since the difference in the size of a cohort from one time period to the next is a function of two things: mortality and net migration. Mortality is the population concept of interest in the production of survival rates, while net migration represents an unwanted source of variation. At the national level one must be concerned only with the net difference between immigration (those entering the country) and emigration (those exiting the country). Determining the level of net migration at the national level is no easy task, as the discussion on migration in chapter

2 indicated, but it is infinitely easier to determine net migration at the national level than it is at a smaller level of geography such as a state or county.

Smaller unit geography involves not only the problem of international migration but the more common problem of net migration from other regions, states, or counties. It is certainly possible to produce survival rates at these smaller areas of geography, but part of the process requires an adjustment for net migration. The process can become quite circular since estimates of net migration are often based on survival rates. In effect, one demographic component (survival) is based on the estimate of the second demographic component (net migration) which is based on the estimate of the first demographic component, and so on. The end product is likely to be of questionable utility.

One possible solution to the confounding influence of mortality and migration in survival rates produced at the subnational level is to generate a composite rate representing both mortality and migration without breaking each component out separately. In this type of strategy, survival refers to the relative proportion of a cohort remaining in a given geographic area over a specified period of time. No effort is made to determine the number of additions to the cohort due to inmigration, nor is there any effort to separate the number of deletions from the cohort by outmigration versus mortality. In an environment of constant mortality and net migration rates, a composite survival rate will operate in precisely the same manner as separate rates reflecting actual survival and net migration. The risk of adopting a composite rate strategy is that current mortality and migration experiences will not remain constant over time. In fact, it is especially likely that net migration will change and the resulting estimates or projections based on the composite rate will be biased. Composite rates including both mortality and migration are best suited to situations where no other alternative can be found.

Life table survival rates present an appealing alternative to census survival rates, especially when one is interested in estimating or projecting the population of smaller areas of geography. Current life tables utilizing a hypothetical cohort, but based on the actual mortality experiences of an area, provide a means of generating a schedule of age specific survival rates that are just as functional as those based on census data. Life table survival rates may be preferable to census survival rates when working with areas of geography below the national level since life table survival rates may be based on the actual mortality experience of the smaller areas of geography. The same level of age detail and separate schedules by race and sex produced through census data also are produced easily through the current life table approach.

## SUMMARY

Survival rates are an essential element of the estimation and projection process and constitute the mechanism through which the mortality experience of a population affects our estimate or projection. Census survival rates are based on data from two successive decennial censuses and are generally produced at the national level. A schedule of age specific survival rates is relatively easy to produce from census data. Separate schedules of census survival rates may be calculated for any number of population subgroups by race or sex. Census survival rates for smaller areas of geography are somewhat more difficult to employ. The calculation and use of smaller area survival rates are made more difficult for two major reasons. Smaller area census survival rates may include bias due to the effects of migration which are more difficult to deal with at smaller geographic levels. The second problem concerns the general problem of bias resulting from the use of a smaller and smaller population base when constructing any type of rate. The smaller the population base which usually constitutes the denominator in the calculation of a rate, the more exaggerated the change in the rate with each unit of change in the numerator.

Life table survival rates employed in the production of population estimates or projections are usually based on a current life table methodology in which actual mortality rates are applied to a hypothetical cohort. The resulting survival rates may be produced in a detailed fashion with age detail ranging from 10- to 5-year cohorts on down to single year detail. Separate schedules may also be produced by race and sex. The major advantage to the life table survival rate strategy is the application of the technique to small areas of geography. Of course, one must still deal with the standard problem of finding suitable mortality data for the life table, but once this problem is solved the survival rates may be produced in a straightforward manner.

# 4

# Census Geography Concepts

Data from the U.S. Bureau of the Census play a major role in the production of population estimates and projections. Census data are often the source of the base population or beginning point in the estimation or projection process and for the calculation of vital rates. In addition, data from two successive decennial censuses may serve as the basis for establishing trends for a variety of population processes. The term *census data* is likely to bring to mind an image of population figures in some degree of detail originating with the Bureau of the Census. What is often unrecognized is the companion concept of *census geography*. Census geography may be thought of as the framework used to organize the tabulation and reporting of census data. All population figures refer to population within a clearly specified geographic area. Census geography refers to the set of physical or statistical areas used to tabulate and report those population data.

Census geography encompasses a variety of areas ranging in size from the entire United States down to the smallest area of a block. The geographic areas themselves also will be found to vary in a number of significant ways. Some geographic areas are legally defined governmental entities, such as the United States, each of the 50 states, individual counties, and legally incorporated cities or towns. Other geographic units are best described as statistical units. Statistical geographic areas also will be found to vary in size ranging from regions such as the South or the Northeast to smaller statistical areas such as census tracts.

In this chapter the major census geography concepts for the 1980 and 1990 censuses are identified and discussed. It is important to be aware of any changes in census geography from one census to the next since many techniques of population estimation or projection require data from two successive census periods. It is also common to find data reported for one area of geography at one level of detail for one census but not for the succeeding or previous census. Major changes in census geography between the 1980 census and the 1990 census will also be discussed due to the importance of data compatibility from one time period to the next.

## MAJOR CONCEPTS OF CENSUS GEOGRAPHY FOR 1980

The general logic of this discussion of 1980 census geography is to begin with the largest levels of geography and to work down to the smallest levels of geography for which census data are reported. In some cases, however, a direct line does not exist from the largest areas to the smallest areas as the focus switches from legally defined geographic areas to statistical geographic areas.

*United States*. The United States comprises the largest geographic area for which census data are reported. This level of geography includes as an aggregate the 50 states and the District of Columbia, which is usually treated as a state for most census reporting purposes. Population reports for the United States may be further specified in terms of total population and total resident population. Some population totals may refer to the total resident population of the United States, meaning all those persons actually present within the legal borders of the United States, while other population totals may include legal residents known to be temporarily out of the country, such as overseas military personnel and their dependents. Additional census data are collected for Puerto Rico and other outlying areas under U.S. sovereignty or jurisdiction such as American Samoa, Guam (where America's day begins), the Northern Mariana Islands, Palau, and the U.S. Virgin Islands. Puerto Rican and outlying area population totals generally are not included in the total U.S. population figures.

*Census Regions and Divisions*. Census regions and divisions represent a statistical level of geography as opposed to a governmental unit. There are four census regions: the Northeast, the Midwest (formally designated as the North Central Region prior to June 1984), the South, and the West. Each census region is composed of two or more census divisions. There are a total of nine census divisions, each of which is made up of a grouping of contiguous states. The constituent parts of the census regions and divisions are as follows:

## Northeast Region

*New England Division*
Maine
New Hampshire
Vermont
Massachusetts
Rhode Island
Connecticut

*Middle Atlantic Division*
New York
New Jersey
Pennsylvania

## Midwest Region

*East North Central Division*
Ohio
Indiana
Illinois
Michigan
Wisconsin

*West North Central Division*
Minnesota
Iowa
Missouri
North Dakota
South Dakota
Nebraska
Kansas

## South Region

*South Atlantic Division*
Delaware
Maryland
District of Columbia
Virginia
West Virginia
North Carolina
South Carolina
Georgia
Florida

*East South Central Division*
Kentucky
Tennessee
Alabama
Mississippi

*West South Central Division*
Arkansas
Louisiana
Oklahoma
Texas

## West Region

*Mountain Division*
Montana
Idaho
Wyoming
Colorado
New Mexico
Arizona
Utah
Nevada

*Pacific Division*
Washington
Oregon
California
Alaska
Hawaii

*States and Equivalent Units.* States and equivalent units are another example of census geography corresponding to legally defined governmental units. Data are collected and reported for each of the 50 states and the District of Columbia, which is treated as a state for most reporting purposes.

*Metropolitan Statistical Areas.* Metropolitan statistical areas (MSAs) are statistical areas of geography defined by the Office of Management and Budget (prior to 1983, metropolitan statistical areas were referred to as standard metropolitan statistical areas [SMSA]). MSAs are based on county-level geography and are comprised of at least one county with a central city of 50,000 or more inhabitants, or an area meeting the Census Bureau definition of an "urban area" of 50,000 or more population and a total MSA population of at least 100,000 persons (75,000 persons in New England). It is not necessary for an MSA to contain a single central city of 50,000 persons. Many areas will qualify as MSAs based on the existence of a "twin cities" area, or a "tri-cities" area which in total will have the minimum population necessary to qualify as an MSA. Counties adjacent to the county containing the central city or urban area will be included in the MSA if at least 50% of the population of the adjacent counties is included in the urbanized area. Outlying (noncontiguous) counties may also be included in the MSA if they have close social and economic links to the area. Specific requirements used to determine the degree of social and economic linkage between an outlying county and the MSA include the amount of commuting of population to the central county and whether the outlying county is metropolitan in character. The population density and percent urban population of the outlying county serve as indicators of its metropolitan character.

Metropolitan statistical areas take their name from the central city serving as the nucleus of the MSA. The boundary of an MSA will not cut through a county boundary; the entire county is either in the MSA or it is not. It is possible for an MSA to cut across state lines and include counties from two or more states. For example the Memphis metropolitan area is officially designated as the Memphis, Tennessee, Arkansas, Mississippi MSA and includes counties in all three of the states indicated. The composition of an MSA may change over time. New counties may be added to the area designated as the MSA as the population of the metropolitan area expands into what were previously rural areas surrounding it. It is also possible for a county to be removed from the MSA if it no longer meets the criteria for inclusion. A total of 323 MSAs were defined at the time of the 1980 census, with an additional 4 MSAs in Puerto Rico.

*Consolidated Metropolitan Statistical Areas and Primary Metropolitan Statistical Areas.* Some areas of the United States are so urbanized that one metropolitan area extends to the beginning of another. Large metropolitan areas of 1 million or more persons made up of two or more separate metropolitan areas are termed consolidated metropolitan statistical areas (CMSAs). When several metropolitan areas meet the criteria to be classified as a CMSA, the individual metropolitan areas that comprise the CMSA are termed primary metropolitan statistical areas (PMSAs) in order to differentiate them from the more typical MSAs. A total of 23 CMSAs were defined based on 1980 census data, and these areas contained a total of 78 PMSAs. There were an additional 12 MSAs with populations of 1 million or more persons, but they did not consist of several identifiable metropolitan areas and therefore did not meet the requirements to be designated as a CMSA. Note that neither CMSAs nor PMSAs were census geographic concepts at the time of the 1980 census.

*Counties and County Equivalent Units.* The county and county equivalent units are some of the most useful units of census geography in the production of population estimates and projections. Counties are the primary political and administrative subdivision of most states. Some states have alternative terminology for essentially the same geographic concept. For example, the state of Louisiana is divided administratively into parishes rather than counties, and the state of Alaska is divided into boroughs and "census areas." County equivalent areas for census purposes include areas termed "independent cities," such as Baltimore, Maryland; St. Louis, Missouri; and Carson City, Nevada; and a number of independent cities in the state of Virginia. The number of county and county equivalent areas varies slightly from census to census. In the 1980 census there were 3,146 county and county equivalent areas in the United States and an additional 78 such areas in Puerto Rico.

*Minor Civil Divisions and Census County Divisions.* Minor civil divisions (MCDs) and census county divisions (CCDs) are each geographic concepts referring to subareas of counties. Minor civil divisions refer to relatively small areas such as towns and townships within counties. Minor civil divisions numbered approximately 25,000 in the 1980 census and are more likely to be found in the New England area. Census county divisions are similar areas defined for approximately 20 states where the MCD concept is not adequate for reporting subcounty population data. Boundaries for census county divisions are defined by U.S. Bureau of the Census personnel in collaboration with local officials.

There were approximately 5,510 CCDs in the 1980 census and an additional 37 census subareas defined for the state of Alaska. Minor civil divisions generally conform to legally defined geographic areas, while census county divisions are more likely to be statistically defined reporting areas that do not conform to legally defined boundaries.

*Incorporated Places.* Incorporated places is another example of a census geography concept conforming to legally defined boundaries. Incorporated places are areas that are legally incorporated within a state, such as cities, towns, villages, or boroughs (exceptions include the use of the term *borough* in New York and Alaska and the term *town* in the New England states, New York, and Wisconsin). There were just over 19,000 incorporated places identified at the time of the 1980 census. Incorporated places will not cross state boundaries, but they may cross MCD or county boundaries. For example, the city of Atlanta, Georgia, is an incorporated place that covers a geographic area encompassing parts of several counties. In some cases it may appear that an incorporated place crosses a state boundary, but this is not the case. A number of cities are located on or near state boundary lines, and the locally inhabited area will cross the state boundary, but those instances actually represent two separate and distinct incorporated places. In some cases the two incorporated places are given very similar names; examples would include Kansas City, Missouri, and Kansas City, Kansas; Memphis, Tennessee, and West Memphis, Arkansas; and Bristol, Tennessee, and Bristol, Virginia.

*Census Designated Places.* Census designated places (CDPs) are areas of closely settled population outside of legally established boundaries. CDPs were previously referred to as unincorporated places. They are areas that are relatively well known locations, usually with a population of at least 1,000 persons and a population density of at least 1,000 persons per square mile, but that have not been legally incorporated as cities or towns. CDPs are defined by the U.S. Bureau of the Census with the help of state and local officials. Census designated places may cross MCD/CCD boundaries or county boundaries but will not cross state boundaries. There were approximately 3,500 CDPs identified in the 1980 census.

*Census Tracts and Block Numbering Areas.* Census tracts are statistical subdivisions of counties. Boundaries for census tracts are generally set by local committees subject to guidelines set by the Bureau of the Census. The boundaries for census tracts are intended to be relatively stable, and an effort is made to maintain consistent boundaries from one census to the next. Census tract population usually ranges from 2,500 to 8,000 with a population of 4,000 considered the ideal size. Census tract boundaries may cross incorporated place and MCD/CCD boundaries but will not cross county boundaries. Census tracts were defined for all metropolitan statistical areas in the 1980 census and for an additional 200 nonmetropolitan counties, resulting in a total number of approximately 43,000 census tracts.

As the population of a census tract increases, it may be split into two or more census tracts. Every effort is made to have the new tracts conform to the boundaries of the original census tract, and a numbering scheme is employed to help identify the new tracts as part of a former single tract. For example, a census tract may be identified with a code number, such as tract 15, in a particular metropolitan statistical area. As the population of that tract increases, it may be split into two tracts identified as 15.01 and 15.02. The combined geographic area of tracts 15.01 and 15.02 will usually conform to the previous area covered by tract 15. Splitting the tract in this manner enables one to match areas of geography from one time period to the next with a minimum of effort.

Block numbering areas (BNAs) are analogous to census tracts and are usually defined for rural areas. BNAs are statistical geographic areas defined for areas that have not been tracted but where census blocks have been designated (see the discussion of census blocks below). In the 1980 census there were approximately 3,400 BNAs. BNAs may cross minor civil division or census county division boundaries and place boundaries, but they will not cross county boundaries.

*Block Groups and Census Blocks.* Census block groups are best understood by first defining the nature of a census block. Census blocks are relatively small statistical areas that are bounded by streets or other physical features. Census blocks are essentially what one thinks of as a typical "city block," an area that is bounded by four streets. Blocks must be bounded by physical features, but things other than streets may serve as a boundary. For example, a block may be bounded on three sides by streets and by a railroad track on the fourth side. Other physical features may serve as block boundaries, such as streams, flood walls, embankments, and so on. Blocks will average approximately 100 persons in population but may range from a population of zero to several thousand. Census blocks are defined for all tracted areas (areas where census tracts have been defined), all urbanized areas, incorporated areas of 10,000 or more population, and additional areas that have contracted with the Bureau of the Census to be blocked. In the 1980 census there were a total of approximately 2.5 million census blocks. The states of Georgia, Mississippi, New York, Rhode Island, and Virginia were completely blocked in the 1980 census. Block boundaries will not cross county or census tract boundaries but may cross minor civil division and place boundaries. Blocks are identified with a numerical code, such as block 101, 102, and so on, and represent the smallest geographic area for which census data are reported.

Block groups represent aggregations of blocks and are defined for census tracts or block numbering areas. Block groups consist of census blocks within a census tract or BNA that begin with the same first digit. For example, blocks 201, 202, 203, and 204 within census tract 12.01 would comprise a block group. Block groups will average about 900 persons in population, and a total of approximately 200,000 block groups were defined in the 1980 census. Boundaries of block groups may cross MCD/CCD, place, urban area, and American Indian reservation boundaries but will not cross county boundaries.

*Enumeration Districts.* Enumeration districts (EDs) are statistical areas analogous to block groups defined for areas that are not blocked. EDs will average a population of 500 inhabitants but may vary considerably in size. Approximately 100,000 EDs were defined for the 1980 census; they represent the geographic area assigned to an individual census enumerator. ED boundaries are drawn so as not to cross any other legal or statistical area boundary.

## ADDITIONAL 1980 CENSUS GEOGRAPHY CONCEPTS

There are several additional geographic concepts that deserve mention in this discussion of census geography. Data are tabulated and reported for areas such as American Indian reservations, Alaska Native villages, congressional districts, local political areas, zip code areas, and a number of specially defined areas under contract with the Bureau of the Census. Several of these areas are of special interest in the production of population estimates and projections and are discussed below.

*American Indian Reservations/Alaska Native Villages.* Census data were tabulated and reported in 1980 for American Indian reservations at both the federal and state level. Data were tabulated for a total of 278 American Indian reservations in 1980. Reports were also generated for approximately 210 Alaska Native villages.

*Congressional Districts.* If one recalls that the constitutional mandate to conduct a census of population every 10 years is for the purpose of apportioning the U.S. House of Representatives, it should be no surprise to learn that data are also tabulated and reported for the 435 congressional districts in the United States.

Data from the census serve as the basis for apportionment of the 435 seats in the House of Representatives and are also used by the individual state legislatures for the purposes of redistricting. It might be useful to point out that the process of apportionment occurs at the federal level and determines the number of congressional seats to which each state is entitled based on total state population, while redistricting occurs at the state level and is the process by which each state legislature creates congressional districts within its borders based on its number of congressional seats. Census data are generally reported for both the current congressional districts (precensus boundaries) and the new congressional districts (postcensus boundaries) drawn after apportionment. Once the postcensus congressional districts have been approved, they remain in place for 10 years until the next census is taken.

*Election Precincts.* Legislation passed in 1975 (Public Law [P.L.] 94-171) provided an opportunity for states to participate in a voluntary program whereby local political areas such as election precincts, wards, voting districts, and similar areas could be defined using census geography concepts. The 1980 census provided the first opportunity to obtain population data for locally defined political areas under the provisions of P.L. 94-171, and many states and local communities will have population data at the local political area level.

State and local areas also may have opted to define a variety of local geographic areas for which census data will be available. Some of the locally defined areas are the result of ongoing Bureau of the Census programs, while others are the result of special tabulations produced on a cost basis by the Bureau of the Census at the request and expense of the local area. Special tabulations are often done for school districts within a given area, and these data may be available for a large number of local jurisdictions.

*Zip Code Areas.* The 1980 census marked the first time that population data were available by postal zip code areas. Budgetary considerations forced a delay in the processing of the 1980 zip code data by the Bureau of the Census; in fact, the cost of data processing was underwritten by a commercial vendor of demographic and marketing data in exchange for exclusive use of the data for a period of time. By the mid-1980s, the zip code data had become available for the general public, and these data are now available for all zip code areas in the United States.

## MAJOR CONCEPTS OF CENSUS GEOGRAPHY FOR
## 1990 AND CHANGES SINCE 1980

The major census geography concepts for the 1990 census remain unchanged from the 1980 census, but there are some important differences to note. Changes since 1980 include types of geographic concepts utilized in the tabulation and reporting of census data and the extent of application of certain types of existing geographic concepts to new areas. An example of the latter change is the tremendous increase in the number of areas where census blocks have been defined in the United States.

*United States.* The geographic concept of the United States remains unchanged from the 1980 census. Data reported at the level of the United States consist of the 50 states and the District of Columbia. Additional data are reported for the outlying areas such as American Samoa, Guam, the Northern Mariana Islands, Palua, and the U.S. Virgin Islands, as was the case with the 1980 census.

*Census Regions and Divisions.* The four census regions remain unchanged since the 1980 census. One should note, however, that the name of the North Central Region was not changed to the Midwest Region until June 1984. Many data products from the 1980 census prepared prior to June 1984 will obviously report the prior name for the Midwest Region, but the actual geographic area for which data are reported remains the same. The nine census divisions remain the same as in 1980, and the states composing the various census divisions are also unchanged since the 1980 census.

*States and Equivalent Units.* This geographic concept is unchanged from the 1980 census. Data are tabulated and reported for each of the 50 states, the District of Columbia, and the outlying areas of the United States.

*Metropolitan Statistical Areas.* MSA geography remains unchanged for the 1990 census; however, many reports from the 1980 census will reflect the former terminology of standard metropolitan statistical area (SMSA) since the revised guidelines for MSAs were not implemented until June 1983. There are currently 267 MSAs including 4 in Puerto Rico. The decline in the number of MSAs compared with the number of SMSAs reported in the 1980 census ($n = 323$) is due to the fact that some of the former SMSAs now meet the guidelines to be classified as primary metropolitan statistical areas.

*Consolidated Metropolitan Statistical Areas and Primary Metropolitan Statistical Areas.* These geographic concepts remain unchanged for the 1990 census. While there were no CMSAs or PMSAs defined as of 1980, many of today's CMSAs and PMSAs were identified as SMSAs in the 1980 census. There is no guarantee, however, that the boundaries have remained the same since 1980. As of the 1990 census there were 21 CMSAs (including 1 in Puerto Rico) and a total of 73 PMSAs (including 2 in Puerto Rico).

*Counties and County Equivalent Units.* These geographic concepts remain unchanged from the 1980 census. As of the 1990 census there were 3,141 county or county equivalent units (such as independent cities or boroughs) in the United States. This total does not include county or county equivalent areas in Puerto Rico or other outlying areas.

*Minor Civil Divisions and Census County Divisions.* The geographic concepts of MCDs and CCDs remain unchanged from the 1980 census. In the 1990 census there were 29,400 minor civil divisions and an additional 5,581 census county divisions defined for areas where the MCD designation is inadequate for reporting subcounty census data.

*Incorporated Places.* The concept of incorporated places remains unchanged from the 1980 census, although a number of new places have been incorporated since the 1980 census and the boundaries of many existing incorporated places have changed since 1980. As of the 1990 census there were approximately 19,300 incorporated places in the United States.

*Census Designated Places.* The concept of census designated places remains unchanged for the 1990 census. Approximately 4,700 census designated places have been delineated by state and local officials following Bureau of the Census guidelines.

*Census Tracts and Block Numbering Areas.* Census tracts are defined in the same way in the 1990 census as in the 1980 census. The total number of census tracts has increased to approximately 49,700 for the 1990 census as compared with approximately 43,000 in the 1980 census, and undoubtedly the boundaries of many census tracts will have changed from 1980 to 1990.

It is with the block numbering areas that we begin to see some divergence between the 1980 and 1990 censuses. The general concept of the BNAs has remain unchanged since the 1980 census, but the 1990 census resulted in a large increase in the number of BNAs. A total of approximately 11,200 BNAs were delineated for the 1990 census compared with an approximate total of 3,400 for the 1980 census. The large increase in the number of BNAs is the result of the entire nation being "blocked" for the 1990 census.

*Block Groups and Census Blocks.* The concepts of block groups and census blocks remain unchanged since the 1980 census; however, the application of census block boundaries to the entire United States has resulted in a tremendous increase in the number of census blocks. The 1990 census data include approximately 6.95 million census blocks compared with an approximate total of 2.5 million in the 1980 census. The enumeration district from the 1980 census, which was analogous to the block group concept for unblocked areas, is now obsolete since the entire nation has been blocked.

## ADDITIONAL 1990 CENSUS GEOGRAPHY CONCEPTS

*American Indian and Alaska Native Areas.* The 1990 census expands the geographic concepts relating to Native Americans and Alaska Native groups. Six geographic concepts comprise the "American Indian and Alaska Native areas" (AI/ANAs). Some of these geographic concepts were previously defined for the 1980 census, while others represent additional areas. The six types of areas include 310 American Indian reservations, including both federal and state reservation areas; 50 American Indian trust lands; 217 Alaska Native village statistical areas; 12 Alaska Native regional corporations; 17 tribal jurisdiction statistical areas which replace the "Historic Areas of Oklahoma" reported in the 1980 census; and 19 tribal designated statistical areas which are areas delineated by federally and state recognized American Indian tribes outside Oklahoma that do not have legally defined reservations.

*Congressional Districts.* As was the case with 1980 census data, 1990 census data will be reported for the existing 435 congressional districts (those resulting from the reapportionment following the application of 1980 census data) as well as for the congressional districts drawn following the reapportionment based on the 1990 census data.

*Election Precincts.* Election precinct data based on locally defined geographic areas are tabulated and reported for the 1990 census. Election precinct or voting ward data are part of a voluntary program, and not all states choose to participate. Data for approximately 149,000 precinct or ward areas are reported for the 1990 census. Some of the local election area boundaries will have changed since 1980, but local election area boundaries should be more stable than the larger congressional district area boundaries.

The 1990 census also afforded state and local areas an opportunity to define a variety of geographic areas and to obtain census results for those areas. Approximately 16,000 school districts have been defined in this program for the 1990 census and these data are available in some form.

Approximately 200,000 "traffic analysis zones" also have been defined nationwide by state and local governments, and these data are also available. The U.S. Bureau of the Census also has expanded its locally defined geographic area program. The "User-Defined Areas Program" allows users to define a geographic area and obtain 1990 census tabulations on a fee-for-service basis. Users do not have to be affiliated or working with a state or local governmental unit. The only major requirement is that the desired geographic area be defined in standard Bureau of the Census geographic concepts.

 *Zip Code Areas.* Zip code areas are also available for the 1990 census. Data for approximately 40,000 zip code areas have been tabulated for the 1990 census. Zip code boundaries are generally stable over time; however, some zip code boundaries will have changed since the 1980 census.

## KEY ISSUES IN CENSUS GEOGRAPHY

Census geography concepts cover a variety of areas including both legally defined governmental units and nongovernmental yet useful statistical aggregations. The geographic concepts range in size from the very large national level to the very small census block level. While it may be technically feasible to produce population estimates or projections for all of the census geographic areas, in some cases it will not be practical to do so. In other cases there may be no practical problem with producing population estimates or projections at a particular geographic level, but some geographic areas will be more useful than others in the production of population estimates and projections.

The feasibility of producing population estimates or projections for any given geographic area is a function of a number of things. One of the major factors will be the type of estimation or projection technique employed. As a general rule, the simpler the technique, the greater its range of application to various levels of geography. An additional factor will be the level of detail desired in the final product. A product with a great deal of detail, such as estimates or projections by age, race, and sex, is better suited to larger areas of geography; a product with little detail, such as reporting only an estimated or projected population total, will have a greater range of application with respect to geographic areas. Again as a general rule, the simpler the level of detail, the greater its range of application.

A final consideration at this point is the consistency of geographic areas from one time period to the next. Many of the methods of population estimation and projection require data from two points in time, usually the two most recent census periods, in order to establish basic population trends. Any estimation or projection technique requiring data from two points in time is best applied to geographic areas that are stable over time. Some geographic concepts have stable boundaries over time while others do not. The nation, census regions, census divisions, states, and counties have relatively stable boundaries over time. A change in county or state boundaries is unusual and any change is usually slight. More often than not the change is the result of a lawsuit filed by one state against another over a relatively minor border dispute. The resulting judgment is more meaningful in symbolic terms than in demographic ones. Incorporated places and census designated places, however, are more likely to have significant boundary changes from one time period to the next. In addition, due to the complete blocking of the nation for the 1990 census, most of the 1990 census blocks and block groups do not have direct 1980 census equivalents. Estimation and projection techniques requiring directly comparable data for an area from two time periods are best limited to the more stable geographic areas.

The national geographic level is a useful one when estimating or projecting population. It is large enough to allow for the most specific detail by age, race, and sex that one would desire, and the national boundaries are stable over time. A number of efforts are made at estimating and projecting the national population. Most of these estimates and projections are produced by the U.S. Bureau of the Census on a regular basis. Detailed estimates by age, race, and sex are produced on an annual basis, and some population estimates reporting total population figures are produced on a monthly basis. Population projections at the national level are produced periodically with varying degrees of detail. U.S. Bureau of the Census estimates and projections are published in Current Population Reports, Series P-25, "Population Estimates and Projections."

Academicians at universities or affiliated research organizations may serve as additional sources of national-level estimates and projections with the latter being more common than the former, and some commercial vendors of demographic and marketing data will produce in-house national-level estimates or projections. In most cases, however, the Bureau of the Census national-level estimates are adopted as a standard. Bureau of the Census national-level projections are usually published in a multiple series format based on several variations of assumptions. The end result is usually a low, middle, and high series, offering users a considerable range in projected population totals. The middle series is most often adopted by users, although there is no reason to choose automatically the middle series over the other two. The Bureau of the Census is not alone in the federal government in the production of population estimation and projection data. Additional projections are produced by the Bureau of Economic Analysis which along with the Bureau of the Census, is a bureau within the Department of Commerce.

Census regions and census divisions are also useful geographic concepts, but they are not the subjects of as many detailed census reports as the geographic levels just above them or just below them in the census geographic hierarchy. For example, the national geographic level of the United States, which is one level above that of regions and divisions, is the subject of a great deal more attention. Similarly, the state level of geography, which is one level below that of regions and divisions, is the subject of more attention.

Census regions and divisions are less likely to be the direct subjects of population estimates and projections. Some federal agencies, including the Bureau of the Census, will produce population estimates and projections at those levels of geography, but most estimation and projection work is done at smaller levels of geography, such as the state level or below. In addition, since census divisions are simply aggregations of contiguous states, and census regions are in turn aggregations of census divisions, it is seldom the case that regions or divisions are the subject of a direct estimation or projection process. One may project the population of a census division by first projecting the population of the individual states that comprise it and then simply summing the population projections for each of the constituent states. A population projection for a census region then may be produced by simply summing the projections for the census divisions that constitute the region. In fact, there is some advantage to producing a population estimate or projection for a region or division by first working with the constituent parts. It seldom will be the case that each component of a larger aggregation will change at the same rate. In the case of a census region, the constituent states will experience population growth at varying rates. For example, the South was a rapidly growing section of the United States during the 1980s, yet much of the growth for the region is accounted for by states such as Florida, Texas, and Georgia. Many other states in the South have had far lower growth rates, and a few have even experienced a population loss in the recent past. By producing population data for the region by first producing data for the constituent parts, one will have data on the total area but will also be able to identify subareas that are growing particularly fast or slow.

Use of the state level of geography provides an area with a sufficiently large population to produce data products detailed by age, race, and sex and provides an area with stable borders. The state level is beyond the threshold where one begins to see a considerable amount of population work by those outside the federal agencies. State population estimates and projections are routinely produced by demographic and marketing firms, and most states have some type of in-house agency producing population estimates and projections. Many substate governmental units also will produce state-level estimates and projections.

A considerable amount of estimation and projection work will be produced at the county level. Estimates and projections often will be produced at the county or county equivalent level due to a variety of reasons, including the population size and relative permanence of county boundaries. While the population size of counties may vary greatly from some counties having populations below 100 persons to the larger counties having populations of over 1 million persons, most counties will have a sufficiently large population to permit the production of detailed estimates and projections. Additional advantages of working with county-level geography include the fact that county boundaries will conform to state boundaries and that county boundaries are relatively stable over time. Just as one may produce population data at the census division level by aggregating state-level data, one also may produce state-level data by aggregating the county data. The resulting data indicate the population of the state as well as where the population is located on a county-by-county basis within the state. The relative stability of county boundaries over time allows one to compute trends from one census period to the next without having to adjust the data for variation in county area. Population estimates for all counties in the United States are produced on an annual basis by the U.S. Bureau of the Census. The Bureau of the Census generally does not produce population projections below the state level, but most states will have an in-house agency that produces population projections.

Once one moves below the county geographic level a variety of problems may be encountered. There is often considerable demand for population estimates and projections at the incorporated place geographic level; however, estimating or projecting population at the level of a city or town often may be difficult. Unlike states and counties, incorporated places do not always have stable boundaries. Cities and towns often annex adjacent territory bringing it into the incorporated limits of their jurisdiction. Again, unlike the boundary changes of a state or county, the boundary changes of an incorporated place are likely to have demographic significance. For example, a boundary change between two states may mean that the border is no longer the center of the river separating the two states but is now set at the right bank of the river. That change certainly has symbolic impact and may even have some economic impact, but it would have little demographic impact. In contrast, cities and towns seldom annex territory for symbolic purposes. Most often the areas chosen for annexation are considered desirable because of their population or economic characteristics.

As a result of annexation some levels of census geography will experience population change over time not only due to demographic forces but also due to changing geographic boundaries. For example, a city's population may grow due to demographic factors such as an increase in the fertility rate or increased migration, but it also may grow due to annexation of territory that was previously outside the city's borders. The population increase due to annexation may be considerable. The change in physical boundaries also makes it difficult to obtain comparable data for the area from two successive censuses. Census data will reflect the current boundaries of the incorporated place—whatever they were at the time of the census. Annual boundary and annexation surveys are conducted by the U.S. Bureau of the Census, but changes in place boundaries are not reflected in previously published census reports. It is possible for one manually to adjust census data to match current boundaries if the annexed areas conform to census geography; however, this is usually a time-consuming process.

An additional problem associated with subcounty areas of geography is a lower population base. The smaller the population of an area, the more difficult it is to produce detailed population estimates and projections. Larger places such as major cities will usually have a sufficiently large enough population to produce estimates and projections in detail. Smaller cities and towns, however, will often lack the population size needed to produce detailed products.

A final consideration when attempting to produce estimates or projections at the place level is that often the boundary defining the end of the political jurisdiction of an area is not consistent with the economic and social impact of the place in question. Suburban area population beyond the legal limits of an urban place is not included in the population total of the place and does not play any role in the estimation and projection of the place's population. The suburban area, however, is an integral part of the social and economic area of the urban place to which it is attached. Of course, to some extent this is a problem that may be encountered at any level of geography. A county boundary may extend through the center of a city. Likewise, a state boundary may pass through a major metropolitan area. In such cases it might be wise to produce two sets of population products—one set conforming to political boundaries and a second set conforming to social and economic boundaries.

Metropolitan statistical areas may combine the advantages and disadvantages of two levels of census geography. Since the MSA is built on county-level geography it is relatively easy to estimate or project the MSA population. In one sense, working with the MSA level of geography represents all of the advantages of working with county-level data. MSAs, however, are also built around a central city or highly urbanized area, which opens the possibility of attempting to estimate or project population at the place level. Attempts to estimate or project the population of an MSA in detail with separate reports for the central city and the surrounding area will suffer from the same problems as any attempt to work with place-level data. It should be pointed out that the major difficulty will be in physical changes in geography from one time period to the next. The central cities of MSAs are sufficiently large to allow for the production of detailed population products since one of the criteria for an MSA is the presence of a large central city. There is still the possibility of changing boundaries for the central city due to annexation. In addition, new counties may be added to, or in some cases deleted from, the area defined as belonging to the MSA.

Most of the geographic levels below the place level represent major challenges in the production of population estimates and projections. Census tracts and their nonurban counterparts, block numbering areas, are often too small in population to allow for highly detailed estimates or projections. Census tracts and block numbering areas are also subject to boundary changes from census to census. This problem is particularly acute with data from the 1990 census since it represents the first census where the entire nation has been defined in census blocks. As a result, many of the 1990 census tracts, and in particular many of the 1990 block numbering areas, do not have a direct counterpart from the 1980 census.

Block groups and census blocks are almost always too small to allow for the production of detailed population products. In the case of 1990 census data, most of the census blocks do not have 1980 census counterparts. Estimation or projection work done at the block group or block level is best done in the most general way possible. The farther one moves beyond estimating or projecting population totals at the block group or block level, the more likely one is to encounter error.

## FINAL CONSIDERATIONS

One of the complicating factors in selecting a level of geography suitable for producing estimates or projections is that often a single methodological technique must be adopted and applied to all areas of a certain type. For example, a particular population projection technique may be selected to project the population of all places in a state or regional planning district even when the projection technique is not suitable for some places. Very often one must accommodate a variety of conflicting demands such as using a single technique versus multiple techniques for all areas to be examined and producing a data product in a highly detailed fashion as opposed to reporting population totals only.

Once a set of estimates or projections has been produced, it may be wise to apply a control figure based on a higher level of geography. The issue here is essentially one of rounding error. In the case of a hypothetical state consisting of 45 counties, one will usually find that the same projection technique applied to each of the 45 counties will sum to a higher projected population total for the state than will be obtained by applying the projection technique to the state itself. In other words, rounding error will result in the sum of the parts (the counties) being greater than the whole (the state). One generally assumes that the results obtained directly for the state are more accurate than the results obtained by summing all of the counties. In these cases one may choose to adopt a control total. A constant is calculated consisting of the state's projected population total divided by the sum of the counties' projected population totals. The fractional value then is used as a multiplier to deflate each of the county population totals. As a result of applying the constant, the sum of the counties will equal the population value obtained independently for the state. The use of a control total may be applied at several levels of geography. For example, subcounty area totals may be controlled to total the county population, county totals may be controlled to total the state population, and state totals may be controlled to total the national population.

## SUMMARY

Census geography plays an important role in the population estimation and projection process. Even when census data are not used in the estimation and projection of population, results are usually reported for areas covered by census geography concepts. Census geography includes both legally defined governmental units, such as the nation, states, counties, American Indian/Alaska Native areas, and incorporated places, and statistical areas, such as census regions, census divisions, metropolitan statistical areas, census tracts, and census blocks. There are relatively few occasions where one will be producing population estimates or projections that are not for areas included in census geography concepts or areas that are not based on census geography concepts. An example of the latter case might be a local planning district that is defined as a certain group of counties or a local school district that is defined in terms of census tracts or blocks.

A major issue in producing estimates or projections at various levels of geography includes matching the methodological technique with the appropriate level of geography. One must be sure that the demands of the estimation or projection technique may be met by the desired level of geography. A technique that results in a highly detailed population product usually will need to be applied to a larger area of geography. Similarly, some techniques require highly detailed input data, and these demands are usually met only by the larger areas of geography. Finally, many techniques will require input data from two historical periods in time. Most often the periods will be the two most recent decennial censuses. It is imperative in these cases that one have comparable data. It is common to find data for a level of geography in one census but not in another. Larger areas of geography are more likely to have comparable data from one census to the next. As a general rule, it is best to match the demands of the methodological technique and the type of desired output to the level of geography best suited to them.

# 5

# Sources and Types of Data for Population Estimates and Projections

The role of demographic and related data in the estimation and projection process cannot be overemphasized. Regardless of one's technical expertise in executing a particular estimation or projection methodology, no population estimate or projection may be produced without meeting first the requisite data demands. The input data are quite literally the raw material from which population estimates and projections are developed. This chapter identifies the basic types and sources of data commonly required by the leading methods of population estimation and projection. Also discussed are the major data products from the 1990 census and the various media through which the data products are disseminated. The discussion begins by identifying the general sources of data for the estimation and projection process.

## MAJOR SOURCES OF DATA

The term *sources of data* in the present context refers to the general strategies that result in the collection, tabulation, and reporting of data useful in the process of population estimation and projection. The term *sources* is not used in the sense of identifying specific entities that provide data, although specific organizations that may serve as a "source" of data are discussed in some sections of the chapter. The four primary sources of data used in the production of population estimates and projections are (1) census data, (2) sample survey data, (3) vital registration data, and (4) special sources of data. Each of the four major sources is described in detail along with examples of the type of data that may be obtained from each source and suggested outlets for obtaining the data.

### Census and Special Census Data

A census is defined as a complete canvass and enumeration of the population. Ideally, all households in the population are identified, and information is collected pertaining to all inhabitants of the geographic area under investigation. A census is conducted in the United States every 10 years in years ending in zero, and special censuses are conducted periodically for smaller geographic areas usually at the request and expense of the jurisdiction making the request. Census data cover a wide range of topics and are vital in the production of population estimates and projections. The primary source of census data in the United States is the U.S. Bureau of the Census, although there are related organizations that also serve as sources for census data. The Bureau of the Census initiated the State Data Center program in 1976 with the goal of establishing an information network at the state level to help disseminate census data. The concept of the state data center is to establish a lead agency within each state to serve as a repository and distribution point for census data, and each state data center in turn establishes its own network of affiliate agencies throughout the state. The State Data Center program has been a successful one that provides local outlets for census data. A fee is usually charged for services involving the processing of data tapes, providing printed reports, or providing printed copies of census reports from media such as microfiche or electronic media. The State Data Center network remains, however, an economical source of census data.

Census data play such a significant role in the production of population estimates and projections that it is worthwhile to review the major data products from the 1990 census. In addition, population projection methodologies often require data from two successive census periods to establish certain parameters or to calculate population growth rates from one time period to the next. It is therefore useful to note data products for 1990 that are comparable to 1980 census data products and to discuss the various media through which census data are made available.

## Dissemination Media for the 1990 Census

Data from the 1990 census are released for public use in several formats, including traditional media such as printed reports, computer tape files, and microfiche; and nontraditional media reflecting new technology, including an on-line computer data retrieval system available through several private vendors, compact disk–read-only memory (CD-ROM) storage devices, and computer flexible diskettes. Printed reports are probably the most familiar medium of census data dissemination for most users.

Computer tape files represent another traditional medium of data dissemination and are generated in two principal forms. The public use micro sample (PUMS) computer tape file represents a randomly selected sample of census returns that are prepared and released for demographic and related research. The PUMS file contains data from individual census records that allow the researcher great flexibility in analyzing and cross-tabulating the data in a variety of ways. The second type of computer tape file containing census data is the summary tape file (STF). The summary tape files represent a much different type of data product than the PUMS files. Summary tape files contain census data in tabulated format, usually in the form of a hierarchical data file. The STF product will contain a particular set of census data concepts prepared in a standard format similar to a printed report. The researcher has no control over the format since the STF does not contain individual census records. The hierarchical nature of the data file means that the same census concepts are contained on the tape for different levels of geography. For example, a particular STF may contain total population by 5-year age groups cross-tabulated by sex for the United States as a whole or for any particular state or group of states. The researcher, however, does not have the flexibility to define his or her own cross-tabulations of data with the STF product. In the present example, one could not retrieve the data from the STF in single years of age or cross-tabulate the age data by race since the data are presented in 5-year age groupings by sex. One way to think of the STF data product is as a printed census table on a computer tape. In most cases the only flexibility offered by the STF products is the ability to retrieve the data for a variety of geographic areas, but one cannot retrieve the data in a different format. In spite of the greater flexibility offered by the PUMS file, the STF data product is used more often in the production of population estimates and projections. The STF data presentation may be more limited, but the data are usually presented in a form required by the commonly used methods of population estimation and projection. The single most frequently used data item from a census in the production of population estimates or projections is the size of the population at the base period. Often the base period must be available in great detail by age, race, and sex. Data from an STF product are usually available to meet the requirements for the base period for all but the smallest areas of geography.

Microfiche is another traditional data dissemination medium through which census results are available. Microfiche consists of sheets of developed microfilm approximately 4 inches by 6 inches in size containing page-size images of census reports for a given geographic area. The microfiche sheets may be loaded into a reader and viewed on a display screen or printed out for a hard copy. Microfiche represents a mid-range product between printed reports and computer tapes that combines desirable features of both. Microfiche provides a method of presenting a great deal of information without taking up the space that would be required to present the same information through printed reports, and yet the information may be retrieved with low-level technology unlike computer tapes which require either a mainframe computer or a personal computer and tape drive mechanism.

Dissemination media for the 1990 census reflecting newer technology include on-line computer services available through several private vendors. The U.S. Bureau of the Census established CENDATA, its on-line computer service presenting census data, in the mid-1980s. Data users may access CENDATA through several private vendors of computer services but not directly through the U.S. Bureau of the Census. Even though CENDATA contains only data available to users in other formats, such as printed reports or data tapes, there were concerns that some members of the public might confuse access to such an on-line data system with access to actual individual census records thus allowing computer users to violate the confidentiality of census data. CENDATA is not a major source of data for the estimation and projection process since the data presented are more likely to be of immediate interest, such as recently released statistics.

Compact disk–read-only memory (CD-ROM) is another dissemination medium for the 1990 census based on newer technology. CD-ROM allows for the storage and retrieval of vast amounts of data in a format that is accessible by personal computers with a CD-ROM drive. Several data products from the 1990 census are available in CD-ROM format, and many data users consider CD-ROM to be a major dissemination medium of the future. There are some disadvantages associated with CD-ROM technology, such as the requirement of a special computer drive capable of reading the disk and access to software capable of manipulating the data. These limitations, however, are more the function of the recent emergence of the technology and will be overcome as more and more data users are attracted by the vast storage capabilities of compact disks. Currently, one CD-ROM can contain up to 600 megabytes (MB) of data in an unindexed configuration or up to approximately 400 MB when fully indexed which aids in the search and retrieval of data from the disk. A fully indexed CD-ROM can hold the equivalent of over 1,000 standard 5 ¼" floppy disks or the equivalent of over 325 high-density 5 ¼" floppy disks. Flexible diskettes (floppy disks) were envisioned as a dissemination medium of the future several years ago; however, very few data products from the 1990 census are available on floppy diskettes given the tremendous storage capabilities of the CD-ROM system. Users who wish to obtain census data on floppy disks likely will have to make special requests either to the U.S. Bureau of the Census directly or to a member agency of the State Data Center network. Selected data files may be transferred from computer tape or CD-ROM to floppy diskette in some cases, although there may be a data-processing charge in addition to the charge for the data.

## Data Products from the 1990 Census

*Apportionment Data.* The amount of data produced in any census of population is truly enormous, and the 1990 census is no exception. Data were collected on census day, April 1, 1990, and then released on a flow basis with most data products being released between 1991 and 1993. The first major official data product from the 1990 census, however, fulfills the constitutional mandate to conduct a census of population every 10 years for the purpose of apportioning the House of Representatives. The Bureau of the Census must deliver to the president of the United States by December 31 of the census year the total population of the United States and of each state and the official apportionment counts. The apportionment counts consist of the number of members of the House of Representatives each state is entitled to based on its population. By April 1 of the year following the census, the Bureau of the Census must deliver to each state legislature and the governor of each state the population counts mandated by the provisions of Public Law (P.L.) 94-171. The P.L. 94-171 data consist of total population; population by race for white, black, Asian and Pacific Islander, American Indian, Eskimo and Aleut, and other; population of total Hispanic origin; and cross-tabulations of data for persons not of

Hispanic origin by race. The P.L. 94-171 data are cross-tabulated for all ages and persons 18 years old and over for the following geographic areas: state, county, minor civil division/census county division (MCD/CCD), place, census tract/block numbering area, block group, and block. States that have defined their voting districts in terms of census geography and have participated in the Bureau of the Census Voting District program will receive the P.L. 94-171 data at the voting district level in addition to the standard geography levels listed under the general provisions of P.L. 94-171. Data for P.L. 94-171 are released on computer tape and paper listings initially, and then on CD-ROM. With the release of the P.L. 94-171 data, the U.S. Bureau of the Census completes its legal obligation with respect to the release of data. A wealth of data products, however, will follow, and some of these are outlined in the following section.

*Data in Printed Reports.* In many respects data released in printed reports are the most accessible to users and are the most convenient to use. Printed reports do not require any additional hardware or software to access unlike data on electronic media or microfiche. Several data products from the 1990 census are of use in the production of population estimates and projections. Three major sets of printed reports are issued: one dealing with data on population and housing, a second dealing with data on population, and a third dealing with data on housing. Each set of printed reports will contain both complete census results (termed 100% items which are asked of every household), and sample items (data obtained from only a portion of households). In most cases only complete census results are of interest in the production of population estimates and projections. One possible exception deals with migration data.

Several population and housing reports may be beneficial in the estimate and projection process. The major differences among the reports are in the type of data presented and the level of geography included. A "Summary Population and Housing Characteristics" report containing data on total population and housing unit counts, and summary statistics on age, sex, race, Hispanic origin, household relationship, number of housing units in the structure, value and rent, number of rooms in each housing unit, tenure, and vacancy characteristics is issued for all local governmental units including American Indian and Alaska Native areas for each state and the United States.

A "Population and Housing Unit Counts" report including data on total population and housing unit counts for the 1990 census and for selected previous censuses is issued for all states, counties, minor civil divisions/census county divisions, places, state component parts of metropolitan statistical areas and urban areas, and selected geographic summary areas such as urban/rural and metropolitan/nonmetropolitan. A report is issued for each state and the United States.

More detailed geographic data may be found in "Population and Housing Characteristics for Census Tracts and Block Numbering Areas." Data from this report will be presented at the relatively small geographic level of census tracts and block numbering areas. One report will be issued for the metropolitan area portion of each state, and a second report will be issued for the nonmetropolitan portion of each state. The entire nation was blocked (defined in terms of census blocks) for the first time for the 1990 census, so data will be available for all areas in this series of reports. Only portions of metropolitan areas and selected other areas were blocked in 1980 so there may not be comparable data from the 1980 census.

A second small geographic–level report on "Population and Housing Characteristics for Congressional Districts of the 103rd Congress" will be issued detailing population and housing data for each congressional district. A report will be issued for each state and the District of Columbia, and additional summary data are available by county, places of 10,000 or more, and minor civil divisions of 10,000 or more for selected states. One limitation of these data is that the congressional districts will be subject to change once the apportionment and redistricting process based on 1990 census results has been completed.

Several publications focusing on the census of population results are of use in the estimation and projection process. A series of reports on "General Population Characteristics" with detailed data on age, sex, race, Hispanic origin, marital status, and household relationship characteristics is issued for states, counties, places of 1,000 or more inhabitants, minor civil divisions of 1,000 or more inhabitants in some states, the state portion of American Indian and Alaska Native areas, and summary geographic areas. A report is issued for each state and the United States.

Three special-level geography reports are issued on general population characteristics: "General Population Characteristics for American Indian and Alaska Native areas," "General Population Characteristics for Metropolitan Statistical Areas," and "General Population Characteristics for Urbanized Areas." Each of these reports, like the previous general characteristics report, is based on 100% data from the 1990 census. One set of printed reports based on sample data from the census of population that may be of interest includes data on migration, income, and the older population for the United States; census regions and divisions; and other selected geographic areas.

A series of reports based on housing data from the 1990 census paralleling those focusing on the population data are available and may be beneficial in the estimation and projection process. A report focusing on "General Housing Characteristics" which provides detailed statistics on the number of housing units in each structure, the value and rent, number of rooms, tenure, and vacancy characteristics is presented for each state and includes data for counties, places of 1,000 or more inhabitants, and minor civil divisions of 1,000 or more inhabitants in selected states. In addition, the state portion of American Indian and Alaska Native areas, and summary geographic areas are covered. A separate report is issued for each state and the United States. Similar reports are available for focusing on "General Housing Characteristics for American Indian and Alaska Native areas," "General Housing Characteristics for Metropolitan Areas," and "General Housing Characteristics for Urbanized Areas."

A variety of additional printed reports are also available, but they are not as useful in the population estimation and projection process. Printed reports represent one of the easiest means to census data, provided one can find a report with the population data necessary for the desired analysis. Reports may be obtained directly from the U.S. Bureau of the Census, one of the affiliate agencies of the State Data Center network, or any number of libraries that serve as repositories for U.S. government documents.

*Data on Computer Tape Files.* In cases where printed reports are not available, one may turn to computer tape files which are more extensive but often are more difficult to deal with. The use of computer tape files obviously requires access to computers, and most often one must have access to a large mainframe computer to process the census data given the size of the data files which often occupy more than one computer tape. In addition, one must have access to appropriate software to access the data since the U.S. Bureau of the Census no longer supports an in-house software package. One advantage of computer tape files is that the data are directly available in machine-readable form which may expedite the production of population estimates and projections in some cases.

Both summary tape files and public use micro sample files are available from the 1990 census, but the STF data products are of greater use in the production of estimates and projections. Summary tape files may be thought of as standardized census reports printed electronically on computer tape but containing much more detail than is usually available in conventional printed reports. In fact, the printed reports for the 1990 census are based on data from the various STF products. Four STF products have been designed for the 1990 census, with two STF series containing 100%

data, and two STF series containing sample data. Each STF contains more than one data file, and is labeled STF 1A, STF 1B, and so on. The STF 1 series and the STF 2 series contain 100% data from the 1990 census and generally will be of more use in the estimation and projection process. STF 3 and STF 4 contain sample data from the 1990 census and have limited use for estimates and projections, although one notable exception is STF 3B which contains data at the zip code level.

Summary tape file 1 includes 100% data on population and housing counts and characteristics and contains four data files. STF 1A contains data for states and state subareas in a hierarchical file structure down to the block group level. Data also will be included for the state portion of American Indian and Alaska Native areas, whole places, whole census tracts/block numbering areas, whole MCDs in selected states, and whole block groups. The hierarchical file structure will allow users to select data at any level of geography included on the tape; for example, one might select population counts at the county level, or for the census tracts defining the county, or for the block groups comprising the census tract. STF 1B provides similar data down to the block level. STF 1C provides similar data at the following geographic levels: United States, census regions, census divisions, states (including by urban and rural population), counties, places of 10,000 or more inhabitants, MCDs of 10,000 or more inhabitants in selected states, urbanized areas, and American Indian and Alaska Native areas. STF 1D provides similar data by state focusing on the congressional districts of the 103rd Congress. Also included in STF 1D are data for counties, places of 10,000 or more inhabitants, and MCDs of 10,000 or more inhabitants in selected states within congressional districts.

The STF 2 series contains 100% population and housing data similar to the STF 1 series but in greater detail, including data by race and Hispanic origin. Three data files are included in the STF 2 series. STF 2A is structured around the metropolitan statistical area (MSA) level of geography. Data are presented for each state at the census tract/block numbering area (BNA) for MSAs and the non-MSA portion of states. Data are presented also at the census tract/BNA level by county, and places of 10,000 or more inhabitants, and for whole census tracts/BNAs.

STF 2B contains similar data presented in a different file structure. Data are presented in an inventory-type file structure with each geographic area presented without linkage to those above or below it, unlike the linkage found in hierarchical file structures. Data are presented for the following geographic areas in STF 2B: states (including summaries for urban and rural), counties, places of 1,000 or more inhabitants, and MCDs of 1,000 or more inhabitants in selected states. Data also will be presented for the state portion of American Indian and Alaska Native areas. STF 3C presents data in a hierarchical file structure for the following geographic areas: United States, census regions, census divisions, states (including summaries for urban and rural), counties, places of 10,000 or more inhabitants, MCDs of 10,000 or more inhabitants for selected states, MCDs of fewer than 10,000 inhabitants in New England MSAs, American Indian and Alaska Native areas, metropolitan statistical areas, and urbanized areas.

Data on STF 1 and STF 2 represent 100% items asked on all census forms, and these data are more likely to be used in the production of population estimates and projections. STF 3 and STF 4 contain data based on a sample of respondents from the 1990 census. A larger amount of data is collected from the sample items, but the content is usually of little use in the preparation of estimates and projections. One possible exception is STF 3B which provides population and housing data at the 5-digit zip code level for each state. There were considerable delays in releasing the zip code data from the 1980 census, but the data proved to be very popular once they were made available. A second exception is a special computer tape file pertaining to migration data containing all intrastate county-to-county migration streams and significant interstate county-to-county migration streams.

In some applications, particularly those involving population projections, it is necessary to have data for an individual level of geography at two points in time. Most often one requires data from the two most recent censuses. The summary tape files for the 1990 census are comparable in content to those released for the 1980 census. Two points, however, should be considered. First, an additional STF product was released for the 1980 census; STF 5 contained an extremely large and detailed cross-tabulation of data for large geographic areas. Second, there is no guarantee of a one-to-one correspondence between geographic areas in 1980 and 1990, and in some cases one may count on significant changes. For example, only a portion of the nation was defined in terms of census blocks in 1980, but the entire nation was blocked for the 1990 census. In addition, smaller areas of geography are subject to changing boundaries over time. Incorporated places such as cities or towns may annex additional territory between the two census periods, and census tracts or block numbering areas may be redefined from one census to another. Caution should be exercised when comparing data from two census periods for what appears to be the same area of geography.

*Data on Microfiche.* Microfiche is a relatively inexpensive, low-technology method of retrieving data similar to that available on the summary tape files. Microfiche is actually generated directly from the summary tape files through a computer transfer process without the need to produce a printed document for conventional microfilming. Again, the 100% data are more likely to be of use in the production of population estimates and projections, and there are two major microfiche products based on 100% data. STF 1A, containing population and housing data in a hierarchical file format, is available on microfiche, as are the data from STF 1B, which presents data in the inventory-type file structure. Comparable data from the 1980 census were released on microfiche, but some of the boundaries for some areas of geography will have changed over the intercensal period.

*Data on CD-ROM.* The release of census data in a CD-ROM format is new for the 1990 census, and the decision process concerning which data files to release will continue for some time. Initial files available on CD-ROM include 100% data on the A, B, and C files from the STF 1 series, as well as sample data on the A, B, and C files from the STF 3 series. Included will be the zip code data on STF 3B. CD-ROM files were not produced for the 1980 census; however, comparable data are available in machine-readable format from the computer STF series for 1980.

Census data often play a key role in the production of population estimates and projections. Frequently, the most recent census data will serve as the source of the base population on which current population estimates or future projections of the population will be based. In some cases, census data may be used to provide estimates of fertility or migration. Census data are available in a variety of formats, with printed reports and computer tapes the more widely used media of dissemination. Data may be obtained directly from the U.S. Bureau of the Census (Data User Services is a good place to begin a search for data) or from the State Data Center network. Not all data needs, however, may be met through census data, and other sources may be used. Sample survey data may be a valuable source in certain applications, and these data are discussed next.

## Sample Survey Data

Sample survey data cover a variety of topics. Since the mid-1950s a number of national surveys designed primarily to measure demographic conditions and processes have been conducted. Examples include the

Growth of American Families Survey; the National Fertility Studies, conducted on several occasions; and the Survey of Fertility and Family Planning (Knowledge, Attitudes, and Practices). While these surveys provide a wealth of demographic data as well as background information on socioeconomic characteristics and values of the respondents, the information from them is of little use in the production of population estimates and projections. The assertion of the limited utility of national survey data is not intended as a criticism of their scope and content; it simply reflects the fact that most national demographic surveys are designed for other purposes. There are, however, two notable exceptions where national demographic surveys do provide data of potentially high value to the estimation and projection process.

One national demographic survey with the potential to contribute to the estimation and projection of population is the Current Population Survey (CPS) conducted by the U.S. Bureau of the Census on a monthly basis. The CPS has been in operation since 1942 when it was designed in response to the need for current information on unemployment during the years of the Depression. Over the years the CPS has been revised in terms of size and scope. The current version of the CPS focuses on employment and unemployment, other characteristics of the general labor force, and the population of the United States as a whole. The total sample size consists of over 70,000 households drawn on a probability basis from each of the 50 states and the District of Columbia.

While some general data are collected each month in the CPS that may be of help in the estimation and projection process, what is of particular interest in the CPS are data from several of the monthly supplements. The CPS contains a monthly supplement on housing vacancy that provides quarterly data on vacancy rates for the United States. The March supplement focuses on demographic characteristics of the population, including information on migration and household composition. The June supplement collects data on fertility, including the number of children ever born and birth expectations. Finally, the October supplement focuses on school enrollments and provides data on school enrollment, college attendance, and high school graduation.

The data provided in the monthly CPS supplements may be beneficial in a number of ways. Housing data from the monthly supplements may be beneficial in several population estimation strategies. Migration data from the March supplement may be useful in both the estimation and the projection process. Fertility data available in the June supplement are of benefit in the projection process, especially since the CPS sampling frame is designed to provide data at the state level. One might use data from the CPS to adjust national-level fertility measures at the state or even substate level in some cases. Larger states will be represented sufficiently in the CPS to provide some analysis below the state level. School enrollment data from the October supplement may be beneficial in both the estimation and projection processes in limited applications.

A second national survey with potential use in the estimation and projection process is the American Housing Survey. The American Housing Survey was begun in 1973 and was initially an annual survey with a sample size of 60,000 housing units. The survey was conducted on an annual basis from 1973 to 1981 with a sample size that fluctuated periodically due to federal budget constraints. Since 1981 the survey has been conducted on a biennial basis (prior to 1984 the American Housing Survey was called the Annual Housing Survey). The sampling frame for the American Housing Survey is designed to provide data at the national level and at the metropolitan statistical area level for selected areas. Currently, 44 MSAs are represented on a rotating basis in the American Housing Survey with 11 MSAs included with each administration of the survey. Data are collected on a variety of housing and demographic characteristics, including some information on recent movers. These data may often prove beneficial in the estimation and projection process, especially in estimating changes in average household size and to some extent in migration volume. One limitation of the American Housing Survey is that reliable state-level data are not available in all cases due to the nature of the sampling frame.


### Vital Registration Data

The vital registration system in the United States operates as a national-level clearinghouse for data collected at the state level on several vital events. The federal government does not actually collect vital event data directly, but rather sets standards for data quality and then collates and reports data from qualifying states. By the mid-1930s, all existing states and some U.S. territories had been admitted to the vital registration reporting system of the United States for births and deaths. Currently, vital registration data on births and deaths are collected for all states, the District of Columbia, and certain U.S. territorial areas.

Vital registration data for the states are collected and reported by the National Center for Health Statistics, with annual data reported in a multivolume publication, *Vital Statistics of the United States*. Of particular interest are Volume I, on natality, and Volume II, on mortality. Monthly data are also published in a *Monthly Vital Statistics Report* series. Data are provided at the summary level for the United States and at the state level, including detail by county, in the annual reports. Monthly data are presented at the national level and the state level. Vital registration data on births and deaths are frequently of use in the production of population estimates and projections. Additional data on marriages and divorces are also collected and reported by the National Center for Health Statistics; these data may have limited uses and may be symptomatic indicators for selected population processes.

Each state operates its own vital registration system; the data are reported by the individual states in annual publications. One advantage of obtaining vital event data directly from the state is that more detailed data are usually reported by the state than are available in the U.S. summaries. One is also likely to have access to vital event data more quickly when obtaining it directly from the state. Local governmental units may serve as an additional source of vital event data. Choosing a source for vital event data that corresponds as closely as possible to the level of geography to be estimated or projected is usually a wise strategy.

## Special Data Sources

The final category of data sources represents a miscellaneous collection of outlets for a number of different types of data. Included in this discussion are specialized data products from the U.S. Bureau of the Census, alternative types of mortality and survival data, examples and sources of symptomatic data for migration, and private sector sources of data.

Most requirements for mortality data may be met through the national vital registration system or through state and local vital registration systems. Alternative sources for mortality-related data, however, are available. The National Center for Health Statistics publishes national and state life tables which can be an invaluable source of data in the production of population projections. Longer range life tables for the United States are produced by the Social Security Administration for its long-term actuarial studies. In addition, census survival rates for various lengths of time are produced and published by the U.S. Bureau of the Census as part of its population projection program. Census survival rates may be found in many of the technical appendices accompanying the Bureau of the Census's published population projections.

U.S. Bureau of the Census population projections are published as part of *Current Population Reports,* Series P-25, on population estimates and projections. The P-25 series presents a wealth of data on population projections for the United States and individual states and on special populations, such as the Hispanic population. Results of the Bureau of the Census's population projections are published periodically; often included in the publication are population projections produced at the state level by members of the Federal State Cooperative for Population Projections (FSCPP). State-level members of the FSCPP often produce population projections for their own state and in detail below the state level. FSCPP members are a good source for locally produced population projections, especially when one requires detail below the state level.

The P-25 series of the *Current Population Reports* also publishes the results of the Bureau of the Census's population estimation program. The population estimation program is somewhat more ambitious than the population projection program. Annual estimates for the United States, all states, and all counties are produced and published by the Bureau of the Census. Subcounty estimates have been published on a biennial basis as well. County-level estimates are produced by the Bureau of the Census as part of its work with the Federal State Cooperative for Population Estimates (FSCPE), which may represent an alternative source of data. Many FSCPE members produce their own population estimates at the state and substate level.

Additional publications of the U.S. Bureau of the Census that may provide helpful information in the population estimation and projection process include the *Statistical Abstract of the United States*, the *County and City Data Book*, and the *Congressional District Data Book*. Much of the content of these publications is indicated by their titles; nonetheless, a few points are worthy of mention. The *Statistical Abstract of the United States* is a good general resource for a variety of data in addition to the general sections on population and vital statistics. Data are often presented at the level of the United States and the individual state. One of the appendices lists all of the metropolitan statistical areas of the United States and identifies the constituent counties of each MSA. The *County and City Data Book* provides general population and economic data at the county level and for selected cities in the United States. The *Congressional District Data Book* provides data for congressional districts but will be of little use if data are needed over time since the geographic composition of many congressional districts changes every 10 years with reapportionment.

Migration data are the most difficult to obtain in the process of producing population estimates and projections. Some sources of migration data based on census results have been identified previously, but alternative sources of migration data are sometimes required. Estimates of international migration are provided by the Immigration and Naturalization Service (INS). The INS maintains records on immigration to the United States and emigration from the United States. One major problem with INS data is that much of the migration to the United States is in the form of undocumented aliens who do not go through the legal entry process. The U.S. Bureau of the Census includes an estimate of approximately 200,000 undocumented immigrants annually into its population estimation and projection models. Raymondo (1988) has provided estimates of the undocumented population at the state level using the Bureau of the Census estimate of 200,000 annual undocumented immigrants and the estimated distribution of the undocumented population from the 1980 census.

Some data are available on migration within the United States, such as the state-to-state migration file based on sample census data or the migration file produced by the Bureau of the Census from Internal Revenue Service data on matched tax returns. Frequently, however, one must turn to symptomatic indicators of migration in the production of population estimates and projections. Any number of variables may serve as symptomatic indicators of migration. Some of the more frequently chosen variables include driver's license applications, motor vehicle registrations, voter registrations, utility hookups, and school enrollments. The difficulty in obtaining access to symptomatic migration data will vary depending on the source. Data gathered by political jurisdictions are often regarded as public information and are readily available, although in some cases it may be difficult finding the correct contact person who will release the data. School enrollment data may be obtained from local school districts or from state-level departments of education, but again it may require some perseverance in finding the correct contact person. Utility data may be more difficult to obtain. Municipal utilities are likely to release data upon request, but privately owned or incorporated utility companies may be more reluctant to release data.

A final type of data that may be of use in the production of population estimates and projections concerns the size of the group quarters population. Individuals included in group quarters are those in institutional settings of some type, such as college dormitories, prisons, long-term health care facilities, military bases, and related types of group housing. Again, some of these data may be readily available, while others may be more difficult to obtain. In the general case, public facilities are more willing than private or incorporated facilities to report population counts for group quarters. College dormitory counts are best obtained directly from the institution as is the population for long-term health care facilities. Prison populations are usually available at the state level from a state department of corrections or related agency. In some cases one may turn to national publications such as the *Statistical Abstract of the United States* for state-level prison populations. A number of federal agencies may provide data on military populations. The Directorate of Information of the U.S. Department of Defense is a good starting point for data on military base populations. In some cases one may even obtain expected future population counts in addition to the current base population. In addition, each branch of the military has an information office that might provide information for its particular bases.

One final source of data that should be mentioned is the private sector. There are a large number of firms that specialize in providing not only general demographic data but demographic products including current population estimates and projections. Data and products are available in a wide variety of formats and geographic levels on a fee-for-service basis. The U.S. Bureau of the Census provides a referral service identifying the names of both private and public data sources in its "National Clearinghouse for Census Data Services" address list. The listing is provided as a public service, but there is no implied "seal of quality" for those organizations included in the listing.

## SUMMARY

Data for population estimates and projections come in a variety of forms from a variety of sources. In many cases, the data required for a particular methodology will be difficult to obtain, but without them there can be no final data product. Basic types of demographic data include the decennial census or a special census, sample surveys at the national or local level, vital registration data, and other specialized types of data.

Census data are available in several primary forms, including printed reports, computer tapes, microfiche, and CD-ROM. Some of the major data products of particular use in the production of population estimates and projections have been identified and discussed in this chapter. Also, some of the key agencies that serve as sources for demographic and related data have been identified. The list is far from exhaustive since the varying nature of the data required by the major techniques of population estimation and projection require one to be innovative in seeking out data sources. The importance of input data in the estimation and projection process cannot be overemphasized, and one should realize that the quality of the end product can be no better than the quality of the data upon which it is based. The phrase often applied to computer data analysis, GIGO (Garbage In, Garbage Out), also applies to the production of population estimates and projections.

# 6

## Methods of Intercensal Population Estimation

Several methods have been developed to estimate population in an attempt to meet the information needs of the business professional, the governmental planner, the marketing specialist, the school administrator, or anyone in need of current population estimates. The methods of population estimation are employed in two broad applications: intercensal estimation and postcensal estimation. More attention by far is given to postcensal estimates, but intercensal estimates are used in some cases. Intercensal estimates result when one has population totals for a particular area from two successive censuses for the census years but does not have population totals for the intervening years. Intercensal estimate methodologies provide a way of estimating the population of the area on a year-by-year basis for the intercensal period and are the subject of this chapter. Postcensal estimates involve estimating the population of an area after the most recent census. Postcensal estimates are more likely to be in demand by planners and other similar users of population data; the major methods of postcensal estimation are the subject of chapter 7.

While one may deal with an intercensal period or a postcensal period, in each case one is dealing with estimates in contrast to projections. Recall that the essential difference between a population estimate and a population projection is that population estimates are made for an area for a specific time in the past. Most often the estimate is for a period in the recent past, such as the previous year; population projections are produced for a period of time in the future. In most cases the methodologies from which one will choose when producing population estimates or projections will differ due to the applicable time frame. In addition, methods of population estimation are more likely to be based on the use of symptomatic data which are likely to move in conjunction or sympathy with population totals. Methods of population projection are more likely to be based on some type of extension or variation of current population trends. All things being equal, a population estimate for a given area for a given point in time is preferable to a population projection for the same area and time period.

## METHODS OF INTERCENSAL POPULATION ESTIMATION

A number of methodological strategies to estimate intercensal population have been developed. The methods vary in their level of complexity, type of data required for their computation, level of detail in the final product, and intended purpose. In addition, many of the methods of producing intercensal population estimates are better described as methodological strategies; that is, there is considerable flexibility in the way certain estimation methods are employed. One common characteristic of population estimation methodologies is that they all in one way or another are based on the classic demographic equation:

$$P_1 = P_0 + B - D + I - O$$

Where:    $P_1$    is the current population

$P_0$    is the population at a previous point in time

$B$    is the number of births since $P_0$

$D$    is the number of deaths since $P_0$

$I$    is the number of inmigrants since $P_0$

$O$    is the number of outmigrants since $P_0$

According to the classic demographic equation, the population at any point in time is equal to the population at a previous point in time plus natural increase (the number of births in the area minus deaths in the area) and net migration (the number of inmigrants minus the number of outmigrants). Not all of the estimation methodologies, however, will deal with the classic demographic equation in as sophisticated a fashion as others.

Not all of the existing methodologies are described in the present discussion. Rather, emphasis is placed on those methods that are used more frequently by those active in population estimation. Included in this discussion of estimation methodologies are intercensal interpolation, assuming arithmetic and compound rates of change, and detailed intercensal estimates through the forward/reverse survival rate method. Major postcensal methodologies are discussed in chapter 7. The discussion of intercensal estimation methodologies begins with an analysis of the interpolation method of producing intercensal estimates.

## THE ROLE OF INTERPOLATION IN INTERCENSAL ESTIMATES

Intercensal estimation most often involves the production of single year population estimates for all years between two census years. For example, we may have the 1980 and 1990 census population for an area but would like to have a year-by-year estimate for years 1981 through 1989. Often some type of interpolation estimation process will be chosen to derive the intercensal estimates. The two observed population totals reported in the two most recent census results are treated as the beginning and ending points for the population, and the interpolation procedure then provides a series of annual estimates. One should note that implicit in an interpolation strategy is the assumption that the population has increased or decreased in a smooth and continuous fashion between the two census years. In many cases the assumption of a continuous population change will be false. Population change often occurs in an irregular fashion with periods of rapid change followed by periods of stagnation. In the case of intercensal estimates, however, the fact that the beginning and end points of the annual population series are represented by actual census results tends to lessen the importance of the estimated population values for the intervening years.

There are two broad uses of interpolation procedures in the production of intercensal population estimates. One use involves the application of one of several alternative interpolation strategies which may be used to actually produce intercensal population estimates on a year-by-year basis. The second broad use of an interpolation procedure provides a method of dealing with what some have termed the "closure problem" with respect to population estimates and the census count. The closure problem is encountered when a series of population estimates is produced that includes an estimate for the most recent census year. Often the census year estimate will be the final estimate in a series of annual estimates. It is unlikely that the population estimate for the census year will equal exactly the population total reported when the most recent census is released.

There is usually a desire to adjust the estimate series when there is a sizeable difference between the estimated population and the enumerated population, and it is often desirable to adjust the entire series of estimates rather than just adjusting the census year estimate. Both uses of interpolation estimates are discussed below, beginning with the former situation of using an interpolation procedure to actually produce intercensal estimates.

## PRODUCING INTERCENSAL ESTIMATES BY INTERPOLATION

There are three major variations of producing population estimates through interpolation. The chief difference among the three variations is the assumption concerning the nature of population growth that has occurred during the period between the two most recent censuses. One may assume a simple rate of population growth between the two most recent census periods as expressed by an arithmetic rate of change, or one may assume a compound rate of growth between the two most recent census periods. The compound rate of growth may be expressed as a geometric rate of change or as an exponential rate of change. A geometric rate of change assumes a compound rate of growth over a specified finite time period, such as compounding annually, quarterly, weekly, and so on. An exponential rate of change assumes a continuous compound rate of growth with the period of compounding infinitely short.

### Arithmetic Rates of Change

An arithmetic rate of change is the simplest approach in producing intercensal population estimates. One begins with the observed population at each of two census years; for example, 1980 and 1990. The population for the earlier period is subtracted from the later period to determine the amount of net change in population between the two census years. The net change in population is then divided by the number of years in the time interval between the two censuses to determine the annual amount of population change between the two time periods. The annual amount of population change is then added to the earlier census total to derive the estimated population for the first year after the census. The annual amount of population change is then added to the previous year's estimate to derive the second year estimate, and so on until all of the intercensal years have been estimated. In the following example, it is assumed that one has population data for the 1980 and 1990 census years.

$$\text{Annual Net Change} = \frac{P_{90} - P_{80}}{n}$$

Where:  $P_{90}$  is the 1990 census population
$P_{80}$  is the 1980 census population
$n$  is the number of years between the two census periods

Population 1980:     72,400
Population 1990:     81,500

$$\text{Annual Net Change} = \frac{81,500 - 72,400}{10} = 910$$

The series of intercensal estimates would be derived by adding 910 persons to the preceding population total on a year-by-year basis as follows:

| Year | Population |
|------|-----------|
| 1980 | 72,400 |
| 1981 | 73,310 |
| 1982 | 74,220 |
| 1983 | 75,130 |
| 1984 | 76,040 |
| 1985 | 76,950 |
| 1986 | 77,860 |
| 1987 | 78,770 |
| 1988 | 79,680 |
| 1989 | 80,590 |
| 1990 | 81,500 |

Population totals for 1980 and 1990 represent hypothetical census values for a particular area, and the population values for years 1981 through 1989 represent estimates based on an arithmetic rate of growth.

Census results are reported as of April 1 in the United States. In many applications the convention for producing population estimates is to use a July 1 date for the estimate years in order to differentiate more clearly a population estimate from an actual census result. When a July 1 date is desired for a series of population estimates, it is necessary to adjust the series since the first estimate occurs 1.25 years past the census date. In order to adjust the above series, one would multiply the annual amount of population increase (910 persons) by 1.25 years (the period elapsed since the base population was enumerated and the first estimate is produced). In the present example, the result of the multiplication is 1,137.5 persons. The estimate for 1981 would then be calculated by adding 1,138 to the base population of 72,400 for an estimate of 73,538. The remainder of the series would be derived by adding the annual amount of net change (910 persons) to the estimated population of the preceding year. The final population value in the series represented by the census count of 1990 will be .75 × 910 (persons) above the 1989 estimate since April 1, 1990, is only three-quarters of a year past July 1, 1989.

In the previous example, the annual net change in population was calculated by subtracting the beginning 1980 population from the ending 1990 population, in order to derive the total net change, and then dividing the total net change by the number of years between the two census periods. The result was an annual net change of 910 persons per year. One may choose to divide the annual net change by the size of the base population (the 1980 population of 72,400) and then multiply by 100 to determine the annual percentage change in population. In this example, the annual percent change would be:

$$\frac{910}{72,400} \times 100 = 1.26\%$$

## Compound Rates of Change

There are two procedures for producing intercensal estimates assuming a compound rate of change. One method assumes a geometric rate of change which involves compound growth over a finite period of time. Usually, one year is chosen as the period of time for compounding. The second method of intercensal estimation assumes an exponential compound rate of change. With an exponential rate of change, the compound growth is assumed to occur on a continuous basis. Rather than having a finite period of time such as a year, half-year, quarter, month, or week over which to calculate the growth rate, an exponential method assumes an infinitely small period of time.

*Geometric Rate of Growth.* The geometric rate of change assumes the population is increasing by a constant amount compounded over a given period of time. In the general case, the formula for a geometric rate of population growth is as follows:

$$P_n = P_0 \times (1 + r)^n$$

Where:  $P_n$   is the end point population
$P_0$   is the initial population
$1 + r$ is the annual rate of growth
$n$    is the number of years between the base population and the estimate period

Assuming census population data for 1980 and 1990, a formula for a geometric rate of growth is as follows:

$$P_{90} = P_{80} \times (1 + r)^n$$

Where:  $P_{90}$   is the 1990 census population
$P_{80}$   is the 1980 census population
$1 + r$ is the annual rate of growth
$n$    is the number of years between the base population and the estimate period

The rate of population growth $(1 + r)$ may be calculated by taking the $n$th root of $P_n/P_0$. For example, if there were two years between the two population observations, then one would take the square root of the result of $P_n/P_0$; if there were three years between the two observations, then one would take the cube root; and so on. In the present case, there are 10 years between the two census observations so one would take the 10th root of $P_{90}/P_{80}$. Readers should note that there are alternate methods for calculating the value of $(1 + r)$ involving logarithmic transformations.

Assume the same 1980 and 1990 census data as in the previous example where:

Population 1980:   72,400
Population 1990:   81,500

Then $P_{90}/P_{80} = 1.1257$; solving for the 10th root of 1.1257, the result is 1.01191. The result of 1.01191 represents the value of $(1 + r)$. The value of $r$ (.01191) represents the proportion of compound annual population growth. Expressed as a percentage, the value would be 1.191% which may be compared to the annual percentage growth rate of 1.26% found in the previous example where an arithmetic rate of population growth was assumed.

Population estimates for the intercensal years are obtained by substituting the appropriate values into the formula:

$$P_n = P_0 \times (1 + r)^n$$

The estimate for 1981 is obtained as follows:

$$P_{1981} = 72{,}400 \times (1.01191)^1 = 73{,}262$$

The estimate for 1982 is obtained as follows:

$$P_{1982} = 72{,}400 \times (1.01191)^2 = 74{,}135$$

Results for the remaining years in the series are presented in Table 6.1 next to the estimates produced previously where an arithmetic rate of growth was assumed. Values for the geometric growth rate have been rounded to the nearest whole number, a common practice in population estimates and projections. The values represent the estimated number of people, so there is little point in reporting fractional numbers to three or four decimal places. The 1981 estimated value of 73,262 persons conveys as much useful information as the seemingly more precise value of 73,262.284 persons.

The population estimates assuming a geometric rate of growth may be adjusted to a July 1 date just as the arithmetic rate of growth estimates were. In the case of the geometric rate estimates, one would simply substitute 1.25 as the exponent $n$ in the term $(1 + r)^n$ rather than an exponent of 1 used in the example above for the first year's estimate. The second year's estimate would use the exponent 2.25 and so on throughout the series. The 1981 estimate would be calculated as follows:

$$P_{1981} = 72{,}400 \times (1.01191)^{1.25} = 73{,}479$$

The higher estimate for 1981 is a result of the fact that 1.25 years have elapsed since the date of the base population compared with the assumption of 1 year in the sample calculations.

*Exponential Rate of Growth.* The exponential rate of growth is the second intercensal estimate strategy based on a compound rate of growth. The exponential rate of growth assumes a continuous period of compounding rather than compounding over a finite period, such as annually, monthly, weekly, and so on. In some ways the exponential rate of growth

**Table 6.1**
**Intercensal Population Estimates With Arithmetic and Geometric Rates of Growth**

| | Population | |
|---|---|---|
| Year | Arithmetic Rate of Growth | Geometric Rate of Growth |
| 1980 | 72,400 | 72,400 |
| 1981 | 73,310 | 73,262 |
| 1982 | 74,220 | 74,135 |
| 1983 | 75,130 | 75,018 |
| 1984 | 76,040 | 75,911 |
| 1985 | 76,950 | 76,815 |
| 1986 | 77,860 | 77,730 |
| 1987 | 78,770 | 78,656 |
| 1988 | 79,680 | 79,593 |
| 1989 | 80,590 | 80,541 |
| 1990 | 81,500 | 81,500 |

is quite similar to what we have seen with the geometric rate of growth, but the calculations may seem a little more cumbersome.

Exponential rates of growth may be expressed as a function of e, the natural logarithm whose value is approximately 2.718. The population at a given time may be expressed as the population at the base period multiplied by e raised to a power reflecting the assumed rate of growth times the time interval since the base period. Using the same hypothetical census data for 1980 and 1990 as above, the 1990 population may be expressed as follows:

$$P_{90} = P_{80} \times e^{rn}$$

Where:  $P_{90}$  is the 1990 census population
$P_{80}$  is the 1980 census population
$e$  is the natural logarithm
$r$  is the growth rate

$n$      is the number of years between the base population and the estimate period

The census data are given, $n$ is equal to 10 years, and e is a constant whose value is approximately 2.718. In order to complete the calculations, it is necessary to find the value of $r$, the growth rate between the two census periods. The calculation for $r$ may seem somewhat cumbersome, but it is simply a matter of substituting the appropriate values into the following formula:

$$r = \frac{\log (P_{90}/P_{80})}{n \times \log e}$$

To solve the formula for $r$, we simply divide the 1990 population by the 1980 population and then take the base 10 logarithm of the result. The resulting term is then divided by the product of the number of years between the two population observations (in this case $n = 10$ years) and the base 10 logarithm of e. Substituting the appropriate values into the formula yields:

$$r = \frac{\log (81,500/72,400)}{10 \times \log e}$$

$$= \frac{\log (1.12569)}{10 \times .43429}$$

$$= \frac{.051419}{4.3429} = .01183$$

The value $r = .01183$ represents the exponential growth rate of the population between 1980 and 1990. Expressed as a percentage, the growth rate is 1.18% compounded continuously over the 10-year period. The exponential growth rate may be compared to the geometric growth rate of 1.19% compounded annually over the 10-year period and the arithmetic growth rate of 1.26%.

Once the value of $r$ has been calculated the intercensal estimates may be computed on a year-by-year basis by substituting the appropriate value of $n$, representing the time between the base population year and the estimate year, into the estimating formula:

$$\text{Estimate} = P_{80} \times e^{rn}$$

The population estimate for 1981 would be obtained as follows:

$$P_{1981} = 72{,}400 \times 2.718^{(.01183)(1)}$$

$$= 72{,}400 \times 1.0119$$

$$= 73{,}262$$

The estimates for the remaining years in the series would be obtained by substituting the appropriate values of $n$ into the formula. For example, the 1982 estimate would be obtained by using $n = 2$, the 1983 estimate would be obtained by using $n = 3$, and so on. The exponential growth rate method is also easily adapted to a July 1 date for the annual estimate period. One would simply adjust the value of $n$ indicating the time of the estimate period beyond the base population. A July 1, 1981, estimate would be calculated by using a value of $n = 1.25$ to reflect an estimate date 1.25 years past the time of the base population.

The remaining values for the annual series based on the exponential growth rate are not presented since they round to values identical to those based on the geometric growth rate assumption. There are situations where the geometric and exponential rates of growth will vary sufficiently to produce different estimates. In the present example, where intercensal estimates are being produced, there is a relatively short time span of 10 years, and the respective growth rates are very similar in magnitude.

## Comparing Results From Arithmetic and Compound Rates of Growth

Since the previous examples deal with intercensal estimates there is no difference between arithmetic and compound rates of growth with respect to the beginning point and the end point in the estimation process. All three types of intercensal estimation strategies examined begin with the population enumerated in the second to most recent census and end with the population enumerated in the most recent census. The results obtained for the simple arithmetic growth rate assumption differ compared to the results from the compound growth rate assumption, but the 10-year interval between the two census observations does not provide enough time for major differences to emerge.

The intercensal estimates obtained with the arithmetic growth rate method change by a fixed absolute amount from year to year but by a variable percentage from year to year. The intercensal estimates obtained with the compound growth rate assumptions change by a variable absolute amount from year to year but by a fixed percentage from year to year. Given the small degree of difference between the two sets of results, there is no real advantage or disadvantage to either strategy. Conventional wisdom suggests that a strategy assuming a compound growth rate is more realistic since human reproduction follows that model, but as we have seen in the case of intercensal estimates the beginning and end points of the series are fixed to equal the observed census results of the two most recent censuses, and there is not that much time for the results of the two strategies to vary that much. There is also the implicit assumption of a relatively smooth rate of change involving gradual growth, or in some cases, gradual decline from beginning point to end point. In reality, intercensal population change is much more sporadic. Periods of growth or decline may be followed by an opposite trend or by a period of stagnation. In such cases, neither method will provide an accurate picture of population change between the two census counts.

The level of geography may play a role in the choice of method with respect to arithmetic versus compound rates of growth. A compound rate of growth is more characteristic of the national experience, because most total population growth is due to natural increase rather than to an increase in net migration. When working with smaller levels of geography, such as a state or county, the role of migration becomes increasingly important with respect to population change. Population growth due to net migration is not necessarily better described by a compound growth rate assumption, and, in fact, growth due to migration is likely to occur in sporadic periods following perceived economic opportunities in the area.

## INTERCENSAL ESTIMATES AND THE CLOSURE PROBLEM

The second broad application of interpolation procedures when dealing with intercensal estimates involves the problem of closure. The closure problem is encountered when a series of intercensal estimates is produced that includes an estimate for the most recent census year that is found to deviate from the actual census count. Most often the estimation methodology employed does not require knowledge of the end point census count in order to construct the estimate series, unlike the intercensal estimate examples discussed previously. The situation is one where a postcensus methodology is used resulting in an independently derived estimate for the next census year which turns out to be too high or too low once the actual census results are released.

The population enumerated in the census traditionally has been accepted as the most accurate number available, and while recent concerns with undercount have caused many to question the quality of the census, the enumerated population is generally accepted over an estimate. In one sense the closure problem is an easy one with which to deal; one simply may choose to use the census result in place of the census year estimate. The problem then becomes one of what to do with the remaining numbers in the estimate series. When the final number in the series representing the census year is adjusted, it often will be out of line with the rest of the series. There will appear to have been a sudden large population change between the year just prior to the census and the census date. In some cases the adjustment will be large enough to represent a reversal in the previous population trend, with the population appearing to grow over the previous 9 years and then dropping in the final year.

The solution to the closure problem is to adjust the entire intercensal series. An adjustment may be made with a relatively simple interpolation process. The difference between the population estimate for the census year and the population enumerated in the census year is found; then, assuming a 10-year intercensal period with annual estimates, each year's estimate in the series is adjusted upward or downward by 10% of the difference between the census estimate and the enumerated population per year. If the estimated population assumes a July 1 date, then the first year's estimate in the series will be adjusted proportionately. The example in Table 6.2 assumes an annual population estimate series with the estimates made for a July 1 date and the census population reported for an April 1 date.

The estimated population for April 1, 1990, of 31,075 persons in this example would have been produced through a postcensal estimation methodology prior to the release of the 1990 census results. Actual (hypothetical) census results reported at a later date indicate an enumerated population of 30,225 persons, or 850 persons below the previous estimate. To adjust the census date estimate by substituting the actual census value would make the April 1, 1990, population lower than the previous year's (1989) estimate. The effect is to suggest that the population of the area suddenly stopped growing and began to decline.

The entire series of estimates may be adjusted by subtracting 10% of the difference between the estimated population on the census date and the

**Table 6.2**
**Intercensal Adjustment**

| Date | Postcensus Estimate | Intercensal Adjustment | Revised Estimate |
|------|---------------------|------------------------|------------------|
| April 1, 1980 | 25,897* | -- | 25,897* |
| July 1, 1980 | 26,225 | - 21 | 26,204 |
| July 1, 1981 | 26,879 | -106 | 26,773 |
| July 1, 1982 | 27,433 | -191 | 27,242 |
| July 1, 1983 | 27,690 | -276 | 27,414 |
| July 1, 1984 | 28,022 | -361 | 27,661 |
| July 1, 1985 | 28,654 | -446 | 28,208 |
| July 1, 1986 | 28,997 | -531 | 28,466 |
| July 1, 1987 | 29,435 | -616 | 28,819 |
| July 1, 1988 | 29,985 | -701 | 29,284 |
| July 1, 1989 | 30,446 | -786 | 29,660 |
| April 1, 1990 | 31,075 | -850 | 30,225* |

\* Indicates hypothetical census result.

enumerated population per year. In this case the difference between the estimated population and the enumerated population is 850 persons, and 10% of that difference is 85 persons. The first adjustment is made for the July 1, 1980, estimate; since that estimate is only one-quarter of a year past the April 1, 1980, census observation, it is only adjusted by 25% of 85, or by 21 persons. The estimate for July 1, 1982, is adjusted by the initial 21 persons plus an additional 85 persons. The estimate for July 1, 1983, is adjusted by the previous 106 persons plus an additional 85, and so on until all of the estimates have been adjusted.

## KEY ISSUES WITH INTERPOLATION TECHNIQUES

The three types of interpolation techniques used to produce intercensal estimates—arithmetic growth assumption, geometric growth assumption, and exponential growth assumption—are relatively easy to calculate, and they have a wide range of application. As illustrated previously, when these methods are used for intercensal estimates, there is not a great deal of difference in the results, so one approach does not have a clear advantage over another. All three of the techniques are versatile in that they may be applied to multiple levels of geography. Even the smallest unit of geography, such as a census tract or block, may be estimated using interpolation procedures. All that is required are beginning and ending census results.

One limitation of an interpolation methodology is that it does not result in detailed population estimates. The interpolation techniques are best suited to the production of total population estimates rather than estimates by race, age, and sex. The interpolation approach is also limited by what are often unrealistic assumptions on the nature of population change between census periods. All three of the strategies we have examined assume, in one form or another, a rather smooth rate of change from one census period to the next which is not often the way populations change. In spite of some limitations, the interpolation approach to producing intercensal estimates is an efficient one.

Each of the interpolation techniques may be used for the development of postcensal estimates. Postcensal estimates are made for years following a census but differ from the intercensal estimates in that they are produced without reference to an end point census value. The use of interpolation techniques to produce postcensal estimates involves applying a previously established growth rate to a base population and extending that growth rate into the future. In effect, the use of interpolation techniques for postcensal estimates results in more of a population projection than a true population estimate. For that reason, the application of interpolation techniques to a base population without reference to an end point census result is discussed in chapter 8 along with other methods of population projection.

## DETAILED INTERCENSAL ESTIMATES: THE FORWARD/REVERSE SURVIVAL RATE METHOD

While the interpolation strategies discussed above have their advantages and play an important role in the production of intercensal estimates, they do not result in detailed population estimates. One strategy for developing detailed intercensal population estimates is the forward/reverse survival rate method. The forward/reverse survival rate method is actually a combination of two methods for developing detailed intercensal population estimates; it involves one method operating in a forward direction and a second method operating in a reverse direction.

The underlying logic of the forward/reverse survival rate method is to take the detailed base population enumerated at the time of the second to last census and to "age" it forward in time to the desired estimate date by subjecting the observed population to a schedule of detailed survival rates. The result is a population estimate at the desired date in as specific a level of detail as made possible by the base population and the available schedule of survival rates. The next stage in the process involves taking the population enumerated at the most recent census and reversing it in time by subjecting it to a schedule of detailed survival rates. Some have termed this process "younging" the population since it is the opposite of "aging" the population as is done in the forward survival rate method (Shyrock & Siegel, 1973). The result of the reverse survival rate method is a detailed population estimate for an earlier period in time. The final population estimate is derived by averaging the results from the forward method with those from the reverse method.

Several sets of data are required in order to produce detailed population estimates with the forward/reverse survival rate method. One begins with the second to most recent census of population for the area whose population is to be estimated. Census population results are produced in a variety of detail; the more detailed the population results, the more detailed the estimates will be. The more detailed the input population, however, the more involved will be the calculations necessary to produce the estimates. One should also keep in mind that the level of detail in the beginning population data should be matched by the schedule of survival rates used in the estimation process. For example, when using population data detailed by age, race, and sex, one should also have survival rates detailed by age, race, and sex. Appropriate detailed survival rates are less likely to be available than are detailed population data, and this is especially true at smaller levels of geography.

One must obtain suitable detailed survival rates following the selection of the detailed population data. As a rule of thumb, it is wise to secure the survival rates prior to determining the level of detail to be used in the population estimates since population data are likely to exist in a wider variety of forms than survival rates. The forward/reverse survival rate method may be used to produce estimates detailed by age, race, and sex, but in the example below only detail by age is presented. In this example, one requires detailed census population data for 1980 and 1990 and a schedule of survival rates by age. Suitable survival rates may be obtained from a life table analysis of the population or from census survival rates (see chapter 3 for a discussion of survival rates). Actually, two sets of survival rates are required for the forward/reverse survival rate method. One set of survival rates representative of the mortality experience of the earlier period (1980 in this example) is required, and a second set of survival rates representative of the later period (1990) is also required. Ideally, the survival rates will correspond to the level of geography and the population to be estimated, but in many cases one will not have survival rates for the precise area to be estimated, especially at smaller levels of geography.

Detailed intercensal population estimates may be produced as an annual series through the forward/reverse survival rate method, but the process can be extremely cumbersome and time consuming. Production of an annual series requires either a set of 1-year survival rates or a 10-year survival rate that has been interpolated to approximate the required level of detail. For example, production of an annual series would require a detailed set of survival rates reflecting 1-year survival, 2-year survival, 3-year survival, and so on. Most often, the forward/reverse survival rate method is used to produce a single set of detailed estimates for the mid-census period. In this example the estimates would be for July 1, 1985.

Adjustments to the data may be necessary at several steps in the estimation process with the forward/reverse survival rate method. Survival rates are most often presented as 10-year survival rates, so these must be adjusted in the present example to reflect a 5-year survival rate. Ten-year survival rates may be adjusted to reflect a 5-year rate by a variety of methods. Two easy approaches are to assume either an arithmetic rate of change or an exponential rate of change. The logic of each approach is similar to the interpolation procedures illustrated above. Assume a 10-year survival rate for a particular age group equal to 0.966637. One can imagine a cohort of individuals beginning at an initial time where 100% of the cohort is alive and then proceeding through time to a point 10 years later when only 96.6% of them are alive. Over the course of the 10-year period, a total of 3.34% of the cohort has expired. The question becomes one of assigning a 5-year survival rate based on the 10-year experience. With an arithmetic rate of change, one would simply assume that half of the mortality losses will occur by the 5-year mark, and thus the 5-year survival rate would be equal to the 10-year survival rate plus half of the expected 10-year mortality.

$$5\text{-Year Survival} = 0.966637 + (.0334/2) = 0.98334$$

The same technique could be applied to each survival rate in the series.

One may choose to assume an exponential rate of change in the survival rates across the 10-year period of time. In the case of an exponential rate of change, the 10-year survival rate may be expressed as a function of the natural logarithm e raised to the power $rn$, where $r$ is the rate of change over the 10-year period and $n$ is the number of years since the base period. In the present example:

$$0.966637 = e^{rn}$$

Where:    $r$    $= \dfrac{\log (0.966637)}{10 \times \log e} = -.003393$

$n$    $=$    5 years

Assuming an exponential rate of change, the 5-year survival rate would be:

$$\text{5-Year Survival} = 2.7183^{(-.003393 \times 5)} = 0.983177$$

The remaining 10-year survival rates in the series could be adjusted in a similar fashion. There is very little difference between the arithmetic assumption and the exponential assumption when estimating 5-year survival rates from the 10-year rates that are given. Suitable results may be obtained from either procedure.

The conventional practice of using a July 1 date for estimates as opposed to the April 1 date, results in the need to make an additional adjustment when using the forward/reverse survival rate method. A cohort such as the 10–14-year-old group as of April 1, 1980, will be the estimated 15–19-year-old group as of July 1, 1985, as we age them 5 years. But we really want the aging process to begin as of July 1, 1980, rather than April 1, 1980, since we are using 5-year survival rates. Between April 1 and July 1, a small portion of the 10–14-year-old group will have "aged" out of the 10–14-year-old cohort, and a small portion of the 5–9-year-old cohort will have "aged" into it. The period of time from April 1, 1980, to July 1, 1980, represents 5% of the time period from the base population date of July 1, 1980, to the estimate date of July 1, 1985; we can use the proportion as a weighting factor to adjust the number of survivors.

One method of adjusting the number of survivors to the estimate date is based on the 0.05 (5%) proportion of time that passes from April 1 to July 1. The number of survivors to July 1, 1985, for any given cohort of individuals as of April 1, 1980, may be expressed as a combination of two

April 1, 1980, cohorts. Using the example of the 10–14-year-old group of April 1, 1980, the survivors aged 15–19 on July 1, 1985, may be expressed as 95% of the survivors of the 10–14-year-old cohort from April 1, 1980, plus 5% of the survivors of the 5–9-year-old cohort from April 1, 1980 (assuming we are dealing with age detail expressed as 5-year age intervals).

Similar types of adjustments must be made for the "reverse" part of the forward/reverse survival rate method. The 10-year survival rates must be adjusted to reflect a 5-year period of time, and the April 1, 1990, base population must be adjusted to reflect the appropriate July 1, 1985, cohort. The adjustments for the 1990 data operate in the same way as the ones for the 1980 data. A 5-year survival rate may be approximated from a 10-year rate by either an arithmetic or exponential adjustment with no clear advantage to either method. The July 1, 1985, cohort may be expressed as a combination of two of the April 1, 1990, cohorts as was done previously, and the weighting factors will be the same.

Once the appropriate base population and the survival rates have been obtained, the estimation process may begin. Hypothetical data are presented in Table 6.3 to illustrate the calculations. Using the forward survival rate method, the 1980 population detailed by age is subjected to a set of detailed 5-year survival rates yielding the number of survivors in 1985. The number of survivors in each age category is then adjusted by weighting the 1985 survivors in a particular age group by 0.95 plus the number of survivors in the immediate cohort younger than it weighted by 0.05. For example, the number of survivors aged 30–34 years in 1985 is calculated by multiplying the 1980 cohort of 25–29-year-olds (1,729 persons) by its 5-year survival rate of 0.993426, resulting in a total of 1,718 survivors in 1985. That result is then weighted by 0.95, which yields 1,632 persons, to which we add 5% of the survivors from the cohort immediately younger than it. There are 1,844 survivors in the 1985 cohort of 25–29-year-olds, and 0.05 (5%) of that group is 92 persons. The total adjusted number of survivors in 1985 is then calculated by adding 1,632 to 92 for a total of 1,724 persons. Calculations for the remaining cohorts are made in a similar fashion.

In the reverse survival rate method, the detailed 1990 population is subjected to a schedule of age specific survival rates. In order to arrive at the number of individuals actually enumerated in the 1990 census, each cohort of the 1990 population is divided by the corresponding survival rate to yield the number of individuals that would have been expected to be alive in 1985. The initial division of the 1990 population by its correspond-

# Table 6.3
## The Forward/Reverse Survival Rate Method

| Forward Method | | | | | | Reverse Method | | | | | | Final Estimate for 1985 | |
|---|---|---|---|---|---|---|---|---|---|---|---|---|---|
| Age 1980 | Age 1985 | Population 1980 | Survival Rate | 1985 Survivors | Adjusted Survivor | Age 1990 | Age 1985 | Population 1990 | Survival Rate | 1985 Survivors | Adjusted Survivors | Age 1985 | Final Estimate |
| births 1980-85 | 0-4 | 2601 | 0.987322 | 2568 | 2552 | 0-4 | N.A. | N.A. | | | | 0-4 | 2734 |
| 0-4 | 5-9 | 2242 | 0.997812 | 2237 | 2254 | 5-9 | 0-4 | 2887 | 0.988716 | 2920 | 2898 | 5-9 | 2391 |
| 5-9 | 10-14 | 2581 | 0.998672 | 2578 | 2561 | 10-14 | 5-9 | 2489 | 0.998073 | 2494 | 2515 | 10-14 | 2743 |
| 10-14 | 15-19 | 2678 | 0.996869 | 2670 | 2665 | 15-19 | 10-14 | 2927 | 0.998822 | 2930 | 2909 | 15-19 | 2892 |
| 15-19 | 20-24 | 2433 | 0.994596 | 2420 | 2432 | 20-24 | 15-19 | 3097 | 0.997168 | 3106 | 3097 | 20-24 | 2882 |
| 20-24 | 25-29 | 1856 | 0.993872 | 1844 | 1873 | 25-29 | 20-24 | 3282 | 0.994928 | 3299 | 3289 | 25-29 | 2314 |
| 25-29 | 30-34 | 1729 | 0.993426 | 1718 | 1724 | 30-34 | 25-29 | 2666 | 0.99428 | 2681 | 2712 | 30-34 | 2205 |
| 30-34 | 35-39 | 1625 | 0.992801 | 1613 | 1619 | 35-39 | 30-34 | 2623 | 0.993966 | 2639 | 2641 | 35-39 | 2175 |
| 35-39 | 40-44 | 1512 | 0.989575 | 1496 | 1502 | 40-44 | 35-39 | 2663 | 0.99363 | 2680 | 2678 | 40-44 | 2013 |
| 40-44 | 45-49 | 1540 | 0.982951 | 1514 | 1513 | 45-49 | 40-44 | 2443 | 0.991066 | 2465 | 2476 | 45-49 | 1864 |
| 45-49 | 50-54 | 1517 | 0.972481 | 1475 | 1477 | 50-54 | 45-49 | 2135 | 0.985592 | 2166 | 2181 | 50-54 | 1739 |
| 50-54 | 55-59 | 1559 | 0.956617 | 1491 | 1490 | 55-59 | 50-54 | 1919 | 0.976184 | 1966 | 1976 | 55-59 | 1754 |
| 55-59 | 60-64 | 1554 | 0.936998 | 1457 | 1458 | 60-64 | 55-59 | 1917 | 0.961416 | 1994 | 1993 | 60-64 | 1661 |
| 60-64 | 65-69 | 1484 | 0.906119 | 1345 | 1350 | 65-69 | 60-64 | 1731 | 0.942774 | 1836 | 1844 | 65-69 | 1580 |
| 65-69 | 70-74 | 1123 | 0.864742 | 971 | 989 | 70-74 | 65-69 | 1631 | 0.913991 | 1784 | 1787 | 70-74 | 1372 |
| 70-74 | 75-79 | 769 | 0.81007 | 623 | 641 | 75-79 | 70-74 | 1501 | 0.875502 | 1714 | 1718 | 75-79 | 1120 |
| 75+ | 80+ | 1009 | 0.639246 | 645 | 672 | 80-84 | 75-79 | 1275 | 0.82525 | 1545 | 1553 | 80+ | 1520 |
| | | | | | | 85+ | 80+ | 779 | 0.74591 | 1044 | 1069 | | |

ing survival rate results in the unadjusted number of survivors in 1985. The 1985 survivors are then adjusted in a process identical to the one used in the forward survival rate method. A weighting factor of 0.95 is applied to the individuals in a particular cohort, and then 5% of the immediately younger cohort of survivors is then added to that number to result in the adjusted number of survivors.

The final panel of Table 6.3 presents the adjusted number of survivors from each method along with the final population estimates for July 1, 1985. Differences in the number of survivors from the forward and reverse methods are due to several factors. Differences in the degree of undercount from one census to the next will contribute to the variation in the results from the two methods. Changing patterns of mortality as reflected in survival rates will also contribute to variation in the results. Finally, the impact of net migration during the intercensal period will have an impact on the results from the two methods. A large net inmigration from 1980 to 1990 will have the result of substantially increasing the 1985 population estimates based on the reverse method, while a large net outmigration would have the opposite effect.

The final population estimates are based on an average of the two sets of adjusted survivors. Calculation of the final estimates represents one final adjustment to the data. Rather than simply average the two sets of survivors from the forward and reverse survival rate methods, it is conventional to weight the two sets of results in reverse proportion to the length of time between the estimate date and the respective census date upon which each set of survivors is based. In this example, the results from the reverse survival rate method are weighted slightly more than the results from the forward survival rate method since the census of April 1, 1990, is fractionally closer to the estimate date of July 1, 1985, than is the census date of April 1, 1980. Proportional weights for the final results are 0.525 for the reverse survival rate method and 0.475 for the forward survival rate method.

## SUMMARY

Intercensal population estimates have a variety of uses and may be produced through a number of methodological strategies. Mathematical interpolation techniques play a major role in the production of intercensal population estimates. One major use of interpolation techniques is the direct production of intercensal estimates. Given census results representing a beginning point and an end point for population size, interpolation may be used to produce an annual series of intercensal estimates. Rates of growth for the estimate series may be based on a simple arithmetic assumption or on a compound rate of growth reflecting either a geometric or exponential rate of change. One may continue to apply the assumed rates of growth beyond the most recent census as a way of producing a set of postcensal population estimates; however, interpolation techniques used in a postcensal situation are described more accurately as population projections rather than as estimates.

The interpolation strategies for producing intercensal population estimates are quite versatile in that they may be applied to any level of geography. The data requirements are minimal, and the calculations are relatively easy. Interpolation methodologies are limited in that they generally produce only estimates of population totals, not detailed estimates. In addition, the use of interpolation in the production of intercensal population estimates assumes that the population change occurring from one census to another has been smooth and continuous.

A second use of interpolation techniques is in adjusting a series of existing intercensal estimates as a way of dealing with the closure problem caused by a disparity between a postcensal estimate for a census year and the actual census result. Interpolation assuming a simple arithmetic rate of change provides a simple and effective way to adjust a series of intercensal estimates. The technique may be applied to any series of estimates at any level of geography. Interpolation adjustment is most often done on intercensal estimates produced through a postcensal methodology, so there is no underlying assumption concerning a smooth and continuous rate of change as there is when interpolation strategies are used directly to produce the estimates.

The final issue in intercensal estimates involves the use of the forward/reverse survival rate method for producing detailed intercensal estimates. The forward/reverse survival rate method is usually applied to the two most recent censuses in order to derive a set of detailed estimates for the mid-census period. Forward survival rates are applied to the base population enumerated in the second to last census, and the results are then averaged with those obtained by the application of reverse survival rates applied to the most recent census. The forward/reverse survival rate method overcomes one of the disadvantages of simple interpolation strategies in the production of intercensal estimates in that detailed population estimates are made possible. The additional detail, however, comes at a cost. Data requirements for the forward/reverse survival rate method are more rigorous than those for simple interpolation methods, and the cal-culations are somewhat more difficult. Still, the forward/reverse survival rate method provides a relatively simple way to produce a detailed set of intercensal population estimates.

# 7

# Methods of Postcensal Population Estimation

Postcensal population estimates are the result of attempts to measure the population of an area in the recent past, and in that respect they are similar to intercensal estimates discussed in chapter 6. The difference between the two is that intercensal estimates are made for a period of time *between* the two most recent census years, while postcensal estimates are made for years *following* the most recent census. Postcensal estimates represent the most current estimate available of population size and characteristics. As such, postcensal estimates are more frequently used for marketing and planning applications.

Several methodologies have been developed to produce postcensal population estimates. The data requirements and complexity of calculations can vary widely among the major postcensal methodologies. Methodological strategies such as proration techniques, simple ratio methods, the censal ratio method, and the vital rates method are relatively simple to calculate and have minimal data requirements. Alternative postcensal estimation strategies such as composite methods, the U.S. Bureau of the Census component method II, the ratio correlation method, the administrative records method, the cohort component method, and the housing unit method involve somewhat more complex calculations and have more extensive data requirements.

As a general rule, the more sophisticated the method of estimation, the more accurate will be the result and the greater will be the detail of the final product. As the level of sophistication increases, however, the more restrictive is the method's range of application. Conversely, the simpler, less demanding postcensal estimation methodologies may be applied in a greater variety of settings and to smaller levels of geography, but the results often will be less accurate and the level of detail in the final data product will be limited. These statements are not intended to be a blanket endorsement of complex and demanding methodologies over simpler and less demanding ones. Application of a demanding methodological estimation strategy without meeting the data requirements, or application of the technique in an inappropriate setting, will result in a worthless final product no matter how complex the method. In some situations one may be in a position to meet only the requirements of a simpler estimation method, and in such cases the best estimate will result from one of the simpler techniques.

This chapter examines some of the more popular postcensal population estimation methods including both simple and complex techniques. As was the case with the intercensal methods discussed in chapter 6, these techniques are better thought of as methodological strategies rather than as single methods since most of them have been applied in a variety of ways. Included in this chapter are proration techniques, simple ratio methods, the censal ratio method, vital rates methods, composite methods, the U.S. Bureau of the Census component method II, the ratio correlation method, the administrative records method, the cohort component method, and the housing unit method. Many of the more complex methods share the underlying logic of the component strategy of producing population estimates. A postcensal population estimation methodology based on the population component strategy will utilize the classic demographic equation in one form or another. The classic demographic equation equates current population to the previous level of population by incorporating changes in the components of population change in the following form:

$$P_1 = P_0 + B - D + I - O$$

Where:   $P_1$   is the current population
          $P_0$   is the population at a previous point in time
          $B$    is the number of births since $P_0$
          $D$    is the number of deaths since $P_0$
          $I$    is the number of inmigrants since $P_0$
          $O$    is the number of outmigrants since $P_0$

To one degree or another the basic logic of the general component model is evident in such postcensal population estimation strategies as composite methods, the U.S. Bureau of the Census component method II, the administrative records method, and the cohort component method. Simpler methods of postcensal population estimation make no attempt to isolate the individual components of population change in the production of population estimates. The discussion of postcensal methods of population estimations begins with the more elementary methods.

## ELEMENTARY POSTCENSAL METHODS OF POPULATION ESTIMATION

### Proration Estimation

Proration estimation is one of the easiest methods of postcensal population estimation, although its ease of application can be misleading. The proration method of population estimation usually is employed as a method to allocate the population of a larger geographic area among its smaller subareas. The method is applied by allocating a portion of the current estimated population of a larger geographic area to a smaller geographic area based on the ratio of the population of the smaller area to the population of the larger area as measured in the latest census. The formula for the proration method is as follows:

$$P_{es} = \frac{P_{cs}}{P_{cl}} \times P_{el}$$

Where:  $P$   is the population
  $e$   is an estimated value
  $c$   is a census result
  $s$   is a geographic subarea
  $l$   is the larger geographic area

Hypothetical data below provide an illustration of the technique:

| Area | 1990 Census Population | 1992 Postcensal Estimate |
|------|------------------------|--------------------------|
| County | 48,945 | 51,250 |
| Census Tract | 2,598 | To be estimated |

$$\frac{P_{cs}}{P_{cl}} = \frac{2,598}{48,945} = 0.053$$

$$P_{es} = 0.053 \times 51{,}250 = 2{,}716$$

In this example of the proration method of population estimation, the latest census results are used to determine the ratio of the population of a census tract to that of the county in which it is located. The current estimate for the census tract is obtained by multiplying the smaller area's proportionate share of the total county population as of the latest census by the current estimate of the population of the county.

The proration method is extremely easy to apply, has minimal data requirements, and may be applied to any level of geography. Application of the proration method is based on the assumption that the proportional relationship of the smaller and larger areas has remained constant since the time of the last census. This is a major assumption and one that is likely to be false as often as it is to be true. A second limitation of the proration method is the requirement of an existing current postcensal population estimate for the larger area. Further, the quality of the result from the proration estimation technique is only as good as the quality of the larger area population estimate. Finally, the proration technique results in a limited data product. An estimate of the total population is the most frequent result from a proration technique, although limited population detail in the form of estimates by race or gender may be obtained. Detailed population estimates by age are beyond the capacity of proration methods. In spite of some serious limitations, the proration technique has its uses and in some cases may be the best method to use, especially when data are limited or one is dealing with a small geographic area.

### Simple Ratio Procedure

The simple ratio procedure is one of several strategies of postcensal population estimation relying on symptomatic data indicators. Symptomatic data are those data that serve as symptoms of population change; ideally, these are data series that change in either a positive or inverse manner in direct proportion to population changes. Any number of data series serve as potential indicators of population change which makes the simple ratio procedure a very flexible tool for population estimation. Logical choices include variables that serve as direct components of population change, such as births and deaths, along with other variables that are more indirect correlates of population change, such as voter registrations, school enrollments, utility hookups, and housing starts.

The logic of producing a postcensal population estimate through the use of a simple ratio technique involves measuring the value of a data series at two points in time along with the size of the population at the earlier point in time. Most often the earlier point in time will be the most recent census year. Once the data series has been measured at the second point in time, a ratio is calculated indicating the change in the data series using the earlier point in time as the base. The change observed in the data series serves as an indicator of change in population. Population change is then measured by multiplying the population observed at the earlier point in time by the value of the ratio for the data series. The result is a current population estimate. One of the strengths of the simple ratio procedure is that multiple indicators of population change (several data series) may be used. Postcensal population estimates are obtained by averaging the various ratios when multiple indicators are used in the simple ratio procedure.

Hypothetical data below are used to illustrate the production of a postcensal population estimate through the simple ratio procedure. The data series used for the illustration are typical of what one ordinarily would select when using this type of technique.

| Variable | A 1990 | B 1992 | C = (B ÷ A) Ratio |
|---|---|---|---|
| Births | 2,125 | 2,250 | 1.059 |
| Deaths | 1,159 | 1,260 | 1.087 |
| School Enrollment | 14,750 | 15,680 | 1.063 |
| New Utility Hookups | 4,022 | 4,505 | 1.120 |
| Population (Census) | 119,780 | | |

Ratios are calculated by dividing the 1992 value of each data series by the 1990 base value. Population for the area has been enumerated in the 1990 census. Any of the four variables used in the example could serve as an indicator of population change by itself by simply multiplying the ratio (column C) indicating change since the base period by the 1990 population value. Any single data series, however, will be subject occasionally to an unusual fluctuation from year to year, so using a single data series might have an adverse effect on the quality of the estimate. A better strategy is to average the results of several data series. This is done by averaging the ratios obtained for each variable and then multiplying the overall ratio by the 1990 base population. The four ratios in this example average to an overall ratio of 1.082. Multiplying the overall ratio by the 1990 base population provides the current population estimate:

$$P_{1992} = 1.082 \times 119{,}780 = 129{,}602$$

One of the strengths of the simple ratio procedure is its flexibility. If one of the ratios for a variable used in the procedure appears out of line when compared with the rest, it is a simple matter to remove it from the calculations. In the present example, the ratio for new utility hookups is somewhat higher than the other three. It is relatively easy to remove this ratio from the overall average; when this is done, the adjusted overall average of the ratios becomes 1.07. Using the adjusted average as the basis of the population, the estimate becomes:

$$P_{1992} = 1.07 \times 119{,}780 = 128{,}165$$

An additional advantage of the simple ratio procedure is that the data requirements for the calculation of the ratios are minimal and usually only require data at two points in time rather than an annual series. One requires data for a variable at the time of the measurement of the base population and data at the time for which the estimate is to be made. There is no need to construct an annual time series for the intervening years if no population estimates for those years are to be made.

The simple ratio procedure is a good choice when data for an area are limited. It may be applied to a variety of levels of geography, and it is a technique that bases a population estimate on changes in variables that one logically can assume are related to population change. Like some of the other less sophisticated postcensal estimation techniques, the simple ratio procedure is limited in output; only estimates of population totals are generally available. Another disadvantage of the simple ratio technique is that while traditional variable choices—births, deaths, voter registrations, utility hookups, among others—are logically related to population change, each of the variables may be affected by other factors. There always will be a tendency for some of the predictor variables to exhibit changes that are independent of population change, and this tendency will be evident even in those variables that would seem most directly related to population. While it is not necessary to track the predictor variables by producing an annual data series when using the simple ratio technique, unusual changes from one year to the next will often be a good indicator that a particular variable is reacting to something other than a population change.

## Censal Ratio Method

The censal ratio method of postcensal population estimation is quite similar to the simple ratio method, but the censal ratio method does have some important distinctions worth examining. Postcensal population estimates produced through the censal ratio technique are based on changes in the ratio of the level of predictor variables to the base population. In most applications some form of adjustment is made based on national trends or some other source. When no adjustments to the ratios are made, the censal ratio technique is essentially the same as the simple ratio technique.

Any number of predictor variables may be used in the censal ratio technique, and one may choose to use more than one predictor variable and average the results to obtain a final population estimate. In the following example, it is assumed that the population of a county is being estimated through the censal ratio technique and that the number of births occurring in the county has been selected as the predictor variable. Data available at the state level will be used for the purposes of adjustment.

The procedure begins by calculating the ratio of births occurring in the base year in the county to the county population enumerated in the base year (in this case 1990). A similar ratio is calculated for the state data in the base year. Data on births and population at the state level for the estimate year are then used to calculate an estimate year ratio of births to population. The difference in the ratio of births to total population at the state level from the base year to the estimate year will be the basis for the adjustment made in the ratio of births to population at the county level. The ability to adjust the ratio of the predictor variable to the population allows one to avoid the often fallacious assumption that no changes in the relationship between the predictor variable and population have occurred since the base year. Once the new ratio of births to population in the estimate year has been calculated for the state, it is divided by the state ratio of births to population previously calculated for the base year. The result indicates the degree of change in the relationship between the predictor variable and population size at the state level, and it becomes the basis for the adjustment to the local area ratio. The local area ratio of births to population is adjusted by multiplying its base year ratio by the state-level adjustment factor just calculated. Finally, the county population estimate is obtained by dividing the number of births at the county level in the estimate year by the adjusted county ratio. A numerical example follows.

### Censal Ratio Method Using Births as a Predictor Variable

(1)   County births (1990) = 2,245
(2)   County population (1990) = 140,313
(3)   Ratio of county births to population (1 ÷ 2) = .0160
(4)   State births (1990) = 76,780
(5)   State population (1990) = 4,877,185
(6)   Ratio of state births to population (4 ÷ 5) = .0157
(7)   State births in estimate year (1992) = 77,985
(8)   State population in estimate year (1992) = 4,935,711
(9)   Ratio of state births to population in estimate year (1992) (7 ÷ 8)
       = .0158
(10)  Adjusted ratio of county births to population (9 ÷ 6) × (3) = 1.006 × .0160
       = .0161
(11)  County births in estimate year (1992) = 2,275
(12)  County population estimate for 1992 (11 ÷ 10) = 141,304

The chief advantage of the censal ratio technique over the simple ratio technique is the ability to adjust the ratio indicating the relationship between the predictor variable and the population size. Any data series will undergo periodic fluctuations due to a variety of factors, and the fluctuations are likely to be more extreme at the local level. The ability to adjust the local ratio based on trends evident in a larger geographic area prevents the data fluctuations in the smaller area from being incorporated into the local population estimate. Of course the ability to adjust the censal ratio value is made possible by the existence of an independently produced population estimate for a larger geographic area and the ability to obtain data on the predictor variable for the larger area for both the base year and the estimate year.

While any number of variables may be used as predictors of population in the censal ratio technique, Shyrock and Siegel (1973) suggest that it is wise to select variables with certain characteristics. Variables for which data are collected and reported at frequent intervals will be preferable to those that are measured less frequently. Variables that have a sufficiently large number of events occurring each year compared with the size of the population are preferable to those with a smaller number of occurrences. Since the censal ratios are calculated by dividing the level of the predictor variable by the population, a predictor variable with a relatively low frequency of occurrence will tend to be overwhelmed when divided by a much larger population. Significant changes in the level of a predictor variable would have an insignificant effect on the level of the censal ratio in such cases. Predictor variables that are relatively stable over time or that change in a predictable fashion should be chosen. Variables subject to extreme fluctuation or variables that are especially sensitive to factors other than population size should be avoided. Variables measuring economic indicators often are subject to large fluctuations that are independent of population size and as such should be avoided.

The censal ratio technique is a very flexible method of producing postcensal population estimates and has wide application. It may be applied to a variety of levels of geography with relative ease. The data requirements are limited, although they are more demanding than those of the simple ratio technique. Like the simple ratio technique, the predictor variables must be measured only at the time of the base population and the desired date of the population estimate. One does not require an annual time series of data for each predictor; however, the existence of an annual time series is beneficial since it enables one to assess the stability of the variable over time.

## Vital Rates Method

The vital rates method proposed by Bogue (1950) may be considered a variation of the censal ratio method designed to overcome some of the problems associated with the censal ratio method. The vital rates method employs the logic of the censal ratio method to produce two preliminary postcensal population estimates utilizing crude birth rates and crude death rates. The two preliminary estimates are then averaged to derive a final population estimate.

Bogue recognized that there were certain disadvantages inherent in using only data on births or deaths to produce a postcensal population estimate. While it is true that the number of births and deaths occurring in an area tends to be proportional to the population size, the birth rate or death rate may change over time due to factors other than population. Changes in net migration and changes in the age structure of the population are examples of two factors that affect both birth and death rates. Changes in birth and death rates within an area, however, tend to occur in an inverse manner—that is, when the birth rate is rising, the death rate is usually declining, and vice versa. Even factors such as migration and age structure tend to have opposite effects on birth and death rates within an area. The changes that may take place in the birth rate or the death rate over time may make using either variable by itself a questionable way to produce a postcensal population estimate, but using the two variables together in the same technique will tend to cancel out whatever biases develop from using either variable alone.

Bogue suggested using the vital rates method for situations where estimates are desired for local areas that make up a larger geographic area for which current population estimates and vital statistics data are currently available. As with the censal ratio method, data from the larger geographic area are used as an adjustment factor for the smaller area estimates. The vital rates methodology may be outlined as follows:

1. Crude birth rates and death rates are calculated for the base year (usually the most recent census year) for both the area to be estimated (the subarea) and the larger area used as a control (the parent area).

2. The crude birth rate of the subarea is expressed as a ratio to the crude birth rate of the parent area, and the same is done for the crude death rates. Expressing the vital rates in ratio form reduces the bias that may occur due to fluctuations in the crude rates between the base year and the estimate date.

3. Any adjustments to the vital rates ratios for the subareas are made based on an analysis of traditional patterns of variation between the vital rates of each subarea and the parent area. The size of the adjustment usually is determined by a statistical analysis of some sort. For example, if a particular subarea is found to have a historically lower crude birth rate than the parent area by some amount, then the subarea's crude birth rate would be adjusted downward at the estimate date.

4. Vital rates for the parent area are then calculated for the estimate year. Completion of this step requires the availability of an independently produced current population estimate of the parent area.

5. The adjusted vital rates ratios from step 3 are multiplied by the current crude vital rates from step 4 to yield the estimated current crude vital rates for the subareas.

6. Two preliminary population estimates are produced by solving for population given all of the other variables in the traditional formula for a crude rate. For example, when the crude birth rate is calculated as:

$$\text{CBR} = \frac{\text{number of births}}{\text{total population}} \times 1,000$$

and all information is given other than total population, it is a simple matter to estimate the current population by dividing the number of births by the crude birth rate and multiplying the result by 1,000. A similar procedure is carried out for the crude death rate. The result is two preliminary population estimates: one based on the crude birth rate and one based on the crude death rate.

7. The population estimates of the local areas are derived by averaging the two preliminary population estimates obtained from the vital rates. Often the final population estimate will be based on a weighted average of the two preliminary estimates rather than a simple average.

8. As a final step, it may be desirable to control the totals of the subareas to the population total of the parent area. Subareas are controlled to the total of the parent area by proportionately adjusting each subarea upward or downward so that the sum of the population of the subareas equals the population of the parent area.

The vital rates method of population estimation overcomes one of the major disadvantages of the censal rate method. The selection of certain predictor variables in the production of postcensal population estimates often will introduce a source of bias into the final result. The vital rates method is no exception, but its use of predictor variables based on the crude birth rate and crude death rate results in preliminary population estimates that tend to cancel out biases that are present when each predictor variable is used separately. The vital rates method would seem to have minimal data requirements; however, it is unlikely that current vital rates data would be available below the county level. In addition, the method assumes the existence of an independently produced population estimate for a parent area.

## ADVANCED POSTCENSAL METHODS OF POPULATION ESTIMATION

The dynamics of population change can be quite complex and are often beyond the scope of simple postcensal population estimation methodological techniques such as proration and variations of censal ratio methods. The need for population estimation strategies offering greater precision and added detail have led to the development of more advanced methods of population estimation. Among them are the housing unit method, the composite method, the U.S. Bureau of the Census's component method II, the administrative records method, the ratio correlation method, and the cohort component method. Each is discussed in turn.

### Housing Unit Method

The housing unit method produces postcensal population estimates by equating population to the number of occupied housing units times the average number of persons per household. The housing unit method is one of the most frequently applied methods of postcensal population estimation and is the primary method of choice for subcounty population estimates. The logic of the method is deceptively simple, which may account for the widespread use of the technique. The following formula represents the logic of the housing unit method for estimating current population:

$$P = (H_o \times O) + I$$

Where:     $P$     is the current population
           $H_o$   is the number of occupied housing units
           $O$     is the number of persons per household
           $I$     is the institutional population

What appears to be a rather simple way to estimate population actually involves two difficult stages. First, the number of occupied housing units in the estimate area must be calculated. Second, the number of persons per household must be calculated. Two major methodological strategies have evolved for calculating the number of occupied housing units in an area. One strategy involves an analysis of building permit and demolition data, while the other strategy involves an analysis of utility data usually based on electric utility meters. Both strategies begin with the number of housing units known to exist at a previous point in time. The most recent census provides an enumeration of occupied housing units and the average number of persons per household which serves as the base data for the housing unit method.

The building permit strategy begins with the number of housing units enumerated in the most recent census and then updates the housing unit base by adding the number of new housing units authorized in the area to be estimated and subtracting the number of housing units demolished in the estimate area. Updating the housing unit base seems like a simple strategy, but there are several problems inherent in the process. The first major problem is that building permits represent an intention to build rather than a completed housing unit ready for occupancy. The use of building permit data is further complicated by the fact that not all of the housing units that are authorized will actually be constructed, and even units that are constructed will not be ready for occupancy for some period of time after the permit has been issued. A problem along similar lines concerns the housing unit base enumerated in the census. Housing units under construction at the time of the census generally are not counted as housing units at the date of the census even though they may soon be completed and ready for occupancy; since they are the result of permits issued prior to the census, they will not be included automatically in the update of housing units. A final problem with respect to updating the housing unit stock by use of housing unit permit data is that not all housing units are alike. One should differentiate construction permits for single family housing units from those for multiple family housing units.

In most cases the problems associated with housing permit data can be overcome. Almost all legal jurisdictions granting construction permits will differentiate between single family units and multiple family units. The lag between the issuance of a construction permit and the completion of a unit may be determined by an analysis of historical data. Generally, one may allow 6 months for the construction of a single family unit and 15 months for the completion of a multiple family unit. Finally, units under construction at the time of the census may be accounted for by examining permit data 6 months prior to the date of the census for single family units and 15 months prior to the census for multiple family units.

The addition of new housing units is only part of the job of updating the housing unit base since the last census. There are also deletions to the housing unit stock in the form of the demolition of existing housing units, and these must be subtracted from the current housing stock in order to estimate the population accurately. Legal jurisdictions require a permit to demolish an existing structure just as they require a permit to build a new one. In such cases, it is a simple matter to take the number of permits issued for the demolition of housing units and to subtract it from the current housing stock. As one might expect, however, there are a few problems associated with the demolition data. First, not all demolitions will be recorded. It is somewhat easier to operate outside the legal process when demolishing an existing structure than it is when constructing a new structure. Generally, it takes much less time to demolish a structure than to construct a new one, and once a structure is demolished there is no need for the parade of inspectors to certify it ready for utility hookups and occupancy as is the case with a new housing unit. In addition, not all housing units in need of demolition are actually demolished. Housing units may pass from the stage of inhabitable to the stage of vacant and abandoned without any paper trail in the town clerk's office. Unfortunately, these two problems of demolition without permit and uninhabitable housing units introduce bias in the same direction in the estimate process in that they both result in an overestimate of the number of current housing units in the area.

Assuming the problems associated with updating the housing stock have been overcome, one is ready to move on to the next phase. Not all housing units are occupied, so one needs to apply an occupancy rate to the existing housing stock in order to derive the number of occupied housing units to be used in the estimate calculations. Older housing units generally will have a higher occupancy rate than newer units. Occupancy rates for both older and newer units may be estimated with census data. At this point in the estimation process, one has estimated the number of occupied housing units for both single family units and multiple family units. The next step is to multiply the estimated number of occupied housing units by the average household size for each respective type of unit. Generally, the single family housing units will have a higher average household size than the multiple family units. Average household size for both types of housing units may be found in the most recent census data. The census data should be viewed, however, as a base figure that will need to be adjusted with the need for adjustment being greater the longer the period of time between the census date and the estimate date. One of the major problems with the housing unit method is that in the past it resulted in inflated population estimates during periods when average household size was declining. Population estimates based on census figures of average household size became increasingly inflated when the decline in household size was not taken into account. Data on current household size from the *Current Population Reports*, Series P-20, "Characteristics of Households," published by the U.S. Bureau of the Census, may be used to adjust the average household size data. Adjustments to the average household size become increasingly important the longer the period of time between the census date and the estimate date.

The estimate of the population in households may be made by multiplying the number of occupied single family and multiple family households by the respective average household size. The final population estimate for the area then is obtained by adding in the number of individuals in group quarters. The group quarters population consists of individuals living outside traditional households and in institutional settings such as college dormitories, military bases, nursing homes, prisons, and similar institutions. Group quarters data are relatively easy to collect from the institution. The major challenge with respect to the group quarters population is identifying the institutions themselves; once the institution is identified, it is generally easy to get a current head count from the administration.

The second major strategy used in the housing unit method involves the use of utility data to update the size of the current housing stock in place of construction and demolition permits. The underlying logic of the method remains the same, the only difference being the use of an alternative type of data series to estimate the number of additions to the housing stock. Electric utility data are the type most often used in the housing unit method. Other types of utility data may be used, such as natural gas service, water and sewer service, or telephone service. Electric utility data, however, have a clear advantage in that almost all households will have electric service, and the service will be billed directly to the household. Water and sewer service is just as likely to be universal as electric service, but water and sewer service for multiple family housing units is often based on a master meter for an entire building with the cost of the service included in the rent.

In the utility data variation of the housing unit method, an updated estimate of the number of households is made by collecting data on the number of new customers from the electric utility. Obviously, cooperation on the part of the utility company is required, but there are a few other complications as well. One of the major problems with using utility data is that the definition of a "customer" for most utility companies is the electric meter itself. In some situations it is not possible to differentiate between a meter that has been added due to a new household and a meter that has been added because a farm operator has decided to run electric service to a barn or pump house and wants a separate electric meter to measure the service. One may also encounter the problem of differentiating between a single family and multiple family unit, although in most cases there will be a separate meter for each housing unit within a multiple unit structure. A final challenge in using utility data is that utility service is not always cancelled at vacant housing units. Utility service will often be maintained at vacant housing units in order to prevent damage from weather or vandalism. The result is an overestimate of the number of households in the area.

Once the size of the housing stock has been updated through the use of the utility data, the estimation procedure continues as before. An occupancy rate is applied to the number of housing units, and an average household size is then multiplied by the number of households. Finally, the group quarters population is added in order to derive the final population estimate. When suitable data are available, it might be wise to calculate a population estimate using each approach and then average the results from the building permit data with those of the utility data for the final estimate.

Either variation of the housing unit method provides acceptable results and is a good choice for producing population estimates, and this is especially true at the subcounty level. The technique has modest data requirements, and the data are generally easy to obtain. Tests of the accuracy of the housing unit method generally have found that the direction of error is toward inflated population estimates. Both variations of the technique tend to produce estimates that are too high, although the utility data variation of the technique has been found to perform somewhat better than the building permit variation. In each case, the greater source of error seems to be in accurately estimating the current number of households in the estimate year rather than estimating the average household size. Variations in the current occupancy rate of households are also likely to be a source of error in the housing unit method, but the occupancy rate is a variable that often goes unadjusted from census results in the housing unit method due to lack of current data. One additional limitation of the housing unit method is that it does not produce detailed population estimates, but at the subcounty level detailed estimates are error-prone anyway. All things considered, the housing unit method is a good economical way to produce population estimates, especially at the subcounty level.

### Composite Method

The composite method, like so many others, refers to an estimation strategy rather than a single method. The general form of the composite method was outlined by Bogue and Duncan (1959) and offers two advantages compared with previous postcensal estimation methods. Bogue and Duncan recognized that commonly used single indicator estimation techniques of the day were better suited to some areas and population subgroups than others and that often the discriminating factor with respect to the effectiveness of a particular estimation technique was the age structure of the population being estimated. The general principle behind the composite method is to develop an overall population estimate through the use of a series of estimation techniques. One key advantage of the composite method is that each segment of the population is estimated by the technique most appropriate for it. The total population estimate is then obtained by summing the various components. A second advantage of the composite method is that it usually results in more detailed population estimates than are produced through single indicator estimation methodologies. Each broad age group is estimated by the technique most appropriate to it and with the data most relevant to it. The result is not only a final population estimate but also a set of preliminary results that provide some age detail and often detail by race and sex.

In most applications, the composite method produces a preliminary population estimate for the following groups: (a) total population aged 45 years and over, (b) females aged 15–44 years, (c) males aged 15–44 years, (d) total population aged 5–14 years, and (e) total population under 5 years of age. Each preliminary estimate is produced with the technique and data most appropriate to it. For example, the total population aged 45 and over is produced through an analysis of age specific death rates. The female population aged 15–44 is produced through an analysis of age specific fertility rates. The population of males aged 15–44 is produced through an analysis of the sex ratio. The population aged 5–14 is produced through an analysis of school enrollment data. Finally, the population under 5 years of age is produced through an analysis of school enrollment data and birth data. A more detailed discussion of the methodological strategy employed in each step follows.

The production of an estimate of the total population over age 45 is accomplished in the following four steps.

1. The process begins with the calculation of age specific death rates by 5- or 10-year age groupings for both the estimate area and the control area at the time of the most recent census. The estimate area is the geographic area for which the population estimate will be developed. The control area is a larger geographic area for which current population and vital event data will be available. Most often the control area used in the composite method is the United States.

2. Age specific death rates with the same level of detail are obtained for the control area for the estimate year.

3. The change in the age specific death rates observed for the control area between the time of the last census and the estimate date is used to provide approximate age specific death rates for the estimate area for the estimate year. It is assumed in step 3 that the direction and degree of change observed in age specific death rates in the control area are similar to what has happened in the estimate area where current vital event data may not be available.

4. The population estimate of the population aged 45 and over is obtained by dividing the number of deaths in the estimate area in the estimate year by the age specific death rate for the estimate area and multiplying that result by 1,000.

This final step is similar to what is done in the vital rates method where given the rate of a vital event per 1,000 population and the number of vital events in a particular year one may easily solve for the population in that year.

The estimate of the number of females aged 15–44 is calculated as follows in a similar fashion except that one relies on age specific birth rates rather than death rates.

1. The process begins by calculating the age specific birth rates for the estimate area and the control area at the time of the most recent census.
2. Age specific birth rates are obtained for the control area for the estimate year.
3. Changes observed in the age specific birth rates between the census date and the estimate date for the control area are used as a basis to estimate the age specific birth rates for the estimate area for the estimate date.
4. The number of females aged 15–44 is estimated by dividing the number of births by the age specific birth rate and multiplying the result by 1,000.

The number of civilian males aged 15–44 is estimated by multiplying the estimated number of females aged 15–44 in the estimate year by the ratio of civilian males to females for the area. The civilian male to female ratio for the estimate area may be calculated as of the most recent census. A final estimate of the total population aged 15–44 is obtained by adding the number of females 15–44 to the number of civilian males aged 15–44 and the number of military personnel in the estimate area.

The 5–14-year-old population may be estimated in several ways in the composite method. The more prevalent strategy is to use a variation of the censal ratio method based on the use of school enrollment data. Postcensal population estimates may be made for a variable period of time following the most recent census. Estimates may be made for as short a period of time as 1 year past the census date or as long as 10 years following the census date. Censal ratios involving school enrollment data are sufficient for estimating the 5–14-year-old cohort for an estimate period up to 6 years past the census date since all of the members of the cohort were alive at the time of the most recent census, with the exception of a small segment of the 5-year-old group. Birth data, however, must be added to the analysis for estimate periods beyond 6 years past the estimate date. The process of estimating the 5–14-year-old population begins by determining the number of children enrolled in school in grades 2 to 7 in the most recent census year. Children in these grades are generally between the ages of 7 and 13 years. The number of children aged 7–13 years in the most recent census is then found. The ratio of the census population aged 7–13 to the school enrollment for grades 2 to 7 in the census year is calculated. The school enrollment in grades 2 to 7 in the estimate year is then determined. The estimated population aged 7–13 in the estimate year is then determined using the same censal ratio technique described previously.

The estimated number of 7–13-year-old children in the estimate year is then compared to the size of its initial cohort in the most recent census. For example, if the estimate year is five years past the most recent census then the estimate year cohort would have been aged 2–8 years at the time of the census. Subtracting the size of the initial cohort from the number of 7–13-year-olds at the estimate date yields an estimate of net migration. Ordinarily, one would "age" the initial cohort to the estimate date by subjecting it to a schedule of mortality rates in order to derive an estimate of net migration, but in this case it is assumed that the normal losses to the cohort due to mortality are offset by the underenumeration of the cohort in the census. The number of net migrants in the 7–13-year-old group is divided by the number of individuals in that cohort counted in the most recent census and then divided by the number of years from the census to the estimate year in order to derive an annual net migration rate.

The final estimate of 5–14-year-olds is calculated by multiplying the census cohort (those members of the 5–14-year-old age group in the estimate year who were living at the time of the most recent census) by the annual net migration rate times the number of years in the estimate period and adding that number to the initial size of the cohort enumerated in the most recent census. For example, if the estimate year is 6 years past the census date, the final estimate of 5–14-year-olds would be made as follows. The census population up to age 9 years, representing those members of the 5–14-year-old cohort who would have been living at the time of the census, is multiplied by the annual net migration rate times 6.25 years, representing the period of time between the census and the estimate date. The resulting product represents the total net migration over the estimate period. The total net migration is then added to the census population of ages 7 and younger, and the resulting sum is the estimated population of 5–14 years at the estimate date.

As the estimate period moves beyond 6 years past the most recent census date, the estimate of the 5–14-year-old group must take into account the number of births for selected years, if possible. In some applications of the composite method, the lack of vital registration data for births at the level of geography for which the estimate is to be made will make inclusion of birth data impossible. In the absence of vital registration data on births, the estimate of the 5–14-year-old cohort will be low, adding to the overall error of the estimate.

The final segment of the population to be estimated in the composite method is the group under age 5 years. The number of children under age 5 is estimated through the use of fertility ratios. The ratio of the number of children under age 5 per 1,000 females aged 20–34 is calculated for the most recent census year. Separate ratios may be calculated by sex of the child and by race of the mother. Control area data may be used to adjust the estimate area ratios to take into account any changing trends in the child woman ratio if desired. The number of females aged 20–34 previously estimated for the estimate year is then used to estimate the number of children under age 5, assuming that changes in the ratio of children aged years and younger to women aged 20–34 in the estimate area will be similar to changing trends in the control area.

The final population estimate of the area is then calculated by summing the preliminary results obtained in each of the previous steps. The two major advantages of the composite method are that each major segment of the population is estimated by the technique and data most appropriate to it and that the resulting estimate provides some detail by age, race, and sex. An additional advantage is that the composite method is flexible and can be adapted to the needs and data availability of the area. Even the broad age groupings may be altered to fit available data as evidenced by some applications of the method using 18–44-year-old and 5–17-year-old cohorts in place of the more traditional 15–44 year and 5–14 year categories first suggested by Bogue and Duncan (1959).

There are some disadvantages associated with the composite method. The composite method does allow for the production of population estimates detailed by age, race, and sex to some degree. The greater the degree of detail in the estimates, however, the greater the degree of error. Further, no method of population estimation is better than the data upon which it is based, and the use of school enrollment data in the composite method can result in some real problems. School enrollment data can fluctuate significantly from year to year even under the best reporting systems. In addition, there is often a question as to what the enrollment figures actually represent. Enrollment figures may refer to any number of concepts, including total annual enrollment, net annual enrollment, enrollment as of a certain date, or some type of attendance concept (Bogue & Duncan, 1959, p. 175). Additional complications with enrollment data include the change in school district boundaries without a corresponding change in the boundaries of the geographic area being estimated and a failure to include private school enrollments on a regular basis. Historically, a large portion of private school enrollments in most communities were in Roman Catholic parochial schools, and the enrollment figures were easily obtained from a diocesan office. The 1970s and 1980s brought about an increase in the number of students enrolled in less conventional private schools, and those enrollment figures are somewhat harder to obtain. Finally, several of the strategies employed in the composite method are based on vital event data at the level of the area to be estimated. The use of strategies such as age specific death rates and age specific fertility rates effectively limit the application of the composite method to the geographic level of the county or above. Detailed subcounty vital event data will seldom be available, and when such data are available they are subject to more proportional year-to-year variation than are data representative of larger geographic areas. Large fluctuations from year to year in the vital event data will translate into a larger rate of error in the final estimate.

## Component Method II

Component method II is one of the major postcensal population estimation methods employed by the U.S. Bureau of the Census. As the title implies, component method II is a type of component method that results in a population estimate through the use of data on the three major components of population: births, deaths, and net migration. The designation "II" reflects the fact that the current method was preceded by an earlier version of the technique. A population estimate is developed with component method II by updating the base population as enumerated in the most recent census, by taking into account births and deaths in the estimate area occurring between the census date and the estimate date, and estimating the amount of net migration in the area.

The major steps of component method II are as follows. The estimation process begins by determining the resident civilian nongroup quarters population as of the most recent census. The civilian nongroup quarters population is calculated by taking the resident population enumerated in the most recent census and subtracting the barracks military population and any other group quarters institutional population in the area, such as prison population, college dormitory population, nursing home population, and similar types of populations. Resident births for the estimate area and resident deaths for the estimate area are then obtained. The initial steps provide information on the base population at the time of the census, increases up to the estimate date due to births, and losses up to the estimate date due to deaths.

The next major component calculated for the population estimate is net migration. Net migration for the area is based on an analysis of the elementary school age population. The estimate of net migration begins by obtaining data on the elementary school enrollment at the time of the census. There is some variation in the application of component method II at this point. Some prefer to use the elementary enrollment for grades 1 to 8, which corresponds approximately to the population aged 6–14 years, while others prefer to use the elementary enrollment for grades 2 to 8, corresponding approximately to the population aged 7–14 years. In some situations the enrollment in grade 1 will fluctuate due to factors other than population, so these data are often excluded from the estimation process.

Presuming we are working with the elementary enrollment for grades 2 to 8 in the census year, the process continues by calculating the ratio of the school enrollment to the population of 7–14-year-olds enumerated in the most recent census. The enrollment for grades 2 to 8 in the estimate year is then obtained and adjusted by the censal ratio just calculated in order to derive the estimated 7–14-year-old population at the estimate date. The census cohort that would be 7–14 years old at the estimate date is then "aged" forward to the estimate date by the application of survival rates. Aging the cohort forward to the estimate date provides an expected 7–14-year-old population, assuming that no migration has taken place. The amount of net migration occurring from the census date to the estimate date is determined by subtracting the expected 7–14-year-old population from the estimated 7–14-year-old population. A net migration rate for the 7–14-year-old population is then obtained by dividing the total net migration by the size of the 7–14-year-old base population. Calculation of the size of the 7–14-year-old base population will vary depending on circumstances. In cases where the estimate year is less than 7 years beyond the most recent census, the base population may be defined as the size of the 7–14-year-old cohort enumerated in the most recent census or the size of that cohort minus one-half of the deaths occurring to it. In the former case, the number of deaths occurring to the cohort is ignored, which will have the effect of slightly reducing the migration rate. In cases where the estimate year is 7 or more years past the most recent census, it is necessary to add the number of births occurring to the 7–14-year-old cohort since the date of the census. Again, deaths to the cohort may or may not be considered.

The net migration rate of the 7–14-year-old cohort is adjusted to reflect the total migration of population under age 65 years based on an analysis of the ratio of migration patterns of the school age population to the total population using data from the Current Population Survey. The under age 65 migration rate is then applied to the under age 65 cohort enumerated in the most recent census in order to obtain the under age 65 net migration. Once the migration for the under age 65 population has been calculated, the population for the under age 65 cohort may be estimated.

The under age 65 population estimate begins by using the age 65 and under cohort population enumerated in the most recent census as a base population. The exact age of the under 65 years cohort at the time of the census will vary depending on how many years have passed between the census date and the estimate date. For example, if an estimate is made 8 years after the census date, the under age 65 cohort at the date of the census was approximately 52 years of age and younger. The estimate process continues by adding to the base population all of the births that have occurred in the estimate area from the date of the census up to the date of the population estimate. The total net migration of the under age 65 population is also added to the base population, although in some cases the net migration total will be negative and thus reduce the size of the under age 65 estimate. Finally, the number of deaths occurring in the area from the census date to the estimate date is subtracted from the base population. In cases where data on resident deaths are not available, one may estimate the number of deaths by applying appropriate mortality rates to the base population.

The population over age 65 is then estimated. One begins with the population of the over age 65 cohort from the most recent census. Again, the exact age of the over age 65 cohort at the date of the census will vary depending upon how much time has passed between the census date and the estimate date. In the general case, the over age 65 cohort from the most recent census consists of those individuals at the date of the census who are or will be age 65 or over at the time of the estimate date. To that base population one simply adds the change in Medicare enrollees from the date of the census to the date of the estimate. The net change in Medicare enrollees will serve as an indicator of both mortality and net migration for the age 65 and over cohort since Medicare enrollment is practically universal.

The final step in estimating the population with component method II is to sum all of the intermediate results. The under age 65 population is added to the age 65 and over population; added to that sum are the military barracks population at the estimate date, if applicable, and the institutional population at the estimate date, if applicable. The result is the total resident population of the area.

Component method II provides reliable results in most applications, but it is somewhat more difficult than some other methods for a variety of reasons. As with component methods in general, component method II has more extensive data requirements than some of the other estimation methods available. Data on births and deaths are readily available at many levels of geography, but data for smaller areas below the subcounty level may be difficult to obtain. Detailed data on births and deaths become especially difficult to obtain as the level of geography becomes smaller. The variation of component method II described here requires access to data on the number of Medicare enrollees for the estimation of the age 65 and over population. Data on Medicare enrollees is available, but the U.S. Bureau of the Census has a somewhat easier entrée to Medicare data than the general public. The acquisition of school enrollment data presents another challenge when using component method II, as well as some of the other methods discussed, since the level of cooperation from school districts will vary. A final concern with component method II is the implicit assumption that the migration patterns of the elementary school age population for the estimate area may be generalized to the under age 65 population based on national trends evident in the Current Population Survey.

### Administrative Records Method

The administrative records method is another of the postcensal population estimation methods employed by the U.S. Bureau of the Census in its annual county population estimate series. The administrative records method is so named due to the major role played in the estimation process by administrative data obtained from the Social Security Administration and the Internal Revenue Service. Essentially, the administrative records method is a variation of the general component model with administrative data from the Internal Revenue Service and the Social Security Administration used for estimating the migration component of the estimation process.

The administrative records method begins with the base population enumerated in the most recent census for the estimate area. In most instances the administrative records method is part of an annual estimation process in which the previous year's estimate serves as the base population for the current year's estimate, but one may think of the most recent census as the ultimate source of the base population. The exact progression of steps in the administrative records method will vary depending on the level of geography to be estimated. For example, estimates made at the state level or county level will result in a strategy utilizing data on Medicare enrollees in order to estimate the size of the age 65 years and over population. Estimates made at the national level will not separate the estimate of the 65 years and over population from the total population.

Once the base population is known, the administrative records method proceeds as any general component method would. The base population is adjusted by adding the number of births occurring from the base period to the estimate date in the area to be estimated and by subtracting the number of deaths. In actual practice only half of the births and deaths are used to update the base population since estimates are conventionally made from July 1 to July 1, and vital event data are reported from calendar year to calendar year. As the estimation process continues from year to year, no vital event data are lost by using only half of the reported births and deaths; rather, a portion of the calendar year natural increase is allocated to one year's estimate and the remainder is allocated to the next or previous year's estimate. The administrative records method also will utilize data on group quarters populations such as military barracks, college dormitories, prisons, and long-term resident health care facilities.

The final step in the administrative records method that differentiates it from the other general component methods is the technique for calculating net migration from the base period to the estimate date. Net migration is estimated through an analysis of matched federal income tax returns for the previous two years. State-to-state and county-to-county migration flows are estimated by matching federal income tax returns for any two successive years. Returns indicating the same address from year to year or different addresses within the same county indicate nonmigrants, while returns with addresses indicating different counties or states indicate migration. The number of total exemptions for the under age 65 population provides data on the volume of migration flow from place to place. One should note that the contents of the individual income tax returns are not provided to the U.S. Bureau of the Census by the Internal Revenue Service. Data are provided only for the purpose of calculating migration flows.

The nature of the year-to-year matching of addresses on tax returns illustrates the need to produce an annual series of estimates with the administrative records method and why the previous year's estimate serves as the base for the current estimate without the need to go back to the most recent census. The administrative records method has performed well in estimating population at the state level as well as the county level. There are two major disadvantages with the administrative records method. The data and computational requirements of the administrative records method are the most rigorous of any postcensal estimation methodology. In fact, the method can be applied directly only by federal agencies with access to the Internal Revenue Service migration data files. In some cases the state-to-state and county-to-county migration data are made available to others, thus permitting a wider application of the method. In the general case, however, the administrative records method is used primarily by federal agencies. The second major disadvantage of the administrative records method is the reliance on Internal Revenue Service data for the calculation of the migration component of the population estimates. Many states with large impoverished urban populations have challenged the validity of the method on the grounds that many of their residents do not file annual federal income tax returns. The point is well taken, and efforts have been made to improve the sensitivity of the methodology with respect to nonfilers of federal income tax returns.

## Ratio Correlation Method

The ratio correlation method is one of the more versatile postcensal population estimation techniques. The ratio correlation method produces postcensal population estimates through the use of a statistical procedure called linear regression. While a thorough explanation of linear regression is beyond the scope of this discussion, a brief description of the linear regression technique is in order.

Linear regression in its simplest case is a statistical technique that allows researchers to predict one variable based on observations of a second variable. The variable to be predicted is referred to as the dependent variable ($Y$), and the variable used to make the prediction is referred to as the independent variable ($X$). Previous observations of values of $X$ and $Y$ are used to determine the statistical relationship between the two variables; given a new observation of $X$, one can use the statistical model to predict the value of $Y$. Linear regression analysis results in the development of an equation for a straight line that best fits the set of previous observations. The basic equation for a linear regression model is as follows:

$$Y' = a + bX$$

Where: $Y'$   is the predicted value of the dependent variable

$a$   is the $Y$ intercept, the point where the prediction line will cross the Y axis

$b$   is the regression coefficient or slope of the regression line

$X$   is the known value of the independent variable

The first step in creating the linear regression model is to calculate the value of $b$, the regression coefficient. The value of $b$ represents the ratio of the change in the value of $Y$, the dependent variable, for each unit change in $X$, the independent variable. A computational formula for $b$ is as follows:

$$b = \frac{n(\Sigma XY) - (\Sigma X)(\Sigma Y)}{n(\Sigma X^2) - (\Sigma X)^2}$$

Where: $n$   is the number of observations

$(\Sigma XY)$ is the sum of each $X$ value multiplied by the corresponding $Y$ value

$(\Sigma X)$  is the sum of the $X$ values

$(\Sigma Y)$  is the sum of the $Y$ values

$\Sigma X^2$  is the sum of each $X$ value squared

$(\Sigma X)^2$ is the square of the sum of the $X$ values

The following data may be used to illustrate the computations of a simple linear regression model.

| $X$ | $Y$ | $XY$ | $X^2$ |
|---|---|---|---|
| 12 | 32 | 384 | 144 |
| 15 | 30 | 450 | 225 |
| 18 | 36 | 648 | 324 |
| 20 | 48 | 960 | 400 |
| 25 | 40 | 1,000 | 625 |
| 28 | 44 | 1,232 | 784 |
| 30 | 45 | 1,350 | 900 |
| 33 | 47 | 1,551 | 1,089 |
| 35 | 50 | 1,750 | 1,225 |
| 35 | 55 | 1,925 | 1,225 |
| $\Sigma = 251$ | $\Sigma = 427$ | $\Sigma = 11,250$ | $\Sigma = 6,941$ |

The value of the regression coefficient $b$ is calculated as follows:

$$b = \frac{10(11{,}250) - (251)(427)}{10(6{,}941) - (63{,}001)}$$

$$= \frac{5{,}323}{6{,}409}$$

$$= .82$$

The value of $b = .82$ indicates that for each unit change in the $X$ variable there is a corresponding change of .82 units in the $Y$ variable. In order to complete the regression equation, one must calculate the value of $a$, the $Y$ axis intercept. The value of $a$ is calculated by taking the mean or simple average of the $Y$ values and subtracting from it the product of the regression coefficient multiplied by the mean of the $X$ values.

$$a = 42.7 - (.82)(25.1)$$

$$= 42.7 - 20.58$$

$$= 22.12$$

Given the value of $a$, the $Y$ intercept, and $b$, the regression coefficient, it is now possible to predict a value for the dependent variable $Y$ by knowing the value of the independent variable $X$. For example, given an $X = 50$, the resulting predicted value of $Y$ is as follows:

$$Y' = 22.12 + .82(50)$$

$$= 63.12$$

In the simplest case, a single independent variable is used to predict the dependent variable; in more complex cases, a set of independent variables may be used to predict the dependent variable through a multiple regression model. The multiple regression equation takes the form:

$$Y' = a + b_1X_1 + b_2X_2 + \ldots + b_nX_n$$

In the ratio correlation method of population estimation, a set of independent variables thought to be symptomatic of population change is used to predict the population of the estimate area. The technique is referred to as the ratio correlation method because ratio transformations of the independent variables, rather than the raw data, are used in the analysis. The ratio approach reduces the impact that an unusually large change in the level of a particular variable will have on the resulting population estimate.

The ratio correlation method is employed to produce postcensal population estimates for geographic subareas that comprise a larger geographic area for which an independent population estimate is available. The most frequent applications would be in the production of state-level population estimates using the United States as the larger geographic area or in the production of county-level population estimates using the state as the larger geographic area. Any number of variables may qualify as suitable independent variables for the regression analysis. Variables indicating the number of births and deaths in the estimate area are logical choices since they comprise two of the major components of population change. Other logical variable choices include symptomatic indicators of migration such as school enrollment, voter registration, automobile registration, driver's license data, and electric utility hookup data, to name a few. Again, there is no single way to apply the ratio correlation method, but in most applications the independent variables are measured at two points in time for both the estimate area and the larger control area and then are expressed as proportional change ratios. Assuming one is producing county-level population estimates in the 1990s using the state as the control area, one would measure the independent variable for the county estimate area and the state in both 1980 and 1990 and express the variable as a proportional change ratio in the following form:

$$X_1 = \frac{\dfrac{\text{county-level population, 1990}}{\text{state-level population, 1990}}}{\dfrac{\text{county-level population, 1980}}{\text{state-level population, 1980}}}$$

The other independent variables would be measured in a similar fashion as would the dependent variable measuring population. The dependent variable would consist of the county-level population in 1990 as a proportion of the state-level population in 1990 with the resulting value divided by the county population in 1980 as a proportion of the state population in 1980.

The steps involved in the ratio correlation method are as follows:

1. Data for the independent variables are collected and expressed as ratios, as demonstrated previously.

2. Population data (the dependent variable) are collected and also presented in ratio form.

3. The multiple regression analysis is performed using the independent variables to derive a predictive model for the dependent variable.

4. Estimate year data for the independent variables are collected for the estimate area and expressed as ratios.

5. The predictive model resulting from the multiple regression analysis is applied to the estimate year independent data resulting in the estimated value of the dependent variable ($Y'$) for the estimate year. The predicted value resulting from the regression analysis represents the estimate year county population expressed as a proportion of the estimate year state population with that quantity divided by the county population in 1990 expressed as a proportion of the state population in 1990. The predicted population value ($Y'$) is of the form:

$$Y' = \frac{\dfrac{\text{county population estimate year}}{\text{state population estimate year}}}{\dfrac{\text{county population 1990}}{\text{state population 1990}}}$$

6. The county-level population for the estimate year then may be calculated through simple algebraic manipulation since all of the other elements in the ratio expression are known quantities.

7. The process is repeated for each subarea until the population of each has been estimated.

8. As a final step, the estimates of the subareas are usually adjusted. In most cases the sum of the subareas will be slightly different than the independently produced population estimate for the larger geographic area. The estimate of each subarea may be proportionally adjusted such that the sum of the subareas will equal the total of the larger control area.

A representative numerical example of the ratio correlation method is presented in Table 7.1. The example assumes that county-level population estimates are produced for a hypothetical state consisting of 10 counties. The number of births and the number of deaths in the county are used as the two independent variables in the model. An independently produced total population estimate for the state of 257,040 persons is used as the basis of adjustment of the preliminary county population estimates. Additional steps may be taken in practical applications of the ratio correlation model. For example, a number of regression analyses may be made with a different combination of independent variables in a search for the combination of independent variables that results in the best predictive model. One also may choose to adjust the estimated population if the base year population consists of census data as of April 1 of a particular year, and the estimate date is to be July 1.

The first section of Table 7.1 presents the base period data for county population (the dependent variable) and the county births and deaths (the two independent variables). Ratios for each variable have been calculated in the form illustrated previously. The ratio transformations provide the input data for the multiple regression analysis that will result in the predictive equation. The second section of Table 7.1 presents the estimate year data for county births and deaths, with each county's data presented in the ratio format. The final section of Table 7.1 presents the multiple regression results indicating the following predictive equation:

$$Y' = -.013748 + 1.193482X_1 + (-0.06386X_2)$$

Ratio transformations of estimate year data for the two independent variables are substituted into the equation to yield the estimate year population ratio. Estimate year population ratios for each county are presented in the final section of Table 7.1. It is a simple matter to transform the county population ratio values into estimate year county population estimates given the 1990 county and state population data and the independently produced estimate of the state population for the estimate year. The transformations of the population ratios to unadjusted county population estimates are presented in Table 7.1 adjacent to the population ratio values. Finally, the county population estimates are adjusted such that the sum of the population of the counties will equal the previously produced state total.

The ratio correlation method is ideally suited to producing postcensal population estimates for geographic subareas such as counties when the population of the larger area is known. One of the strengths of the ratio correlation method is its flexibility since a wide variety of variables may be used as independent variables in the multiple regression model. In many cases the data for a particular variable may appear erratic, indicating that the measurement of the variable is no longer reliable or that there has been some type of change in the way the data are collected and reported. In other cases a variable simply may no longer be available. The advantage of the ratio correlation method in these cases is that one may delete the erratic or

**Table 7.1**
**The Ratio Correlation Method**

Base Year Population Data

| County | Population 1980 | 1990 | Population Ratio (Y) |
|---|---|---|---|
| 1 | 25000 | 26500 | 1.013730 |
| 2 | 23000 | 23800 | 0.989613 |
| 3 | 16000 | 17000 | 1.016121 |
| 4 | 15000 | 14500 | 0.924470 |
| 5 | 30000 | 31000 | 0.988227 |
| 6 | 35000 | 39000 | 1.065646 |
| 7 | 8000 | 8200 | 0.980257 |
| 8 | 42000 | 45000 | 1.024659 |
| 9 | 12000 | 10000 | 0.796957 |
| 10 | 35000 | 37000 | 1.010997 |
| State | 241000 | 252000 | |

Base Year Independent Variable Data

| County | Births 1980 | Births 1990 | Birth Ratio ($X_1$) | Deaths 1980 | Deaths 1990 | Death Ratio ($X_2$) |
|---|---|---|---|---|---|---|
| 1 | 405 | 430 | 1.033422 | 223 | 237 | 1.015803 |
| 2 | 420 | 440 | 1.019689 | 231 | 242 | 1.002304 |
| 3 | 240 | 241 | 0.977395 | 125 | 133 | 1.016158 |
| 4 | 212 | 200 | 0.918245 | 117 | 110 | 0.902589 |
| 5 | 468 | 460 | 0.956701 | 257 | 253 | 0.940390 |
| 6 | 560 | 620 | 1.077626 | 291 | 353 | 1.161104 |
| 7 | 112 | 115 | 0.999411 | 65 | 67 | 0.982371 |
| 8 | 690 | 700 | 0.987446 | 400 | 406 | 0.970610 |
| 9 | 150 | 145 | 0.940895 | 90 | 88 | 0.940267 |
| 10 | 540 | 550 | 0.991364 | 313 | 319 | 0.974462 |
| State | 3797 | 3901 | | 2112 | 2208 | |

154

Estimate Year Independent Variable Data

| County | Births 1993 | Births 1990 | Birth Ratio (X₁) | Deaths 1993 | Deaths 1990 | Death Ratio (X₂) |
|---|---|---|---|---|---|---|
| 1 | 460 | 430 | 1.034241 | 239 | 237 | 1.007194 |
| 2 | 450 | 440 | 0.988763 | 250 | 242 | 1.029606 |
| 3 | 225 | 241 | 0.902605 | 140 | 133 | 1.052676 |
| 4 | 190 | 200 | 0.918451 | 115 | 110 | 1.041961 |
| 5 | 485 | 460 | 1.019333 | 236 | 253 | 0.929689 |
| 6 | 650 | 620 | 1.013570 | 359 | 353 | 1.012452 |
| 7 | 115 | 115 | 0.966790 | 70 | 67 | 1.045969 |
| 8 | 755 | 700 | 1.042752 | 405 | 406 | 0.994204 |
| 9 | 135 | 145 | 0.900115 | 90 | 88 | 1.014124 |
| 10 | 570 | 550 | 1.001946 | 311 | 319 | 0.971664 |
| State | 4035 | 3901 | | 2215 | 2208 | |

Multiple Regression Analysis of Birth and Death Ratios to Predict Population

| Constant | -0.13748 |
|---|---|
| Std Err of Y Est | 0.060633 |
| R Squared | 0.479777 |
| No. of Observations | 10 |
| Degrees of Freedom | 7 |

| | Regression Coefficients | Standard Error |
|---|---|---|
| b₁ = | 1.193482 | (1.031742) |
| b₂ = | -0.06386 | (0.684353) |

| County | Predicted Estimate Year Population Ratio | Estimate Year Population Unadjusted | Estimate Year Population Adjusted |
|---|---|---|---|
| 1 | 1.032548 | 27909.79 | 28177 |
| 2 | 0.976840 | 23713.77 | 23940 |
| 3 | 0.872539 | 15129.83 | 15274 |
| 4 | 0.892135 | 13194.67 | 13321 |
| 5 | 1.019706 | 32243.11 | 32551 |
| 6 | 1.007543 | 40080.07 | 40463 |
| 7 | 0.949571 | 7942.26 | 8018 |
| 8 | 1.043536 | 47898.33 | 48356 |
| 9 | 0.872029 | 8894.70 | 8981 |
| 10 | 0.996274 | 37599.40 | 37959 |
| State | | 254605.93 | 257040 |

unavailable variable from the predictive model and substitute it with another variable. Such flexibility is not seen in most of the other methods of postcensal estimation examined previously.

## Cohort Component Method

The cohort component method of postcensal population estimation represents a true component estimation methodology and has the potential of providing the most detailed estimates with respect to age, race, and sex of any estimation methodology. The cohort component method is conceptually simple but relatively difficult to apply due to the data requirements. One may follow a single year cohort strategy, which is the most demanding in terms of data requirements and calculations, or a modified cohort strategy using a 5 or 10 years of age cohort definition. Assuming the single year of age cohort strategy, postcensal population estimates are produced through the cohort component method by the following three equations. The first equation estimates the population of the 0–1-year-old cohort, the second equation estimates the population of the 1–2-year-old cohort, and the third equation estimates the population for all other age cohorts.

(1) $$P_0^1 = B - f_0 D_0 + .5M_0$$

Where:  $P_0^1$      is the population from age 0 to 1 year

       $B$      is the number of births in the year

       $f_0$      is a separation factor indicating the proportion of deaths to the 0–1-year-old cohort

       $D_0$      is the number of deaths to the 0–1-year-old cohort

       $.5M_0$      is one-half of the net migration to the 0–1-year-old cohort

(2) $$P_1^{t+1} = P_0^1 - [(1 - f_0)D_0 + .5D_1] + .5(M_0 + M_1)$$

Where:  $P_1^{t+1}$      is the population from age 1 to 2 years

       $P_0^1$      is the population from age 0 to 1 year

       $(1 - f_0)D_0$      is the number of deaths to the 0–1-year-old cohort not allocated to the population estimated by equation (1)

       $D_1$      is the number of deaths to the 1–2-year-old cohort

       $.5(M_0 + M_1)$ is one-half of the net migration to the 0–1-year-old cohort

$$(3) \qquad P_{a+1}^{t+1} = P_a^t - .5(D_a + D_{a+1}) + .5(M_a + M_{a+1})$$

Where:    $P_{a+1}^{t+1}$         is the population for a given single year

             $P_a^t$           is the cohort population 1 year earlier

          $.5(D_a + D_{a+1})$ is one-half the number of deaths to the cohort the previous year

          $.5(M_a + M_{a+1})$ is one-half of the net migration to the cohort the previous year

While equations (1), (2), and (3) may look rather formidable, they actually represent quite simple ideas. Equation (1) simply indicates that the population of the 0–1-year-old cohort may be estimated by taking the births in the estimate year, subtracting those infant deaths belonging to the estimate year's birth cohort, and adding one-half of the net migration of the 0–1-year-old cohort. Equation (2) describes the estimation process for the 1–2-year-old cohort. One begins with the population 0–1 year of age, subtracts those deaths to the 0–1-year-old cohort that were not attributed to the 0–1-year-old estimate in equation (1) plus one-half of the deaths to the 1–2-year-old cohort, and then adds one-half of the net migration of the 0–1-year-old cohort. Equation (3) provides a generalized estimation equation for any cohort where the population for any cohort beginning at age 2 years or older is equal to the population of the cohort 1 year earlier minus one-half the deaths to the cohort plus one-half the net migration. The cohort component method may be applied to single year of age cohorts, or the equations may be modified to represent 5 or 10 years of age cohorts.

The explanation of the cohort component estimation equations is deceptively simple since the data requirements are extensive. To complete the estimation process successfully, one must have annual vital event data for births and deaths by single year of age and estimates of net migration by single year of age. Data availability will vary by level of geography, but data on births should be readily available for most levels of geography at the county level and above. Data on deaths by single year of age are less likely to be reported at smaller levels of geography. In the case of data on deaths by age, the problem really is one of reporting rather than theoretical availability. Age at death is routinely collected and reported on death certificates, but it is seldom reported in that fashion on a routine basis. The real problem with respect to data availability is with migration data. Actual migration data simply do not exist in most cases. In most cases the migration component of the basic population equation must be estimated by one of the methods described earlier. The technique of using school enrollments as seen in component method II is a viable option as is the use of administrative records data or survey data. Further, the data requirements expand considerably if population estimates with detail by race and sex are desired.

The cohort component technique is the method of choice if highly detailed estimates are desired. One solution to the problem of lack of data, especially for migration, is to estimate current levels of migration based on previously measured trends. Technically, the adoption of the strategy of extending previous trends to estimate current migration shifts the cohort component technique from a population estimation methodology to a population projection methodology, even if the date of the estimate is in the recent past. Many products of a cohort component technique that are presented as population estimates are actually short-range population projections based on an extension of past trends.

## SUMMARY

Most of the leading methods of postcensal population estimation have been discussed in this chapter. Each method has its strengths and weaknesses, and each is suited to certain situations better than others. The simpler methods of postcensal population estimation, such as proration techniques, simple and censal ratio techniques, and the vital rates method, have limited data requirements and may be applied to a wide range of geographic areas. The utility of these techniques, however, is limited in some respects since the level of detail in the output of the estimate is usually limited to population totals. Further, many of the simple techniques require either the existence of an independently produced population estimate for a larger control area or the existence of vital event data for both the estimate area and the larger control area.

More complex methods of population estimation, such as composite methods, component method II, the administrative records method, the ratio correlation method, the cohort component method, and the housing unit method, offer greater detail in the output and in many cases increased accuracy, but a price is paid in terms of more extensive data requirements and a methodology that is more difficult to apply. The methods that are based on the general component model have an inherent logic that is appealing; the estimates are produced through an analysis of the three components of population change: births, deaths, and net migration. The difficulties of meeting the data requirements, especially in terms of the migration component, may quickly dampen one's enthusiasm for a component methodology. The ratio correlation method offers great flexibility in terms of the choice of input data, but like some of the simpler methods of population estimation it requires the existence of an independently produced population estimate for a larger control area.

The range of application with respect to level of geography is generally more narrow when using any of the more complex methods of postcensal population estimation. The underlying logic of the methods will hold up quite well at any level of geography, but most of the more complex methods simply have data requirements that cannot be met at smaller levels of geography below the county level. One exception is the housing unit method, the method of choice in many cases where subcounty population estimates are desired. Several of the more complex methods offer a greater level of detail in the population estimates, but for highly detailed estimates the method of choice is usually a cohort component procedure.

The choice of a method of postcensal population estimation for a particular application is often far from simple. Major factors in the decision include the level of geography and the desired detail in the estimates. One must often pass over what would seem to be the ideal choice due to a lack of data. Finally, one should keep in mind that there is often no single ideal method for a given situation. Often the best strategy is to produce a set of population estimates with several different methods and then average the results.

# 8

## Methods of Population Projection

The useful life of population data can be exceedingly short. In many cases, no sooner than the ink has dried on the latest census results, planners, marketing professionals, and data users of all types are asking the question "But what will the population be 10 years from now?" In the extreme case, the release of the latest census results is sometimes irrelevant from a data application standpoint, with the census results viewed as only the basis for a new round of speculation over the population at a later point in time.

The demand for future population information is met through the generation of population projections or a related data product. By now it should be clear that there are major differences between population projections and population estimates. The two more important differences are that in general (1) population estimates are made for a date in the recent past, while population projections are made for a date in the future, and (2) population estimates tend to be produced with current data based directly on the major components of population change or with current data regarded as symptomatic of the components of population change, while population projections tend to be based on extensions or alterations of previously observed trends in the major components of population change. What may be less clear is the distinction between a population projection and a population forecast. The difference between a population projection and a population forecast has been explained in a variety of ways, but the key distinction is that population projections present future population values based on the extension of current population trends or on assumptions of changes in current population trends with no expectation that the future population will equal the projected value. A population projection is more the result of logic expressed in the form of "If current trends continue, the population in 10 years will be . . . ," or "If fertility levels decline by 8% and mortality levels decline by 5% over the next 10 years, then the population will be . . . ." In either case there is no expectation on the part of a demographer producing the population projections that current trends will continue or that fertility and mortality trends will actually change. The population projection, then, is best characterized as a data product based on a set of assumptions or a set of alternative assumptions.

A population forecast is the result of a methodological process similar to that of population projection, but the population forecast is based on assumptions that are thought best to represent future conditions. The results of a population forecast are therefore presented with a high degree of expectation that they will be realized. An additional source of confusion is found in situations where a multiple set of population projections is presented. Often population projections will be presented in terms of three series: (1) a series reflecting high-growth assumptions, (2) a series reflecting moderate-growth assumptions, and (3) a series reflecting low-growth assumptions. All too often the users of population data will view the middle series of projections as a population forecast and adopt those results as the most likely to reflect future conditions. In most cases there is no more justification in adopting the middle series of projections as a forecast than for adopting any other series.

This chapter discusses the major methodological strategies for producing population projections as well as the central issues in selecting a particular methodology. Most of the major methods of population projection in use today fall into one of the following four categories: (1) ratio allocation methods, (2) mathematical methods, (3) econometric methods, and (4) the cohort component method. Each of the four general strategies shares the same general logic of population projection, which is to begin with the known population at a given point in time, the base population, and to subject that population to the forces of population change over the projection period. The specific manner in which the forces of population change are applied to the base population, however, may vary considerably from method to method.

Ratio allocation methods provide a way to allocate the projected population of a larger area among the constituent subareas that comprise the larger area. Ratio allocation methods will require the existence of an independently produced population projection for the larger control area.

Mathematical methods involve the extension of a particular rate of growth into the future. Ratio allocation and mathematical methods are two of the simpler types of population projection methodologies. Econometric methods represent a different approach to the production of population projections. Econometric methods produce population projections through a statistical model of the economy. Population projections are usually based on a projection of future employment in an area. Econometric methods are usually the most complex methods one can adopt for the production of population projections, and yet they do not result in highly detailed projections. Cohort component methods are much more demanding than ratio allocation and mathematical methods in terms of data requirements and methodological complexity. Cohort component methods, like their estimation counterparts, project the population by an analysis of the three major components of population change: births, deaths, and net migration. Cohort component methods can result in as detailed population projections as one would normally require.

Several issues play a role in the selection of a particular type of projection methodology. The desired level of detail by age, race, and sex in the final data product is often a major factor in the selection of one type of methodology over another. The number of years in the projection period also will play a role in the choice of methodology. Finally, the availability of input data for the projection model often will determine the choice of a projection methodology. Each of the four major types of population projection strategies has its own strengths and weaknesses and can provide acceptable results under certain circumstances. Each of the major types of projection methodologies is discussed in turn below.

## RATIO ALLOCATION METHODS

Ratio allocation methods of population projection provide a way to allocate or distribute the projected population of a larger area among its constituent subareas. For example, the projected population of the United States might be allocated to the individual states that comprise it, or the population of a single state might be allocated to its counties. In either case there is the requirement of an existing population projection for the larger area.

Applications of the ratio allocation technique generally fall into one of two basic categories, although the technique can become as simple or as complex as one would like to make it. Essentially, one is given a population projection for a geographic area made up of identifiable subareas and proceeds to allocate the population projected for a given date among the subareas based on a set of operating assumptions. One general strategy is to assume that the subarea's share of the total population at an earlier date will remain constant over the length of the projection period. The other general strategy is to assume that some pattern of changing share is more appropriate, and the subarea will be allocated an increasing or decreasing share of the total projected population. The most recent census is usually the basis for determining the subarea's share of the total projected population when a constant share approach is chosen. For example, a particular census tract in a county may be observed to contain 7.5% of the total population of the county at the time of the most recent census. A projection of the tract's population is easily obtained by multiplying the projected population of the county by .075, assuming that the tract's share of the county population will remain constant over time. The underlying assumption in this case is that the rate of growth in the census tract will equal the rate of growth of the county.

In other cases one may have reason to assume that a subarea's share of the larger area's population will change over the projection period. Again, census data are a logical starting point for determining the subarea's changing share of the total population, but a longer period of observation is usually required. One might examine the relationship between the subarea's share of total population over time and then derive a measure of the average percentage increase of the total population. For example, a particular county's share of the state population may have increased from 4.0% of the total in 1970, to 4.5% of the total in 1980, to 5.0% of the total in 1990. The projection of the county's population for the year 2000 might be based on the assumption that the county's share of the state population will continue to increase by 0.5% over the 10-year period, so the year 2000 population projection for the county will be 5.5% of the state's projected population.

Undoubtedly, the ratio allocation technique can be applied in more complex ways than demonstrated here. The relationship between the population of a subarea and a larger area may be expressed in a variety of ways, and any of them may be used as the weighting factor when projecting the subarea's population. Essentially, the ratio allocation technique is often just a form of a censal ratio technique seen earlier for producing population estimates. In spite of its simplicity, the ratio allocation technique does have several advantages and may be a wise choice in many applications. The technique does require the availability of an existing population projection for the larger area, but beyond that the data requirements are minimal. The ratio allocation technique is especially well suited to small area geographies that are not easily projected by other methods. The technique has its disadvantages as well. One of the major disadvantages is that the projections resulting from a ratio allocation method are only as good as the population projection for the larger area. In addition, the subarea's share of the total population almost certainly will change over time, which among other things will mean that the ratio allocation technique will not be as practical for longer projection periods.

## MATHEMATICAL METHODS

The primary methods of mathematical population projection involve applications of mathematical extrapolation, which is the extension of a mathematically defined trend. The logic of mathematical methods of population projection follows closely the discussion of mathematical methods of intercensal population estimation by interpolation presented in chapter 6. In fact, there is no discussion of mathematical approaches to postcensal population estimation in chapter 7 since the analogue to mathematical interpolation in the postcensal case—mathematical extrapolation—essentially constitutes a population projection. There are situations where the application of a particular mathematical technique creates at best a vague distinction between a population estimate and a population projection. For example, the current date may be 5 years past the most recent census, and a mathematical method involving extrapolation is to be used to produce a population value for a date 3 years past the most recent census. In this case one is producing a population value for a time in the recent past that is consistent with the definition of a population estimate; however, the technique being used does not rely on current data pertaining to the major components of population change or even on symptomatic data, a case more suggestive of a population projection. While one may choose to characterize the application of a mathematical model in this case as either a population estimate or a population projection, the situation more accurately is defined as a short-term population projection even though the reference date is in the recent past.

There are two major types of methods of mathematical population projection, and each type has several variations. One major type involves mathematical extrapolation, or simply extending a mathematical trend into the future. The mathematical extrapolation methods are similar to the

methods of intercensal population estimation utilizing mathematical interpolation discussed in chapter 6, and one may use the same three types of
assumptions. That is, given a growth rate for a population, one may assume
an arithmetic rate of growth or a geometric rate of growth, with geometric
rates of growth expressed as a function of periodic compounding or
continuous compounding. The second major type involves fitting a growth
rate to a curve. Three frequently chosen alternatives are the Gompertz
curve, the Pearl-Reed curve, and a modified logistic curve. In each case a
mathematical constant is used to place an upper limit on the amount of
growth that may take place during the projection period. Each of the three
curves results in a growth pattern characteristic of a logistic curve which
takes the form of an elongated S-shaped pattern suggestive of a period of
slow gradual growth followed by a period of rapid growth and then
culminating in a final period of no growth.

The two major strategies for projecting population by a mathematical
technique are very similar. In each case a rate of growth is assumed and
extrapolated into the future. The major difference between the two
strategies is that a limit representing the maximum growth possible for
a population is incorporated into the techniques based on the application
of a growth curve. The simple mathematical extrapolation techniques
and the curve fitting techniques result in three population growth
scenarios. Mathematical extrapolation assuming an arithmetic rate of
growth will result in a constant growth pattern which will appear as a
straight line projection when graphed. Mathematical extrapolation assuming a geometric rate of growth will result in a projection line with
an increasing rate of growth over time and will appear as an upward
curve when graphed. The application of a logistic curve to a set of data
will result in a variable rate of population change with an increasing
rate of growth in the early period and a decreasing rate of growth in the
later period. Logistic curve projections will result in an S-shaped
projection curve when graphed, although in some cases the projection
curve is quite elongated making the S-shape difficult to discern. Figure
8.1 presents graphic representations of three series of population projections based on arithmetic, exponential, and logistic rates of growth. All
three series begin with a base population of 81,500 and extend for a
110-year time period. The projection curves reflect the data presented
in Table 8.1 which provides the results of population projections based
on an arithmetic, geometric, exponential, and logistic methodology. The
geometric data series is not graphed due to its similarity to the exponential series.

**Figure 8.1**
**Population Projections**

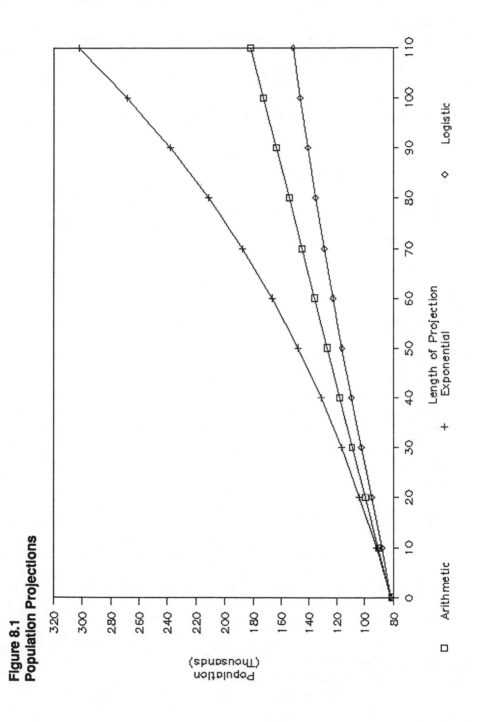

Population (Thousands)

Length of Projection

□ Arithmetic    + Exponential    ◇ Logistic

## Table 8.1
## Population Projections Under Alternative Growth Assumptions

| | Growth Assumption | | | |
|---|---|---|---|---|
| Years Beyond Base Period | Exponential | Geometric | Arithmetic | Logistic |
| 0 | 81,500 | 81,500 | 81,500 | 81,500 |
| 10 | 91,808 | 91,744 | 90,600 | 88,344 |
| 20 | 103,420 | 103,275 | 99,700 | 95,291 |
| 30 | 116,501 | 116,256 | 108,800 | 102,271 |
| 40 | 131,237 | 130,868 | 117,900 | 109,215 |
| 50 | 147,836 | 147,317 | 127,000 | 116,054 |
| 60 | 166,535 | 165,833 | 136,100 | 122,725 |
| 70 | 187,598 | 186,677 | 145,200 | 129,170 |
| 80 | 211,326 | 210,140 | 154,300 | 135,340 |
| 90 | 238,055 | 236,552 | 163,400 | 141,193 |
| 100 | 268,165 | 266,285 | 172,500 | 146,700 |
| 110 | 302,083 | 299,754 | 181,600 | 151,841 |

### Arithmetic Rates of Change

Projecting population through an arithmetic rate of change is quite similar to the intercensal population estimation technique based on interpolation. One begins with a base population, such as the most recent census enumeration, and then adds a constant amount of population increase to the base amount with the resulting total becoming the new base population as the process continues over the length of the projection period. The following formula represents the process:

$$P_t = P_{t-1} + I$$

Where:  $P_t$  is the population at time $t$
        $P_{t-1}$ is the population at the previous time
        $I$    is the amount of net change since time $t$

Recall that an annual amount of net change may be calculated as follows:

$$\text{Annual Net Change} = \frac{P_{90} - P_{80}}{n}$$

Where:  $P_{90}$ is the 1990 census population
        $P_{80}$ is the 1980 census population
        $n$    is the number of years between the two census periods

Using data from the example in chapter 6 of an intercensal population estimate, the amount of change per year may be calculated.

Population 1980:    72,400
Population 1990:    81,500

$$\text{Annual Net Change} \quad = \quad \frac{81,500 - 72,400}{10} \quad = \quad 910$$

One may project the population into the future by adding the annual amount of change to the base population, which in this case is defined as the most recent census result. One may proceed on an annual basis by adding 910 persons to the most recent census count, and then 910 additional persons to that total, and so on; or one may choose to project the population on a 10-year basis by adding 9,100 persons to each previous total spaced 10 years apart.

As with population estimates, population projections are conventionally calculated and reported as of a July 1 date in contrast to census results which are reported as of April 1 in the United States. The same techniques employed to adjust the results of population estimates to reflect a July 1 date also may be used to adjust population projections. In the case of a population projection that has used the most recent census enumeration as its base population, one may either adjust the census result to reflect a July 1 date or adjust the projection results. In some cases it is not critical that an adjustment be made. The longer the period of time for which projections are produced, the less critical the need to adjust the base population. The 3-month adjustment from April 1 to July 1 may have a significant impact on a population estimate produced 1 or 2 years past the census date, but the same 3-month period will have practically no effect on a 20- or 30-year projection period.

## Compound Rates of Change

Mathematical methods also may be used to produce population projections based on an assumed rate of population change. Two procedures are common, and each assumes a type of compound growth rate. One approach assumes a rate of change compounded over a finite time period, while the other approach assumes a continuous compounding based on an exponential rate of change. Each strategy is similar to the methods of intercensal population estimation discussed previously, but the results of compound rates of growth are more dramatic in the case of population projections. In the case of intercensal estimates, the presence of a fixed end point in the form of the most recent census results determines the final estimated value. The population is free to grow without the restriction of an end point in the case of projections, and the result is the classic exponential curve reflecting an increasing amount of growth over time.

*Geometric Rate of Growth.* Population projections based on a geometric rate of growth assume the population is increasing by a constant rate of growth compounded over a given period of time. In the general case, the formula for a geometric rate of population growth is as follows:

$$P_n = P_0 \times (1 + r)^n$$

Where:   $P_n$   is the projected population at time $n$
         $P_0$   is the initial population
         $1 + r$ is the annual rate of growth
         $n$     is the number of years between the base population and the projection period

Growth rates may be assumed for purposes of population projections, or one may calculate a growth rate based on a past period. For example, the two most recent census periods may be used to calculate the rate of population growth $(1 + r)$ by taking the $n$th root of $P_0/P_{0-n}$ (where $P_0$ is the most recent census and $P_{0-n}$ is the census $n$ years earlier). For example, if there were 2 years between the two population observations, then one would take the square root of the result of $P_0/P_{0-n}$; if there were 5 years between the two observations, then one would take the fifth root; and so on. Assuming one is working with the 1980 and 1990 census data, there are 10 years between the two census observations, so one would take the 10th root of $P_{90}/P_{80}$. Using the same hypothetical census results as in chapter 6 for the demonstration of intercensal estimates will yield the following results:

Population 1980:     72,400
Population 1990:     81,500

Then $P_{90}/P_{80} = 1.1257$; solving for the 10th root of 1.1257, the result is 1.01191. The result of 1.01191 represents the value of $(1 + r)$. The value of $r$ (.01191) represents the proportion of compound annual population growth.

Population projections may be calculated by substituting the appropriate values into the formula, assuming that the 1990 population is used as the base:

$$P_n = P_0 \times (1 + r)^n$$

The projection for the year 2000 is obtained as follows:

$$P_{2000} = 81{,}500 \times (1.01191)^{10} = 91{,}744$$

The projection for the year 2010 is obtained as follows:

$$P_{2010} = 81{,}500 \times (1.01191)^{20} = 103{,}275$$

Results for the remaining years in the series are presented in Table 8.1 along with population projections based on an arithmetic rate of change, an exponential rate of change, and a logistic rate of change.

*Exponential Rate of Growth.* Population projections based on an exponential rate of growth operate in a fashion very similar to geometric rates of growth. A growth rate for the projection series is adopted based either on past trends or a judgmental assumption concerning future growth. The difference between the geometric and the exponential rate of growth is simply that the exponential rate of growth assumes continuous compounding over time. The net effect is to increase the size of the population projection given the same assumed rate of growth operating over the same period of time. In most cases, however, the difference between a geometric rate of growth based on annual compounding and an exponential rate of growth based on continuous compounding is quite small. As the data in Table 8.1 indicate, the differences in the size of the projected population after a 110-year period are still relatively small.

As was the case with population estimates, exponential rates of growth may be expressed as a function of e, the natural logarithm. The projected population for any given time may be expressed as the population at the base period multiplied by e raised to a power reflecting the assumed rate of growth times the time interval between the base population date and the projection date. An illustrative formula for population projections based on an exponential rate of change may be represented as follows:

$$P_n = P_0 \, e^{rn}$$

Where:   $P_n$   is the projected population
         $P_0$   is the base population
         e    is the natural logarithm
         r    is the growth rate
         n    is the number of years between the base population and the
              projection date

Population projections based on an exponential rate of growth are presented in Table 8.1 with an assumed rate of growth of 0.01191%, which is the same rate of growth used in the geometric growth rate application. The 0.01191% rate is the rate calculated in the example of intercensal population estimates in chapter 6. One may choose to assume a particular rate of population change for the projection period or calculate a rate of change based on past trends. One may calculate a rate of growth occurring between two previous time periods through the following formula:

$$r = \frac{\log (P_t/P_{t-n})}{n \log e}$$

Where:   $P_t$    is the population at time $t$
         $P_{t-n}$  is the population $n$ years earlier
         e     is the natural logarithm

Once the value of the growth rate has been calculated or assumed, one may proceed to project the population. Using the hypothetical 1990 census result of 81,500 as the base population, the projection to any date may be made by substituting the appropriate values into the formula. For example, the population projection for the year 2000, which is 10 years beyond the base population date, may be calculated as follows:

$$P_{2000} = 81,500 \times 2.718^{(.01191)(10)}$$

$$= 81,500 \times 1.1265$$

$$= 91,808$$

The population projections for the remaining years in the series are obtained by substituting the appropriate values of $n$ into the formula. It is also an easy matter to adjust the projection date to reflect a July 1 date as is conventional with estimates and projections, but again the projection period is usually long enough that adjustments are not that critical. The remaining projections for the series are presented in Table 8.1. One should

note that the projections based on the geometric rate of growth and the
exponential rate of growth are very similar even at the end of the projection
period.

*Logistic Curve Fitting.* The final mathematical methodology for producing population projections discussed in this section deals with the use of
logistic curves. While the world's population growth since the late 15th
century has generally followed an exponential pattern of population
growth, and may be projected by such a pattern, the population of most
areas does not grow exponentially. Often, areas will experience a brief
period of rapid, or exponential, growth, but that will be followed by a
gradual reduction in the growth rate. Logistic curves are based on exponential growth functions just as the previous technique was; however, logistic
curve techniques such as the Gompertz curve and the Pearl-Reed curve
apply constraints to the growth rate with the result being a growth pattern
resembling the classic *S*-shaped population growth curve. While the
Gompertz curve and the Pearl-Reed curve have their advantages in certain
situations, one is more likely to see a modified exponential curve used in
population projections.

The classic logistic or exponential curve is described by the following
equation:

$$Y = \frac{k}{1 + e^{a+bx}}$$

Where:    $Y$    is the projected value of the population
            $k$    is a constant representing the maximum value that the curve
                may attain (the upper asymptote)
            $e$    is the natural logarithm
            $x$    represents the time period of the projection
            $b$    is a constant representing an incremental change ratio for
                successive periods of $x$
            $a$    is a constant equal to the difference between $Y$ and $k$ when $x$ is
                equal to zero

The parameters $k$, $a$, and $b$ operate to constrain the growth projected by
the equation. The parameter $k$ represents the upper limit of growth. More
specifically, $k$ is equal to the upper asymptote, a value that the curve will
approach but never attain. The parameter $b$ is a constant representing a
change ratio based on changing values of $x$ (the length of time between
the base period and the projection period). The parameter $a$ represents the

difference between the projected population value and the upper asymptote when $x$ is equal to zero.

Several methods are available to fit logistic curves to historical population data in order to derive a population projection equation. One must solve for the values of $k$, $b$, and $a$, and then a population projection may be calculated for any given value of $x$. Shyrock and Siegel (1973) describe a procedure for deriving a "modified exponential curve" which is fitted to a variable representing transformed values of population rather than being fitted directly to the population data. In the modified exponential curve method, the population data are presented as reciprocal values times 100,000, represented as the transformed variable $Z$. The exponential curve is then fitted to the transformed population data in the following form:

$$Z = a + bc^x$$

Where:   $Z$           is the reciprocal of the population multiplied by 100,000
         $a$, $b$, and $c$   represent constants derived from partial summation and
                     partial differences for groupings of historical data

The method is described with a detailed example in Shyrock and Siegel (1973, pp. 382–383) and represents a simplified way to fit a logistic curve to historical data. Not all historical series, however, may be fitted by the modified exponential curve method.

The population projections resulting from a logistic curve will appear as an elongated $S$-shaped curve. Table 8.1 presents population projections for a 110-year period beginning with the same base population value of 81,500 as the previous projection examples. The graphic representation of the logistic projection series is presented in Figure 8.1 along with the arithmetic and exponential series. In the case of the logistic series, the historical data were not ideally suited to a logistic fit, so the resulting curve is highly distorted. Still, one can see the effect of a gradual reduction in the growth of the population as evidenced by the flattening of the curve and the increasing distance between the logistic curve and the arithmetic curve at any given point.

## Mathematical Methods in Perspective

Mathematical methods are valuable tools in the production of population projections. Arithmetic methods, compound growth methods, and logistic curve methods are each applicable to a wide variety of geographic levels and may be applied after meeting relatively few data requirements. Populations at even the smallest geographic levels may be projected with the mathematical techniques; in fact, one of the mathematical methods may be the best choice for small geographic areas. The arithmetic and compound growth methods are especially free of extensive data requirements, but the use of logistic curve techniques will require more data. Each of the methods is flexible in terms of the length of the projection period. As the examples in Table 8.1 indicate, the methods may be used to project population far into the future. It is also worthy of note that major differences do not emerge in the results for the projections from the four types of alternative assumptions presented in Table 8.1 until 30 to 40 years into the projection period. Projections beyond 20 to 30 years go beyond most planning purposes.

Mathematical methods suffer from some disadvantages. In many applications the underlying growth assumptions implicit in the mathematical models are not realistic for the areas to be projected. The population of very few areas will grow at an exponential rate for any length of time, especially small areas of geography. Small geographic areas are more likely to encounter a ceiling effect where the population may grow rapidly and then slow after most of the available land in the area has been developed. In some cases an area will experience several cycles of rapid growth, especially if it is an area in high demand. Typically, the area will grow until it is close to its maximum density given the prevailing housing pattern; then housing patterns will change, having the effect of raising the population density and leading to a new cycle of growth. Unfortunately, cyclical patterns are not built into the assumption matrix of population projection methodologies.

Perhaps the greatest disadvantage of mathematically based population projections is the lack of detail in the final product. All of the mathematically based methodologies result in projections of the population total and do not offer any detail by basic characteristics such as age, race, or sex. For smaller areas of geography the lack of detail may not be a problem since detailed projections for small areas tend to be subject to a great deal of error. Detailed projections usually are desirable for larger areas of geography, so mathematical methods of population projection tend to be limited. It may be advantageous, however, to apply a mathematical method when projecting the population of a larger area and to use the result as a control total in another methodology such as an econometric or cohort component technique.

## ECONOMETRIC MODELS

The relationship between econometric models and population projections is an interesting one. Econometric models have been used to project population, but more often one will find that population projections have been used as an input variable in the econometric model. It is useful to examine the basic logic of econometric models in order to understand the manner in which they may be employed in the production of population projections.

Econometric models cannot logically be put into any single category any more than other methods of population projection can, but some general similarities may be described in order to provide an idea of the operation of econometric models. Most econometric models consist of a set of interrelated equations designed to predict or "model" certain aspects of the economy. A typical econometric model may consist of hundreds of equations and be based on data for over a thousand variables. Often the equations are in the form of multiple regression equations, of which a simplified version is described in chapter 7 in the ratio correlation method of postcensal population estimation. In the case of econometric models, one creates a separate multiple regression equation to predict some aspect of the economy (the dependent variable) using a set of independent variables that seems both to be related logically to the dependent variable and that provides a good fit to the historical data.

The econometric model, then, consists of the set of equations with each equation designed to predict some aspect of the economy. The variables defining each equation are of two possible types: exogenous variables and endogenous variables. Exogenous variables are those that originate outside the econometric model but are used as input data in some of the predictive equations. Endogenous variables are those whose values are generated by the econometric model, and then are used as input data in other predictive equations. Usually, the econometric model is a type of simultaneous equation model, which means that the equations are solved "simultaneously," or at the same time. In actual fact, the equations are solved simultaneously only in the sense that the solution is found in a single computer run. The individual equations actually are solved in some order of priority since the result of one equation may be part of the input data for another equation.

The use of population projections in an econometric model may be explained more clearly by discussing the dual role that population may play in econometric modeling. In some applications, population projections serve as exogenous variables. That is, a set of independently produced population projections is used as input data for some of the equations in the model. In such an application, it is appropriate to say that population data are used to predict some aspect of the economy, or one might say that a particular equation in the model is driven by population. For example, if one is to forecast per capita income at a future date, one must have a forecast for total income for the area and total future population. In other applications, however, the population data are endogenous to the model, and equations in the econometric model are used to forecast population. In this latter case, an econometric model truly is used to project population, although there is no standard set of equations used to project population in an econometric model. Population often is defined as a function of employment. In periods when an increase in employment is forecast, it is assumed that an increase in population will result if the size of the work force is not sufficient to meet the demand created by the number of expected jobs. Conversely, an oversupply of working age population relative to the number of available jobs in the area is expected to result in a reduction of population. It should be obvious that net migration is the chief mechanism through which economic forces impact population. The econometric models generally are not geared toward forecasting the other components of population change such as fertility and mortality.

Population projections resulting from an econometric model will be presented in some degree of detail at least with respect to age. Generally, projections will be produced in three broad age groups: the 18–64-year-old group, the 0–17-year-old group, and the age 65 and older group. The three age groups may be thought of as the working age population, the pre-working age population, and the retired population. Given the nature and overall purpose of econometric models, it is unlikely that population projections will be produced in any greater degree of age detail or with detail by race or sex. The working age population is usually projected as a function of expected employment with some adjustment made for an expected amount of unemployment. The number of employed and unemployed will provide a projection of the civilian labor force. In most applications, the projections for the pre-work force population (0–17 years of age) and the retired population (65 years of age and older) are based on the ratios of those respective age groups to the work force population as measured in the most recent census.

A major advantage of econometric modeling in the production of population projections is the underlying logic of the relationship between employment and population. Logically, one would expect a strong relationship between employment opportunities in an area and net migration, and over time population shifts will occur in response to economic factors. The population projections resulting from an econometric model, however, are seldom worth the time and effort needed to develop them. Econometric models are easily the most demanding, both in terms of data requirements and technical expertise, of any of the population projection methods currently in use. Unfortunately, from the standpoint of the demographer, most of the effort required to produce an econometric model is geared toward results other than population projections. The emphasis on factors other than population is not a weakness of econometric models but simply reflects the fact that econometric models are developed primarily for other purposes.

The quality of the projections resulting from an econometric model is open to question. The projections for population are no worse than those for the economic variables forecast by the model, but they are not likely to be any better. The detail in the projections usually is limited to the three broad age groups, and in a sense only the working age population is projected with any level of sophistication since the pre-work force population and the retirement age population are usually based on ratios to the work force population. There seldom will be any detail by race or sex in population projections resulting from an econometric model. Finally, one should realize that the production schedule and forecast period of an econometric model are different than those of most population projections. Econometric models do not extend routinely beyond a 5-year period, a relatively short time frame for population projections. Of course, some econometric models will provide a long-range forecast, but in most cases the forecast period is short. Further, econometric models tend to be produced on a regular schedule. It is not uncommon for a 5-year economic forecast to be produced every year, and in some cases a 5-year forecast may be produced every quarter. Population projections, in contrast, tend to be produced with a longer projection period and are updated less often.

## COHORT COMPONENT METHOD

The cohort component method of population projection is analogous to the cohort component method of postcensal population estimation described in chapter 7. A cohort component strategy of population projection is based on the logic of a general population component methodology which examines separately the three components of population change: fertility, mortality, and net migration. One should note that, while mortality is regarded as one of the components of population change, the converse of mortality—survival—is applied in the cohort component method. The components of population change are then applied to each cohort of the population under study resulting in a detailed set of population projections. The specific logic of a cohort component method of population projection is relatively simple. One begins with a base population, usually the most recent census result. The base population is projected forward in time by the application of net migration rates, mortality rates, and fertility rates. Of course, there are several major issues associated with the development and application of rates for each of the components of population change, and these are discussed in turn.

Migration has long had the well-deserved reputation of being the most troublesome of the components of population change. In the case of a cohort component methodology, it is necessary to derive a set of net migration rates with the same degree of detail by age, race, and sex as will be presented in the population projections. In some applications of the cohort component method, the result can be a quite detailed set of net migration rates. The conventional strategy for producing detailed migration rates involves an analysis of population data from the two most recent censuses and a set of detailed survival rates. An example of the derivation of net migration rates is presented in Tables 8.2 and 8.3. In Table 8.2 the 1980 population for a hypothetical area of geography is presented in detail by age, race, and sex. Age is presented in 5-year cohorts, which is about as detailed as one would require for even the most extensive population projections. Some projection series may present results detailed by single year of age, an uncommon strategy adopted only occasionally for the largest geographic areas.

The calculation of net migration rates begins by aging the population enumerated in the second to most recent census 10 years forward to the date of the most recent census. In the example presented in Table 8.2, the 1980 population is detailed by 5-year cohorts by race and sex and then aged 10 years into the future to 1990 through the application of 10-year life table survival rates. Each cohort of the population is multiplied by its corresponding 10-year survival rate, resulting in the number of members of each cohort expected to survive 10 years to the date of the next census. Survival rates should be chosen that represent as closely as possible the mortality experience of the population projected at the time period under study.

## Table 8.2
## Calculation of the 1990 Expected Population Through Application of Life Table Survival Rates to the 1980 Population

| Age in 1980 | 1980 Census Population | | | | Life Table Survival Rates for the 1980 to 1990 Period | | | | Age in 1990 | 1990 Expected Population | | | |
|---|---|---|---|---|---|---|---|---|---|---|---|---|---|
| | White Male | White Female | Nonwhite Male | Nonwhite Female | White Male | White Female | Nonwhite Male | Nonwhite Female | | White Male | White Female | Nonwhite Male | Nonwhite Female |
| 0-4 | 3253 | 3161 | 1394 | 1347 | 0.9887 | 0.9911 | 0.9791 | 0.9833 | 0-4 | 2701 | 2577 | 1525 | 1457 |
| 5-9 | 3562 | 3435 | 1596 | 1554 | 0.9861 | 0.9892 | 0.9743 | 0.9795 | 5-9 | 2585 | 2469 | 1387 | 1327 |
| 10-14 | 3843 | 3705 | 1853 | 1953 | 0.9963 | 0.9973 | 0.9940 | 0.9960 | 10-14 | 3217 | 3133 | 1364 | 1324 |
| 15-19 | 3758 | 3638 | 1721 | 1952 | 0.9943 | 0.9973 | 0.9937 | 0.9970 | 15-19 | 3512 | 3398 | 1555 | 1523 |
| 20-24 | 3454 | 3321 | 964 | 1181 | 0.9880 | 0.9958 | 0.9872 | 0.9951 | 20-24 | 3829 | 3695 | 1841 | 1945 |
| 25-29 | 3166 | 3086 | 640 | 718 | 0.9840 | 0.9950 | 0.9771 | 0.9920 | 25-29 | 3737 | 3628 | 1710 | 1946 |
| 30-34 | 2601 | 2536 | 585 | 766 | 0.9842 | 0.9946 | 0.9690 | 0.9889 | 30-34 | 3413 | 3307 | 951 | 1175 |
| 35-39 | 2414 | 2647 | 604 | 860 | 0.9844 | 0.9936 | 0.9631 | 0.9854 | 35-39 | 3116 | 3071 | 625 | 712 |
| 40-44 | 2701 | 2767 | 660 | 1009 | 0.9809 | 0.9905 | 0.9524 | 0.9785 | 40-44 | 2560 | 2522 | 566 | 758 |
| 45-49 | 2667 | 2560 | 679 | 757 | 0.9704 | 0.9839 | 0.9317 | 0.9659 | 45-49 | 2377 | 2630 | 582 | 847 |
| 50-54 | 2343 | 2315 | 603 | 776 | 0.9512 | 0.9735 | 0.8996 | 0.9482 | 50-54 | 2649 | 2741 | 629 | 988 |
| 55-59 | 2093 | 2227 | 629 | 784 | 0.9220 | 0.9581 | 0.8533 | 0.9220 | 55-59 | 2588 | 2518 | 633 | 731 |
| 60-64 | 1868 | 2020 | 472 | 658 | 0.8803 | 0.9355 | 0.7953 | 0.8845 | 60-64 | 2228 | 2253 | 543 | 736 |
| 65-69 | 1382 | 1732 | 457 | 595 | 0.8170 | 0.9027 | 0.7358 | 0.8457 | 65-69 | 1930 | 2134 | 537 | 723 |
| 70-74 | 988 | 1232 | 263 | 369 | 0.7295 | 0.8551 | 0.6724 | 0.8016 | 70-74 | 1644 | 1889 | 376 | 582 |
| 75-79 | 681 | 992 | 181 | 222 | 0.6211 | 0.7831 | 0.5827 | 0.7284 | 75-79 | 1129 | 1564 | 336 | 503 |
| 80-84 | 368 | 570 | 75 | 139 | 0.4954 | 0.6741 | 0.4653 | 0.6226 | 80-84 | 720 | 1053 | 177 | 296 |
| 85+ | 222 | 420 | 86 | 117 | 0.2722 | 0.3886 | 0.2858 | 0.4026 | 85+ | 423 | 777 | 105 | 162 |

The 1990 expected population represents the expected number of survivors from the 1980 population, assuming that no migration has taken place. For example, the 964 nonwhite males aged 20–24 years enumerated in 1980 are subjected to a 10-year survival rate of 0.9872 to yield an expected number of 951 nonwhite 30–34-year-olds in 1990, assuming that no migration has taken place. The expected 1990 population is calculated for each cohort by race and sex in a similar fashion with the exception of the two youngest groups: the 0–4-year-old cohort and the 5–9-year-old cohort. The expected 1990 population for the two youngest cohorts is calculated by the application of a fertility measure to the 1980 population. In this case, a general fertility rate (GFR) of 53.8 births per 1,000 women aged 15–44 is applied for the white population, and a general fertility rate of 74.1 births per 1,000 women aged 15–44 is applied for the nonwhite population. The births then must be allocated to the male or female group based on an assumed sex ratio. Finally, the births are subject to an appropriate survival rate representing a length of exposure corresponding to the period of time since birth.

The expected 1990 population is compared with the observed 1990 population with the difference between the expected and observed population attributed to net migration. Table 8.3 presents the expected 1990 population and the observed 1990 population along with the set of 10-year net migration rates that have been calculated. The net migration rates are based on the difference between the observed and expected population for each cohort by race and sex. Each migration rate is calculated by taking the observed population and subtracting the expected population from it. The difference is the estimate of the amount of net migration occurring between 1980 and 1990. The amount of net migration is then converted into a net migration rate by dividing the amount of net migration by the expected 1990 population and then adding a value of 1.00 to the result. The net migration rates by age, race, and sex are presented in Table 8.3 rounded to three decimal places. A value greater than 1.00 indicates that the observed population in 1990 is greater than the expected population, so there is an assumption of net inmigration. Conversely, a value less than 1.00 indicates that the observed population is less than the expected population, so there is an assumption of net outmigration over the 10-year period.

Net migration is not the only factor that may be responsible for the difference between the size of the expected population and the observed population. Some of the difference between the expected population and the observed population is undoubtedly due to changes in mortality rates

**Table 8.3**

**Calculation of 1980 to 1990 Migration Rates Through Comparison of Observed 1990 Population With Expected 1990 Population**

| Age | 1990 Observed Population White Male | White Female | Nonwhite Male | Nonwhite Female | 10-Year Migration Rates White Male | White Female | Nonwhite Male | Nonwhite Female | 10-Year Survival Rates for Projection Period White Male | White Female | Nonwhite Male | Nonwhite Female | 2000 Projected Population White Male | White Female | Nonwhite Male | Nonwhite Female |
|---|---|---|---|---|---|---|---|---|---|---|---|---|---|---|---|---|
| 0-4 | 3047 | 2924 | 1903 | 1913 | 1.128 | 1.135 | 1.248 | 1.313 | 0.9979 | 0.9984 | 0.9965 | 0.9975 | 3249 | 3106 | 2145 | 2099 |
| 5-9 | 3435 | 3114 | 1902 | 2017 | 1.329 | 1.261 | 1.371 | 1.441 | 0.9986 | 0.9990 | 0.9979 | 0.9988 | 3611 | 3364 | 2292 | 2299 |
| 10-14 | 3441 | 3247 | 1791 | 1731 | 1.070 | 1.036 | 1.313 | 1.307 | 0.9958 | 0.9982 | 0.9958 | 0.9982 | 3430 | 3312 | 2366 | 2506 |
| 15-19 | 4428 | 4060 | 2091 | 2307 | 1.261 | 1.195 | 1.345 | 1.258 | 0.9926 | 0.9974 | 0.9907 | 0.9969 | 4559 | 3924 | 2603 | 2903 |
| 20-24 | 4344 | 4110 | 1659 | 2073 | 1.134 | 1.112 | 0.901 | 1.066 | 0.9920 | 0.9974 | 0.9859 | 0.9951 | 3666 | 3359 | 2341 | 2259 |
| 25-29 | 4466 | 4245 | 1546 | 1922 | 1.195 | 1.170 | 0.904 | 0.988 | 0.9922 | 0.9970 | 0.9828 | 0.9933 | 5541 | 4838 | 2786 | 2892 |
| 30-34 | 3754 | 3640 | 1136 | 1222 | 1.100 | 1.101 | 1.194 | 1.040 | 0.9922 | 0.9963 | 0.9803 | 0.9913 | 4889 | 4560 | 1474 | 2198 |
| 35-39 | 2929 | 2932 | 691 | 887 | 0.940 | 0.955 | 1.106 | 1.246 | 0.9892 | 0.9941 | 0.9732 | 0.9876 | 5296 | 4952 | 1374 | 1885 |
| 40-44 | 2496 | 2462 | 632 | 851 | 0.975 | 0.976 | 1.116 | 1.123 | 0.9821 | 0.9900 | 0.9601 | 0.9799 | 4097 | 3991 | 1330 | 1260 |
| 45-49 | 2358 | 2623 | 620 | 840 | 0.992 | 0.997 | 1.065 | 0.991 | 0.9699 | 0.9833 | 0.9394 | 0.9676 | 2724 | 2783 | 744 | 1092 |
| 50-54 | 2621 | 2669 | 632 | 936 | 0.989 | 0.974 | 1.005 | 0.948 | 0.9505 | 0.9729 | 0.9078 | 0.9522 | 2390 | 2379 | 677 | 936 |
| 55-59 | 2364 | 2388 | 617 | 688 | 0.914 | 0.948 | 0.975 | 0.941 | 0.9252 | 0.9599 | 0.8773 | 0.9339 | 2269 | 2573 | 620 | 806 |
| 60-64 | 1855 | 2077 | 521 | 700 | 0.832 | 0.922 | 0.960 | 0.952 | 0.8852 | 0.9393 | 0.8330 | 0.9039 | 2465 | 2528 | 576 | 845 |
| 65-69 | 1552 | 1930 | 533 | 790 | 0.804 | 0.904 | 0.993 | 1.093 | 0.8293 | 0.9096 | 0.7875 | 0.8791 | 1998 | 2174 | 528 | 605 |
| 70-74 | 1136 | 1576 | 359 | 574 | 0.691 | 0.834 | 0.955 | 0.986 | 0.7588 | 0.8650 | 0.7360 | 0.8440 | 1367 | 1798 | 417 | 602 |
| 75-79 | 692 | 1150 | 257 | 387 | 0.613 | 0.736 | 0.764 | 0.769 | 0.6603 | 0.7850 | 0.6497 | 0.7708 | 1035 | 1588 | 417 | 759 |
| 80-84 | 364 | 620 | 136 | 200 | 0.590 | 0.589 | 0.770 | 0.677 | 0.5298 | 0.6609 | 0.5439 | 0.6572 | 595 | 1137 | 252 | 478 |
| 85+ | 241 | 544 | 97 | 185 | 0.570 | 0.700 | 0.921 | 1.143 | 0.3972 | 0.5164 | 0.4291 | 0.5351 | 448 | 1102 | 223 | 432 |
| Total | 45523 | 46311 | 17123 | 20223 | | | | | | | | | 53630 | 53469 | 23165 | 26855 |

Total Population 1990: 129,180

Total Population 2000: 157,119

over the 10-year intercensal period. A reduction in mortality rates taking place during the 10-year intercensal period will have the effect of overestimating mortality to the 1980 population and reducing the number of expected survivors to 1990. The direction of bias is to overestimate inmigration when mortality rates are falling. Conversely, in periods when mortality rates are rising, or more commonly when mortality rates have been selected that are too low for the area under study, the number of survivors to 1990 will be overestimated, and the direction of bias is to underestimate inmigration.

An additional factor that may operate to introduce bias in the amount of net migration estimated by comparing the expected population with the observed population is a change in census coverage or undercount between the two census periods. Ironically, undercount itself is not a problem; the problem stems from changes in the degree of undercount from one census period to the next. In periods when the degree of undercount is diminishing, the effect is to count individuals in the most recent census who were missed in the previous census, and the direction of bias is to overestimate inmigration. In periods when the degree of undercount is increasing, the effect is to miss individuals in the most recent census who were enumerated in the previous census, and the direction of bias is to overestimate outmigration. Unfortunately, the effects of net migration, changing mortality rates, and changes in census coverage each play a role in the difference between the size of the expected population and the observed population, and there is no foolproof way to isolate each of the individual effects. Bias in the estimate of net migration may be minimized by applying mortality rates that seem best to fit the population under study and by adjusting the census population in extreme cases of changes in the degree of census coverage.

The calculation of net migration rates is one of the more difficult steps in the cohort component method. In many respects, the calculation of the remaining two components of population change—mortality and fertility—is somewhat easier by comparison. A set of detailed mortality rates must be derived for use in the cohort component model, and, as was the case with migration, the detail of the mortality rates must match that of the final population projections. The degree of difficulty in obtaining suitable mortality rates will vary depending on a variety of situational factors. One possible source of mortality rates is a life table analysis or census survival analysis specific to the population being projected. In some respects an individually tailored life table analysis or census survival analysis represents the ideal source of mortality rates for a population since the resulting mortality rates represent the actual mortality experiences of the population under study.

In some cases, however, it may not be possible to calculate mortality rates specific to the population under study, and in other cases it may not be wise to do so. In the former case, the problem is likely to be one of data availability. Detailed mortality data by age, race, and sex must be available for the level of geography being projected if one is to produce a life table analysis specific to the level of geography. Similarly, if one is producing a set of population projections at the county level for an entire state, then the mortality analysis must be carried out for each specific county. In many cases the data simply will not be available, and one must turn to an alternative source for survival rates. In the latter case, when the population base is small it might not be wise to produce a local mortality analysis. As the level of geography becomes smaller and the population size is reduced, the likelihood of bias is introduced into the mortality rates due to the problem of small numbers. A small population base may be overly sensitive to a relatively small change in mortality. A change in one or two deaths either way during the reporting period may have a major impact on the resulting mortality rate. Therefore, as the level of geography becomes smaller, it is advisable to avoid the use of mortality rates specific to the area. In the case of county-level geography, alternative sources of mortality rates and the survival rates that will be produced from them for inclusion in the cohort component model would be state-level mortality data which should be readily available. In the absence of state-level data, one could turn to national-level data, although local deviation from national norms can be extreme in some cases.

Fertility is the final variable included in the cohort component model, and in most respects it is the easiest of the three population parameters with which to deal. Any number of measures of fertility may be selected for use in a cohort component model, and, while one still requires a detailed measure of fertility, the level of detail required is much less extensive compared with that of migration or mortality. Detail with respect to a fertility measure refers to fertility differentials by race more than anything else. It is possible to select a set of age specific fertility rates by race and apply them in the cohort component model, but such a level of detail really is not necessary. A simpler measure of fertility such as the general fertility rate, which measures the number of children born per 1,000 women aged 15–44 years in the population, will provide acceptable results in the population projection model.

Once the migration rates and survival rates have been calculated and a measure of fertility has been selected, the population projection process can proceed. Table 8.4 presents the results of a 10-year population projection through the use of a cohort component model. The population enumerated in the 1990 census is presented in detail by 5-year age cohorts by race and sex and serves as the base population. Detailed 10-year net migration rates are presented along with detailed 10-year survival rates. The base population, the net migration rates, and the 10-year survival rates form the basis of the majority of the population projections presented for the year 2000. Each cohort is multiplied by its respective net migration rate and 10-year survival rate to yield the projected population of the cohort in the year 2000 when the members of the cohort will be 10 years older. For example, the 632 nonwhite males aged 40–44 years in 1990 are subjected to the 10-year net migration rate of 1.116 and the 10-year survival rate of 0.9601 to yield the expected number of 677 nonwhite males aged 50–54 years in the year 2000.

The population projections to the year 2000 for all other cohorts are carried out in a similar fashion with the exception of cohorts at each end of the age distribution. The projection for the 85 years and older cohort for the year 2000 represents the survivors from three separate 1990 cohorts: the 75–79-year-old cohort, the 80–84-year-old cohort, and the 85 and over cohort. The other exception is found in the two cohorts at the initial ages of the population distribution. The number of 0–4-year-old individuals and the number of 5–9-year-old individuals are the result of the application of the fertility measure to the base population in addition to the net migration and survival rates. The general fertility rate was used in this application of the cohort component model. The same GFR is used in the projections as was used in the earlier stage for the net migration rates. A GFR of 53.8 for whites and a GFR of 74.1 for nonwhites is applied in the projection model. The projected number of births for whites and nonwhites is allocated to the male and female categories based on assumed sex ratios. The projected number of births is then subjected to net migration and survival rates appropriate to each cohort. The 5–9-year-old cohort is subjected to a full 10-year net migration rate and survival rate, while the 0–4-year-old cohort is subjected to a 5-year period of exposure for net migration and survival. Five-year net migration and survival rates may be approximated by taking the square root of the observed 10-year rates.

Taken together, Tables 8.2, 8.3, and 8.4 represent the typical steps one would take in producing detailed population projections through a cohort component method. A 10-year projection is presented, but it is a simple

**Table 8.4**
**Detailed Population Projections: 1990 to 2000 Through the Cohort Component Model**

| | 1990 Expected Population | | | | 1990 Observed Population | | | | 10-Year Migration Rates | | | |
|---|---|---|---|---|---|---|---|---|---|---|---|---|
| Age | White Male | White Female | Nonwhite Male | Nonwhite Female | White Male | White Female | Nonwhite Male | Nonwhite Female | White Male | White Female | Nonwhite Male | Nonwhite Female |
| 0-4 | 2701 | 2577 | 1525 | 1457 | 3047 | 2924 | 1903 | 1913 | 1.128 | 1.135 | 1.248 | 1.313 |
| 5-9 | 2585 | 2469 | 1387 | 1327 | 3435 | 3114 | 1902 | 1912 | 1.329 | 1.261 | 1.371 | 1.441 |
| 10-14 | 3217 | 3133 | 1364 | 1324 | 3441 | 3247 | 1791 | 1731 | 1.070 | 1.036 | 1.313 | 1.307 |
| 15-19 | 3512 | 3398 | 1555 | 1523 | 4428 | 4060 | 2091 | 1915 | 1.261 | 1.195 | 1.345 | 1.258 |
| 20-24 | 3829 | 3695 | 1841 | 1945 | 4344 | 4110 | 1659 | 2073 | 1.134 | 1.112 | 0.901 | 1.066 |
| 25-29 | 3737 | 3628 | 1710 | 1946 | 4466 | 4245 | 1546 | 1922 | 1.195 | 1.170 | 0.904 | 0.988 |
| 30-34 | 3413 | 3307 | 951 | 1175 | 3754 | 3640 | 1136 | 1222 | 1.100 | 1.101 | 1.194 | 1.040 |
| 35-39 | 3116 | 3071 | 625 | 712 | 2929 | 2932 | 691 | 887 | 0.940 | 0.955 | 1.106 | 1.246 |
| 40-44 | 2560 | 2522 | 566 | 758 | 2496 | 2462 | 632 | 851 | 0.975 | 0.976 | 1.116 | 1.123 |
| 45-49 | 2377 | 2630 | 582 | 847 | 2358 | 2623 | 620 | 840 | 0.992 | 0.997 | 1.065 | 0.991 |
| 50-54 | 2649 | 2741 | 629 | 988 | 2621 | 2669 | 632 | 936 | 0.989 | 0.974 | 1.005 | 0.948 |
| 55-59 | 2588 | 2518 | 633 | 731 | 2364 | 2383 | 617 | 688 | 0.914 | 0.948 | 0.975 | 0.941 |
| 60-64 | 2228 | 2253 | 543 | 736 | 1855 | 2077 | 521 | 700 | 0.832 | 0.922 | 0.960 | 0.952 |
| 65-69 | 1930 | 2134 | 537 | 723 | 1552 | 1930 | 533 | 790 | 0.804 | 0.904 | 0.993 | 1.093 |
| 70-74 | 1644 | 1889 | 376 | 582 | 1136 | 1576 | 359 | 574 | 0.691 | 0.834 | 0.955 | 0.986 |
| 75-79 | 1129 | 1564 | 336 | 503 | 692 | 1150 | 257 | 387 | 0.613 | 0.736 | 0.764 | 0.769 |
| 80-84 | 720 | 1053 | 177 | 296 | 425 | 620 | 136 | 200 | 0.590 | 0.589 | 0.770 | 0.677 |
| 85+ | 423 | 777 | 105 | 162 | 241 | 544 | 97 | 185 | 0.570 | 0.700 | 0.921 | 1.143 |

matter to extend the projection period farther into the future. To extend the projections another 10 years to the year 2010, one simply would use the projected population for the year 2000 as the base population and apply the schedule of net migration, 10-year survival, and fertility rates to the projected 2000 population. The process may be repeated any number of times with a population being projected 10 years into the future and then becoming the new base population for the next step in the projection process.

Several additional issues should be addressed involving the cohort component model; to some extent they are issues that may affect any type of population projection. As the length of the projection period is extended, it may become necessary either to alter some of the underlying assumptions in the model with respect to the major components of population change or to generate a series of population projections based on alternative assumptions. The components of population change are certainly going to vary over time. Life expectancy has increased over the past 100 years and it is realistic to assume that the trend will continue, so it might be advisable to factor in an increase in the underlying survival rates in the projection model for extended projection periods. Similarly, one might find it advisable to alter the fertility assumptions implicit in the model, especially as the length of the projection period increases. The white-non-white differentials with respect to vital rates have diminished over time. One might find it advisable to have white-nonwhite survival rates and white-nonwhite fertility rates converge toward the end of an extended projection period.

An alternative way to handle changes in the underlying assumptions is to issue several series of population projections with each series based on a different set of assumptions. For example, one series could be based on constant mortality, migration, and fertility assumptions; a second series could be based on a "high-growth" scenario assuming constant fertility but reduced mortality; and a third series could be based on a "low-growth" scenario assuming reduced fertility and constant mortality. The number of permutations is not endless, but it may seem that way at times, especially if one alters the net migration assumptions in addition to those of fertility and mortality. Both the strategy of using a single population projection series based on changing assumptions over time and the strategy of using a multiple series based on alternative assumptions have their advantages and disadvantages. The single series reduces the potential for confusion but leaves one faced with difficult decisions as to how and when to alter the underlying assumptions in the model. Conversely, a multiple series based on a variety of alternative growth scenarios removes the necessity of deciding how and when to alter the underlying assumptions but in the process may provide too many alternatives. A multiple series of population projections is often taken as a statement in the form of "We have no idea what the population will be in the future, but here are twelve different possibilities."

A recent series of Hispanic population projections released by the U.S. Bureau of the Census (1986) began with a U.S. base population of 15.8 million persons of Hispanic origin in 1982 and projected the population forward to the year 2080 using just three different projection series: a low series, a middle series, and a high series. By the year 2080 the difference between the projection for the lowest series (34.6 million persons) and the highest series (140.7 million persons) was over 100 million persons. Undoubtedly, the series of projections will prove to be accurate; by the year 2080 the Hispanic population of the United States will in all likelihood be between 34.6 million and 146.7 million persons, but the range is so great that we really do not know much more than we did before we examined the projections. Multiple series of population projections often will have the same effect—offering so many choices or so great a range that the projections become less meaningful.

An additional issue that may arise in a cohort component method, or any method that produces population projections detailed by age, concerns the problem of special population and group quarters. The typical situation might involve the presence of a relatively large college or university population in a county. The college population represents a relatively permanent presence at a fixed age in the population distribution of the county. In a typical population projection strategy, the college age population would represent a "bulge" in the population distribution appearing in the cohorts aged 15–19 years, 20–24 years, and, possibly, 25–29 years. In the absence of any special provisions, the college age population would be subject to the normal forces of age, migration, and mortality and would move up the population distribution to older and older cohorts as the projection process continues. In a very real sense, however, the college age population does not age or migrate with respect to the remainder of the population distribution of the area. The individuals may age, but as they do they also graduate or leave and are then replaced by a new group of students in the same two or three age cohorts. It is therefore necessary at times to adjust the normal population projection model to account for the presence of special populations.

One strategy for adjustment is to subtract the approximate number of individuals in a special population from the appropriate age groups; then to subject the remainder of the population to the normal forces of age, migration, mortality, and fertility; and then to add the number of members in the special population back into the total in the same age groups from which they were initially subtracted. In this manner the special population remains a constant size and age which is reflective of its presence in the actual age distribution of the population.

College populations are not the only type that may require adjustment in the population projection model. Prison populations, military bases, and nursing homes are additional examples of group quarters populations that may require special treatment. It should be noted, however, that group quarters populations do not always require a special adjustment. As the size of the base population increases, the need to adjust for the presence of group quarters or special populations will decrease. Adjustments are necessary only when the special population represents a significant percentage of the total population.

The cohort component method is one of the more demanding methods of population projection in many respects. The method may be applied to a variety of levels of geography, but as the size of the level of geography decreases, the availability of data may decrease as well. The data requirements of the cohort component method are extensive, but so too are the resulting projections. No other population projection methodology can match the level of detail with respect to age, race, and sex.

## SUMMARY

Population projections fill a vital need for those charged with the task of planning for the future. Projections concerning population size, composition, and distribution in varying degree of detail may be provided by one method or another. This chapter has discussed the four major strategies of population projection: ratio allocation techniques, mathematical methods, econometric models, and cohort component methods. Each has its major advantages and disadvantages, and each may be a wise choice of methodology in certain applications.

Ratio allocation methods and mathematical methods are two of the less sophisticated general strategies for producing population projections. Ratio allocation methods provide a way to allocate or distribute a larger area's population projection among its constituent subareas. The share of each subarea of the total population projection is usually determined by a previously observed relationship between the population of the subarea and the population of the larger area. The ratio allocation method of population projection is analogous to a censal ratio method of population estimation. In each case, an independently produced population value must be available, and the share of the total allocated to the subarea is based on previously measured relationships between the subarea and the larger area. While the ratio allocation method lacks a high level of sophistication, it does have its uses. The lack of extensive data requirements allows the method to be applied to almost any level of geography. For very small levels of geography, such as the census tract level, the ratio allocation method may be the best choice. The method is limited in that there are no guarantees that previously observed relationships between the population of the subarea and the larger area will remain constant over time. Ratio allocation methods are also limited in that the level of detail in the final population projection is usually limited to population totals.

Mathematical methods are also relatively simple to apply in most situations. Mathematical techniques include extrapolation methods involving the extension of a particular growth rate into the future and curve fitting techniques. The mathematical extrapolation techniques are easy to apply. One begins with a base population and applies a rate of growth subject to certain assumptions. The rate of growth may be based on a previously observed growth rate for the area, or it may be assumed for the purposes of the projection period. Curve fitting techniques usually involve the fitting of a logistic curve to previously observed growth patterns, and then the curve is extended into the future. The most common applications of fitting a logistic curve include the adoption of mathematical constants which act as constraints on the maximum amount of growth that may take place. The application of constraints on growth is an attractive feature of the curve fitting strategy. Growth at any level will not continue indefinitely, and high growth in particular is subject to reduction over time. One of the disadvantages of some of the mathematical methods is the often unrealistic assumption that a particular rate of growth will continue over the entire projection period. Mathematical extrapolation methods based on an exponential rate of growth are especially unrealistic, so methods involving some type of upper limit in the projection process are attractive alternatives. Of course, not all previous population growth patterns lend themselves to the application of logistic curves. In general, the mathematical methods have few data requirements and, like ratio allocation methods, may be applied to geographic areas of almost any size.

Econometric models are perhaps the most demanding in terms of data and technical expertise of any of the methods of population projection presented in this chapter. Unfortunately, the quality of the results from econometric models does not always match the demands of the approach. This is not an indictment of econometric models; it is simply a realization that in most cases econometric models are not designed primarily to produce population projections. The main function of econometric models is to model and forecast economic variables and relationships, and much of the effort and data are directed toward these ends. Econometric models do have an attractive element of logic underlying their efforts to project population. The measurement and projection of migration remains one of the most difficult aspects of population projection. The approach prevalent in most econometric models is to allow migration to be driven by an equation or a series of equations dealing with employment and the expected size of the working age population. The idea of employment opportunities driving migration and ultimately population is an attractive one, but the lengths one must go are often not worth the results. Econometric models do result in population projections with some degree of detail. In most cases, projections will be produced in three broad age groups: the pre-working age population, the working age population, and the retirement age population. Application of econometric models is somewhat limited in terms of geographic areas. Geographic areas below the state level tend not to be the subject of econometric modeling, so the econometric approach is usually applied at the state level or above.

Cohort component methods represent the final population projection strategy discussed in this chapter. Like econometric models, the cohort component approach can be quite demanding in terms of data requirements and technical expertise. The underlying logic of the cohort component method is easily the most appealing of the methods examined in this chapter, since cohort component strategies base projections of future population directly on the components of population change: fertility, mortality, and net migration. No other method of population projection can approach the cohort component method's potential for providing highly detailed population projections by age, race, and sex. The analysis of the separate components of population change and the high level of detail, however, come at a high price in terms of data requirements and technical expertise. The level of detail desired in the final population projection product must be matched in many of the intermediate calculations. For example, net migration and survival rates must be produced in as great a level of detail as the final population projections. At smaller levels of geography, required data may not be available, and in other cases the data may not be reliable for some of the intermediate steps. One may attempt to solve the lack of data problem by applying migration rates or survival rates for a larger area of geography, but in the process the validity of the end product may be questioned. The cohort component method is flexible and may be applied to a variety of geographic areas; generally, there are no problems in applying the cohort component method at the county level or above. Lack of data can become a problem below the county level, and at very small levels of geography the extensive detail produced by most cohort component methods is simply not practical. Cohort component methods, however, represent the usual method of choice when highly detailed population projections are required.

Each of the methods discussed in this chapter has its uses. In the general case, smaller geographic areas are better projected by the simpler methods such as ratio allocation or mathematical methods. Larger areas and situations that require more detailed population projections are better suited to the econometric models or the cohort component method. A final issue concerns the length of the projection period. Any of the methods may provide acceptable results for relatively short projection periods of no more than 10 to 20 years. For longer projection periods, the more sophisticated methods will yield better results. It is more appropriate to consider long-range projections as illustrative of what the future may hold rather than as guarantees of what it will hold.

# 9

# Population Estimates and Projections: Putting It All Together

This chapter is concerned with several topics that are intended to put the process of population estimation and projection into perspective. Included in this chapter are a discussion of some of the practical issues involved in selecting a method of population estimation or projection, the overall merits and limitations of the major methods of estimation and projection discussed in the book, an evaluation of the quality of the results of the major methods of population projection and postcensal population estimation, and suggestions on when one should update population projections. The discussion begins with an analysis of the major methods of postcensal population estimation.

## ISSUES IN POSTCENSAL POPULATION ESTIMATION

Selecting a method of postcensal population estimation involves several issues, including geographic level of the area to be estimated, available data, technical demands of the method, and accuracy of the method. The accuracy or quality of a population estimate is a critical factor and will be addressed first.

### Accuracy of Methods of Estimation

In general, the results of the simpler methods of estimation, such as the mathematical methods including proration, the various ratio procedures, and the vital rates method, are not as good compared with the results from the more advanced methods, such as the housing unit method, ratio correlation method, administrative records method, and component method II. The accuracy of the housing unit method began to deteriorate in the 1970s, but the problem seemed to be due more to improper assumptions concerning average household size than to any inherent flaw in the method. The record of accuracy among the advanced methods employed by the U.S. Bureau of the Census for its county-level estimates has been mixed over time. In the early 1970s, component method II provided superior results compared with composite methods and the ratio correlation method. In the 1980s, results from the ratio correlation method were slightly better than either the administrative records method or component method II.

The following two generalizations may be made for all types of estimation methodologies. First, one will find that the larger the area being estimated, the more accurate will be the result. For a variety of reasons, larger areas of geography are estimated more accurately than smaller areas. Much of the volatility of population change associated with small areas tends to be averaged out when the level of analysis increases to a larger area. Second, the greater the degree of population change in an area, the greater the degree of error in the estimate. Areas that are changing rapidly are more difficult to estimate, and this applies to rapid net losses of population as well as to net gains in population. The population of areas that change in a moderate, steady fashion is simply easier to estimate.

## Merits and Limitations of Methods of Estimation

The simpler methods of population estimation, such as proration, the simple ratio procedure, the censal ratio method, and the vital rates method, have several advantages. First, the methods are relatively easy to apply and do not require a great deal of technical expertise. Second, they are characterized by limited data requirements, and the data requirements that do exist are usually easily met. Finally, the simple methods may be applied to a wide range of geographic areas including small areas. The major limitation of the simpler methods is that they do not produce results as accurate as those from the more complex methods.

The more advanced methods of postcensal population estimation have several advantages as well. First, the more advanced methods have been shown to produce more accurate results compared with the simpler methods. Additional advantages and limitations are better delineated on a method-by-method basis. The housing unit method is especially well suited to small geographic areas, especially those below the county level. The housing unit method has been shown to be very accurate provided one can meet the data requirements.

Component method II, the ratio correlation method, and the administrative records method each have a clear track record due to their use by the U.S. Bureau of the Census. While some differences exist in the accuracy among the three, they each are relatively reliable methods of population estimation. A major limitation of each of the methods is the extensive amount of data required and the high level of technical expertise required. Of the three methods, the ratio correlation is the most flexible in terms of data requirements and requires a slightly lower level of technical expertise. Component method II has extensive data requirements and requires a fair amount of technical expertise. The administrative records method requires data on matched federal income tax returns from the Internal Revenue Service, which severely restricts the application of the method. All three methods may be applied at small levels of geography, such as the county level, and in some applications may even be used to produce population estimates for areas below the county level.

The composite method and the cohort component method provide quality estimates if the data requirements can be met. Like other more complex methods, the composite method and the cohort component method have extensive data requirements and require a high level of technical expertise. The main advantage of each of these methods is that they result in population estimates with considerable detail by age and by race and sex if desired. The composite method is designed to produce population estimates for five major age groupings of the population with each age group estimated with data and by a technique that is best suited to it. The cohort component method produces estimates in the greatest level of detail with respect to age, race, and sex of any method of postcensal population estimation. While the cohort component method requires a high level of technical expertise, it is no more demanding than the composite method, and, in general, better results are obtained with it.

## Choosing a Method of Population Estimation

There is no single method of population estimation that is best for all situations, so choosing a methodology must be based on several situational factors. The proration method is best suited to allocating an estimate for a larger geographic area among its constituent subareas in cases where one does not or cannot produce an independent estimate for the subareas. The mathematical methods such as the simple ratio procedure, censal ratio method, and vital rates method are all good choices when faced with limited data. Any of these simpler methods may be applied to a variety of geographic levels.

Situations demanding greater accuracy in the population estimates will require the use of a more sophisticated methodology. The housing unit method is an excellent choice when faced with the need to produce reasonably accurate estimates for relatively small areas, such as the subcounty level. Component method II and the ratio correlation method are each wise choices for producing accurate population estimates at the county level or above. The methods are demanding in terms of data and expertise, but the skills required to produce estimates with these methods are easily acquired. The data requirements of the administrative records method preclude its use by most outside the federal government.

The cohort component method and the composite method are the obvious choices when one requires detailed population estimates. Of the two, the cohort component method is the better choice for most situations and will result in estimates of far greater detail by age, race, and sex. The required data and technical expertise necessary to apply the cohort component method are not significantly greater than those of the composite method, and the results are usually better.


## ISSUES IN POPULATION PROJECTION

### Accuracy of Methods of Projection

The accuracy associated with methods of population projection generally parallels the situation with methods of estimation. Better results tend to be found for the projection of larger areas of geography than for smaller areas. Results tend to be better for areas that have experienced population change at a steady, moderate pace compared with areas that have experienced an extreme rate of net change (either population growth or population decline). Further, results tend to be better for shorter projection periods than for longer projection periods. One may categorize methods of population projection in a manner similar to population estimates in that there are simpler methods and more advanced methods. Unlike the tests of accuracy of population estimates, there is no clear indication that the more advanced methods of population projection produce consistently superior results compared with the simpler methods of projection.

## Merits and Limitations of Methods of Projection

Chapter 8 presents a discussion of four broad categories of population projection, including ratio allocation methods, mathematical methods, econometric models, and the cohort component method. Ratio allocation and mathematical methods are simpler methods, while econometric models and the cohort component method are more complex. Ratio allocation methods provide a way to allocate the population projection of a larger geographic area to the subareas that comprise it. This is a relatively simple way to produce a population projection for small areas of geography that may not be projected in any other manner. The limitation of ratio allocation methods is that they require access to an existing population projection for a larger area, and the resulting projections for the subareas will be at best only as good as the larger area's projection. Mathematical methods produce population projections by applying a growth rate in some manner to a base population. The mathematical methods are relatively easy to apply and require very little input data, and the results are often quite good, especially for short-range projections. Their major limitation is that they are not designed to produce detailed population projections.

Econometric methods and the cohort component method are more complex and require much more extensive input data and technical expertise. Of the two, econometric methods probably are more complex in that one must have or create an econometric model in order to generate the population projections. The logic of the econometric approach is appealing, but the results often are not worth the effort. Detailed projections for several broad age categories are available with econometric models. Econometric methods may be applied to any level of geography for which one has a suitable econometric model, but in most cases the econometric approach is not used below the state level. The cohort component method can provide the most detailed projections with respect to age, race, and sex. The data requirements may be extensive, but not as great as the econometric approach, and the results are generally better. The cohort component method may be used at a variety of geographic levels but is probably best suited to the county level or above.

### Choosing a Method of Population Projection

Any of the major methods of population projection are suitable for producing short-range projections of limited detail. The less sophisticated methods probably are better choices for very small levels of geography. As the length of the projection period increases, or if highly detailed projections are required, one is usually better served by a technique that incorporates the dynamics of population change into its methodology, such as the econometric model or the cohort component method. The cohort component method is the obvious choice for projections of great detail by age, race, and sex.

### The Need to Update Projections

Several factors determine the need to update a set of population projections. All other things being equal, a population estimate for a given date will be superior to a population projection, so it is certainly time to update projections when current estimates have caught up with the projection date. In addition, the release of current estimates of the population may reveal a change in trends indicating that the most recent projections are in need of revision. Projections should be updated when better input data are available. The release of the latest census figures generally results in a rash of population projection activity, since the census figures provide an updated source for the base population. Finally, projections should be updated when there is a clear planning need for more current numbers.

## SUMMARY

This chapter has attempted to put the population estimation and projection process into perspective, and in the process it was intended to serve as a summary statement for the other chapters in the book. The issues discussed, such as the merits and limitations of the various estimation and projection techniques, selecting a methodology, and updating a projection series, can be understood best by a consideration of the topics examined in the previous chapters.

Population estimates and projections play a vital role in the planning and decision-making process of so many fields. As populations continue to grow, the need to have an accurate estimate of what the population is today and what it is likely to be tomorrow can become only more important. This book was intended to bring into focus the methods available to meet that need.

# References and Suggested Readings

Ascher, W. (1981). The forecasting potential of complex models. *Policy Sciences, 13,* 247–267.

Atchley, R. (1968). A short-cut method for estimating the population of metropolitan areas. *Journal of the American Institute of Planners, 34,* 259–262.

Barclay, G. W. (1958). *Techniques of population analysis.* New York: Wiley & Sons.

Bogue, D. J. (1950). A technique for making extensive population estimates. *Journal of the American Statistical Association, 45,* 149–163.

Bogue, D. J., & Duncan, B. (1959). A composite method for estimating postcensal population of small areas by age, sex, and color. *Vital Statistics Special Reports, 47*(6).

Bowles, G. K., & Tarver, J. (1965). *Net migration of the population, 1950–60 by age, sex, and color.* Economic Research Service, U.S. Department of Agriculture. Washington, DC: U.S. Government Printing Office.

Corner, I. E. (1987). Household projection methods. *Journal of Forecasting, 6,* 271–284.

Dorn, H. F. (1950). Pitfalls in population forecasts and projections. *Journal of the American Statistical Association, 45,* 311–334.

Faber, J. F. (1982). Life tables for the United States: 1900 to 2050 (Actuarial Study No. 87). Washington, DC: Office of the Actuary, Social Security Administration.

Gonzales, M., & Hoza, C. (1978). Small area estimation with applications to unemployment and housing estimates. *Journal of the American Statistical Association, 73,* 7–17.

Greenberg, M. (1972). A test of combinations of models for projecting the populations of minor civil divisions. *Economic Geography, 48,* 179–188.

Greenberg, M. R., et al. (1978). *Local population and employment projection techniques.* New Brunswick, NJ: Rutgers University Center for Urban Policy Research.

Hamilton, C. H. (1965). Practical and mathematical considerations in the formulation and selection of migration rates. *Demography, 2,* 429–443.

Hamilton, C. H., & Perry, J. (1962). A short method for projecting population by age from one decennial census to another. *Social Forces, 41,* 163–170.

Haub, C. (1987). Understanding population projections. *Population Bulletin, 42*(4). Washington, DC: Population Reference Bureau.

Irwin, R. (1977). Guide for local area population projections. (Technical Paper 39). U.S. Bureau of the Census. Washington, DC: U.S. Government Printing Office.

Isserman, A. (1977). The accuracy of population projections for subcounty areas. *Journal of the American Institute of Planners, 43*, 247–259.

Keyfitz, N. (1981). The limits of population forecasting. *Population and Development Review, 7*, 579–593.

Land, K. C. (1986). Methods for national population forecasts: A review. *Journal of the American Statistical Association, 81*, 888–901.

Land, K. C., & Schneider, S. H. (Eds.). (1987). *Forecasting in the social and natural sciences.* Dordrecht, Netherlands: Reidel.

Lee, E. S., & Goldsmith, H. F. (Eds.). (1982). *Population estimates: Methods for small area analysis.* Beverly Hills, CA: Sage Publications.

Makridakis, S., & Wheelwright, S. (Eds.). (1987). *The handbook of forecasting* (2nd ed.). New York: Wiley & Sons.

Martin, J., & Serow, W. (1978). Estimating demographic characteristics using the ratio-correlation method. *Demography, 15*, 223–233.

Meade, N. (1988). Forecasting with growth curves: The effect of error structure. *Journal of Forecasting, 7*, 235–244.

Mitra, S. (1967). The pattern of age-specific fertility rates. *Demography, 4*, 894–906.

Morrison, P. A. (1971). *Demographic information for cities: A manual for estimating and projecting local population characteristics.* Santa Monica, CA: Rand Corporation.

Namboodiri, N. (1972). On the ratio-correlation and related methods of subnational population estimation. *Demography, 9*, 443–453.

National Center for Health Statistics. *Vital statistics of the United States: Vol. 1. Natality.* Hyattsville, MD: Public Health Service.

National Center for Health Statistics. *Vital statistics of the United States: Vol. 2. Mortality.* Hyattsville, MD: Public Health Service.

National Center for Health Statistics. (1990a). Advance report on final natality statistics, 1988. *Monthly Vital Statistics Report, 39*(4).

National Center for Health Statistics. (1990b). Advance report on final mortality statistics, 1988. *Monthly Vital Statistics Report, 39*(7).

National Center for Health Statistics. (1990c). *Vital statistics of the United States, 1987: Vol. II, Sec. 6. Life Tables.* Hyattsville, MD: Public Health Service.

National Research Council. (1980). *Estimating population and income of small areas.* Washington, DC: National Academy Press.

O'Hare, W. (1976). Report on a multiple regression method for making population estimates. *Demography, 13*, 369–379.

Pittenger, D. B. (1976). *Projecting state and local populations.* Cambridge, MA: Ballinger Publishing.

Raymondo, J. C. (1987). Who's on first? *American Demographics, 9*(11).

Raymondo, J. C. (1988). How to count illegals, state by state. *American Demographics, 10*(9).

Raymondo, J. C. (1989a). How to estimate a population. *American Demographics, 11*(1).

Raymondo, J. C. (1989b). How to choose a projection technique. *American Demographics, 11*(2).

Rives, N. W., Jr., & Serow, W. J. (1984). *Introduction to applied demography*. Beverly Hills, CA: Sage Publications.

Rogers, A. (1985). *Regional population projection models*. (Scientific Geography Series, Vol. 4). Beverly Hills, CA: Sage Publications.

Shyrock, H. S., Siegel, J. S., & Associates. (1973). *The methods and materials of demography*. U.S. Bureau of the Census. Washington, DC: U.S. Government Printing Office.

Siegel, J. S. (1972). Development and accuracy of projections of population and households in the United States. *Demography, 9*, 51–68.

Smith, S. (1984). *Population projections: What do we really know?* (BEBR Monographs, No. 1). Gainesville, FL: Bureau of Economic and Business Research, University of Florida.

Smith, S. (1986). A review and evaluation of the housing unit method of population estimation. *Journal of the American Statistical Association, 81*, 287–296.

Smith, S. (1987). Tests of forecast accuracy and bias for county population projections. *Journal of the American Statistical Association, 82*, 991–1012.

Smith, S., & Lewis, B. (1980). Some new techniques for applying the housing unit method of local population estimation. *Demography, 17*, 323–339.

Smith, S., & Sincich, T. (1990). The relationship between the length of the base period and population forecast errors. *Journal of the American Statistical Association, 85*, 367–375.

Smith, S., & Sincich, T. (1991). An empirical analysis of the effect of length of forecast horizon on population forecast errors. *Demography, 28*, 261–274.

Starsinic, D., & Zitter, M. (1968). Accuracy of the housing unit method in preparing population estimates for cities. *Demography, 5*, 475–484.

U.S. Bureau of the Census. (Annual Publication). *Statistical abstract of the United States*. Washington, DC: U.S. Government Printing Office.

U.S. Bureau of the Census. (General Series). *Current population reports*, Series P-20, Characteristics of households. Washington, DC: U.S. Government Printing Office.

U.S. Bureau of the Census. (General Series). *Current population reports*, Series P-25, Population estimates and projections. Washington, DC: U.S. Government Printing Office.

U.S. Bureau of the Census. (Periodic Publication). *Congressional district data book*. Washington, DC: U.S. Government Printing Office.

U.S. Bureau of the Census. (Periodic Publication). *County and city data book*. Washington, DC: U.S. Government Printing Office.

U.S. Bureau of the Census. (1983). Provisional projections of the population of states, by age and sex: 1980 to 2000. *Current population reports*, Series P-25, Population estimates and projections. (No. 937). Washington, DC: U.S. Government Printing Office.

U.S. Bureau of the Census. (1984). Projections of the population of the United States. *Current population reports*, Series P-25, Population estimates and projections. (No. 952). Washington, DC: U.S. Government Printing Office.

U.S. Bureau of the Census. (1985). Census geography—Concepts and products. (Factfinder CFF, No. 8, revision, August 1985). Washington, DC: U.S. Government Printing Office.

U.S. Bureau of the Census. Spencer, G. (1986). Projections of the Hispanic population: 1983 to 2080. *Current population reports*, Series P-25, Population estimates and projections. (No. 995). Washington, DC: U.S. Government Printing Office.

U.S. Bureau of the Census. (1987). United States population estimates and components of change: 1970 to 1986. *Current population reports*, Series P-25, Population estimates and projections. (No. 1006). Washington, DC: U.S. Government Printing Office.

U.S. Bureau of the Census. (1989). *1990 census of population and housing tabulation and publication program.* Washington, DC: U.S. Government Printing Office.

U.S. Bureau of the Census. Wetrogan, S. I. (1990). Projections of the population of states by age, sex, and race: 1989 to 2010. *Current population reports*, Series P-25, Population estimates and projections. (No. 1053). Washington, DC: U.S. Government Printing Office.

U.S. Bureau of the Census. (1991). Census geography—Concepts and products. (Draft, Factfinder CFF, No. 8, revision, January 1991). Washington, DC: U.S. Government Printing Office.

Willekens, F. J. (1990). Demographic forecasting; State of the art and research needs. In C. A. Hazeu & G. Frinking (Eds.). *Emerging issues in demographic research.* New York: Elsevier Science.

Zitter, M., & Shyrock, H. (1964). Accuracy of methods of preparing population estimates for states and local areas. *Demography, 1*, 227–241.

# Index

Administrative records method, 146–
48; advantages and limitations of,
147–48
Age specific death rate (ASDR), 22–25
Age specific fertility rate (ASFR), 17–
18
American Housing Survey, 93
Annexation, 76–77
Apportionment data, 85. *See also*
Public law 94-171
Arithmetic rate of change, 168–69

Base population, 12
Bogue, Donald, 131, 138, 142

CENDATA, 84
Census (*see also* United States Bureau
of the Census)
—data: computer tape files, 83; compact disk-read-only memory (CD-
ROM), 84, 91; microfiche, 84, 91;
printed reports, 83; public use micro
sample (PUMS), 83, 88–89; summary tape files (STF), 83, 88–89
—decennial, 12, 82
—geography: Alaska Native villages,
68, 72; American Indian reservations, 68, 72; block groups, 67, 71;
block numbering areas, 66, 71;
blocks, 67, 71; census county
divisions (CCD), 65, 71; census
designated place, 66; census tracts,
66, 71; changes 1980 to 1990, 70–
72; congressional districts, 68, 72;
consolidated metropolitan statistical
area (CMSA), 65, 70; counties, 65,
71; divisions, 62, 70; elections
precincts, 69, 72; enumeration districts, 68; incorporated places, 66,
71; metropolitan statistical areas
(MSA), 64, 70; minor civil divisions
(MCD), 65, 71; places, 66, 71;
primary metropolitan statistical areas
(PMSA), 65, 70; regions, 62, 70;
states, 64, 70; United States, 62, 70;
zip code areas, 69, 73
—special, 12
Censal ratio method, 129–30; advantages and limitations of, 130–31
Census tracts, 66, 71. *See also* Census
geography
Census survival rate: advantages and
limitations, 44–46; calculation, 44;
defined, 43
Child woman ratio, 14–16
Closure problem, 101, 110–12

Cohort component method: in popula-
    tion estimation, 156–58; in popula-
    tion projection, 178–87
Component method II, 143–46
Composite method of population es-
    timation: advantages and limitations,
    138, 142–43; calculation of, 138–43
Coverage error, 36
Crude birth rate (CBR), 13–14
Crude death rate (CDR), 19–22
Crude net migration rate, 32–36
Current Population Survey, 92

Data (see also Vital registration data):
    National Clearinghouse for Census
    Data Services, 97; sources, 81
Demographic equation, the basic, 3,
    100, 124
Duncan, Beverly, 138, 142

Econometric models, 176–178
Extrapolation in population projec-
    tions, 165; advantages and limita-
    tions, 175

Federal State Cooperative Program for
    Population Estimates (FSCPE), 95
Federal State Cooperative Program for
    Population Projections (FSCPP), 95
Fertility
—age specific fertility rate (ASFR): ad-
    vantages and limitations, 18; calcula-
    tion, 17–18; defined, 17
—child woman ratio: advantages and
    limitations, 15–16; calculation, 14–
    15; defined, 14
—crude birth rate (CBR): advantages
    and limitations, 13–14; calculation,
    13; defined, 13
—general fertility rate (GFR): ad-
    vantages and limitations, 17; calcula-
    tion, 16–17; defined, 16
Forward/reverse survival rate method,
    113–19. See also Intercensal popula-
    tion estimates

Geometric rate of growth (see also
    Population projections):

compared with arithmetic rate of
    growth, 109–10; continuous com-
    pounding, 104–6, 166, 169–70; ex-
    ponential rate, 106–9, 171–73;
    periodic compounding, 166, 170–71
General fertility rate (GFR), 16–17
Gompertz curve, 166, 173

Housing unit method, 134–38

Infant mortality, rates of: conventional,
    25–26; neonatal, 27; postneonatal,
    27; true infant mortality rate, 26
Intercensal component method of
    migration rates, 34–35
Interpolation, 101–2, 113
Internal Revenue Service (IRS), 30, 96,
    146
Immigration and Naturalization Service
    (INS), 96

Life expectancy, 54
Life table: abridged, 49; complete, 49;
    current, 48; defined, 47; explained,
    50; generational or cohort, 48

Metropolitan statistical area (MSA), 64–
    70. See also Census geography
Migration
—data problems, 30
—data sources, 29
—defined, 28
—emigration, 30
—immigration, 30
—inmigrant, 31
—internal, 30
—international, 30
—measures of: crude net migration
    rate, 32–36; intercensal component
    method, 34–35; migration ratio, 33–
    36
—net migration, 3, 31, 34, 100
—outmigrant, 31
—population balancing equation, 34–
    35
Migration ratio, 33–36
Modified logistic curve, 166, 174
Mortality

—age specific death rate (ASDR): advantages and limitations, 24–25; calculation, 12–23; defined, 22
—Crude death rate (CDR): advantages and limitations, 22; calculation, 20–21; defined, 19–20
—Infant mortality rate (IMR): calculation, 25–26; conventional vs true, 25–26; defined, 25
—neonatal infant mortality rate, 27
—postneonatal infant mortality rate, 27

National Center for Health Statistics, 94
National Clearinghouse for Census Data Services, 97
Natural increase, 3, 34, 100

Pearl-Reed Curve, 166, 173
Population estimates
—accuracy of, 193–94
—characteristics of, 4–6
—choosing a methodology, 195–96
—growth rates; arithmetic change, 102–4; compound change, 104–6; exponential, 106–9; geometric, 104–6
—intercensal, 4, 100
—merits and limitations of methodologies, 194–95
—methods of: administrative records, 146–48; censal ratio, 129–31; cohort component, 156–58; component method II, 143–46; composite method, 138–43; forward/reverse survival rate, 113–19; housing unit, 134–38; interpolation, 102–13; proration, 125–26; ratio correlation (regression), 148–53; simple ratio procedure, 126–28; vital rates, 131–33
—postcensal, 4, 100, 124–25
—similarities and differences to population projections, 2–3
Population forecasts, 7, 161–62
Population projections
—accuracy of methods, 196–97
—characteristics of, 9
—choosing a methodology, 8, 198
—compared with population forecasts, 7, 161–62

—growth rates: arithmetic change, 168–69; exponential change, 171–73; geometric change, 166–71
—merits and limitations of methodologies, 197–98
—methods of: cohort component, 178–87; econometric models, 176–78; mathematical extrapolation, 165, 175; ratio allocation, 163–65
—types of methodologies, 7–8
Proration method of postcensal population estimation, 125–26; advantages and limitations of, 126
Public law 94-171 (P.L. 94-171), 69, 85–86

Radix, 48. See also Life table
Ratio allocation method of population projection, 163; advantages and limitations, 164–65
Ratio correlation method of population estimation, 148–53; advantages of, 153
Reverse survival rate of migration, 36; advantages and limitations, 38–40; calculation of, 36–37; similarity to intercensal component method, 36

Shyrock, Henry, 130, 174
Siegel, Jacob, 130, 174
Simple ratio method of postcensal population estimation, 126–28; advantages and limitations of, 128
Social Security Administration, 94, 146
Special populations (group quarters), 188
SMSA. See MSA
State Data Center Program, 82, 88
Stationary population, 54. See also Life table
Survival rates: advantages and limitations, 58–59; census vs life table, 58; life table, 55–58
Symptomatic data, defined, 3

Undercount. See Coverage error
United States Bureau of the Census, 94–95

Vital rates method of postcensal population estimation, 131–33; advantages
   and limitation, 133

Vital registration data: monthly vital
   statistics report, 94; vital statistics of
   the United States, 93

## ABOUT THE AUTHOR

JAMES C. RAYMONDO is Associate Professor of Sociology and Chairman of the Division of Social Sciences at Union College in Barbourville, Kentucky. He has published scholarly articles on issues in the study of population. Raymondo worked previously as a demographer producing population projections at the state, county, and metropolitan level for the state of Alabama.